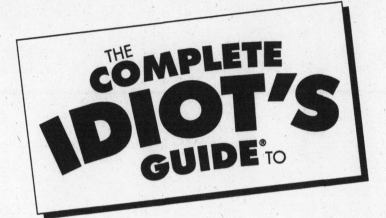

Active Trading

D0731077

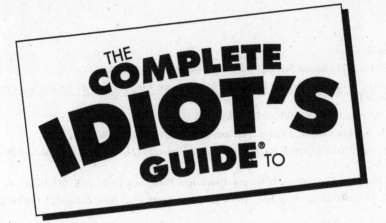

THE COMPLETE IDIOT'S GUIDE® TO

Active Trading

by Ken Little

ALPHA

A member of Penguin Group (USA) Inc.

ALPHA BOOKS

Published by the Penguin Group

Penguin Group (USA) Inc., 375 Hudson Street, New York, New York 10014, USA

Penguin Group (Canada), 90 Eglinton Avenue East, Suite 700, Toronto, Ontario M4P 2Y3, Canada (a division of Pearson Penguin Canada Inc.)

Penguin Books Ltd., 80 Strand, London WC2R 0RL, England

Penguin Ireland, 25 St. Stephen's Green, Dublin 2, Ireland (a division of Penguin Books Ltd.)

Penguin Group (Australia), 250 Camberwell Road, Camberwell, Victoria 3124, Australia (a division of Pearson Australia Group Pty. Ltd.)

Penguin Books India Pvt. Ltd., 11 Community Centre, Panchsheel Park, New Delhi—110 017, India

Penguin Group (NZ), 67 Apollo Drive, Rosedale, North Shore, Auckland 1311, New Zealand (a division of Pearson New Zealand Ltd.)

Penguin Books (South Africa) (Pty.) Ltd., 24 Sturdee Avenue, Rosebank, Johannesburg 2196, South Africa

Penguin Books Ltd., Registered Offices: 80 Strand, London WC2R 0RL, England

Publisher: *Marie Butler-Knight*
Editorial Director: *Mike Sanders*
Senior Managing Editor: *Billy Fields*
Senior Acquisitions Editor: *Paul Dinas*
Development Editor: *Michael Thomas*
Senior Production Editor: *Janette Lynn*
Copy Editor: *Jennifer Connolly*

Cartoonist: *Chris Sabatino*
Cover Designer: *Rebecca Harmon*
Book Designer: *Trina Wurst*
Indexer: *Angie Bess*
Layout: *Brian Massey*
Proofreader: *Mary Hunt*

This book is dedicated to all those who work hard at trading for a living. It is a difficult way to earn a living, but it can be financially and emotionally rewarding for those willing to do the hard work success requires. It's like my grandfather used to say: "If it was easy, everybody would do it."

Contents at a Glance

Contents

Introduction

Study after study proclaims that attempting to "beat the market" is a losing strategy. Many financial professionals and writers, me included, encourage people to make quality investments that they can hold for the long term.

New studies have shown that most people who invested in actively managed mutual funds would have done better if they had put their money in a low-cost index fund instead.

Why, then, write a book about active investing? There are several reasons.

Active investing is not about "beating the market." It is about making a profit one trade at a time over a short period, rather than waiting for years to see if your investment pays off.

More important, active trading is not about what "most people" should do. The truth is most people should not attempt active trading. They will not have the financial resources, determination, or patience to learn how to make money at it. The statistics speak for themselves: by some counts, 80 percent of the people who attempt active trading as a full-time career do not succeed. Interestingly, that is about the same percentage of failure for starting your own business, which is what becoming a full-time active trader amounts to.

Active trading comprises a group of strategies to pursue profits in the markets, just as growth and value investing are strategies. There is nothing unseemly or of less value about active trading. It provides liquidity and there is little evidence that retail active traders have much influence on prices.

Active trading is an umbrella term for several different strategies that involve holding a position for a limited amount of time ranging from seconds to months. Throughout the book, I use the term short-term trading instead of day trading. The reasoning is that day trading is limited to one particular style and I want to emphasize that today's active trader has several strategies that can be used as market conditions and opportunities dictate.

I also focus on trading stocks because they are still very popular with active traders and most readers will have some familiarity with them. Many of the strategies discussed apply to other securities; however, it would take a very large book to detail how to trade them all. Thanks to the Internet and technology, you can trade a wide variety of domestic and foreign securities from the comfort of your home.

With this convenience comes the explicit understanding that you must take responsibility for your actions. You will not have a professional looking over your shoulder telling you what to do or correcting your mistakes. You will also not have that person taking a big bite of your investment capital whether you have a winning trade or not. When you lose, you must learn from your mistakes. When you have a winning trade, you must also learn why the trade worked to confirm your trading strategy. Active trading is a process of constantly learning because the market is constantly changing. No one will ever be smarter than the market, but if you are a faithful student, it will reward hard work.

What to Expect

This book is an overview of what active trading is and how it works. It is not an attempt to sell you on active trading (or anything else for that matter). If you decide to learn more, there are several important topics that are only discussed briefly in this book and will require a much more detailed examination. Maybe the most important area you will need to study is technical analysis, which looks at patterns in price movements and volume. Short-term active traders rely heavily on technical analysis to spot price trends and reversals.

You will also need to study futures, options, and other derivatives in depth along with the forex market to gain a better understanding of these markets. You may find products or markets to trade that are better suited to your style than stocks or bonds.

The most dangerous thing you could do would be to put down this book and attempt to become an active trader with no other preparation. However, if you are determined to be your own boss and have the patience to do what is necessary in preparation work, an exciting career in active trading may be yours.

How to Use This Book

This book is divided into five parts:

Part 1, "The Active Trading Game," defines active trading and describes the several different strategies that make up this form of trading. We'll also explore the ways in which active trading differs from investing.

Part 2, "Markets and Products for Active Trading," takes you on a tour of the markets and securities that active traders use to profit in all types of market conditions.

Part 3, "Active Trading Tools," describes the technology and information services and providers that make active trading possible. What resources you need at all levels of active trading are outlined.

Part 4, "Strategies for Active Traders," discusses what each of the four main active trading strategies entails and how they find profits in the market.

Part 5, "What It Takes to Be an Active Trader," walks you through the legal, financial, and tax consequences of being an active trader. It also discusses some of the personality traits that may help and some that may hinder your success.

Extras

Throughout the book, you will find these sidebars, which will add to your understanding of active trading:

Trading Tip

These boxes feature insider information on making the most of active trading tools and techniques.

Margin Call

Here you'll find warnings about the pitfalls and dangers of active trading.

def·i·ni·tion

These sidebars contain definitions of industry terms.

Market Place

Advice for getting the most out of your active trading strategies can be found here.

Acknowledgments

A special thanks to Andrew Wilkinson with Interactive Brokers (www. interactivebrokers.com), who provided the majority of charts used in this book as screen shots from its trading system. The black-and white-reproductions don't do the charts justice. I don't endorse any products or services, but if you are serious about active trading, there is a good reason I chose Interactive Brokers to help with this book. It would be worth your time to consider its services when you are looking for a direct access provider.

Thanks again to Paul Dinas of Alpha Books for another chance to test his patience. Also thanks to Mike Thomas and Jennifer Connolly and the rest of the Alpha team that make me look good.

Trademarks

All terms mentioned in this book that are known to be or are suspected of being trademarks or service marks have been appropriately capitalized. Alpha Books and Penguin Group (USA) Inc. cannot attest to the accuracy of this information. Use of a term in this book should not be regarded as affecting the validity of any trademark or service mark.

Part 1

The Active Trading Game

Active trading is a broad term that identifies people who look for short-term profit opportunities in trading securities on price changes. Many active traders do this full-time, while others use the strategies to augment traditional long-term investing plans.

Active trading strategies can be defined by how long (or short) the trader holds the security. This holding period ranges from seconds for short-term traders to months for position traders. In between these two extremes, momentum and swing traders catch and ride price movements.

Chapter 1

What Is Active Trading?

In This Chapter

◆ Several short-term trading strategies

◆ Assuming a higher degree of risk

◆ Using leverage to enhance capital

◆ Active trading as a supplement to investing

Most investment advice suggests that the best strategy for the average investor is to "buy and hold." The idea is to identify great companies, buy the stock at a reasonable price, and hold it for years. An active trader, however, is more concerned with short-term profits from price changes in stocks and has little interest in what the company does or its future prospects.

Active trading is more risky because traders deal in volatile price changes over short time periods and often use leverage (short-term borrowing) to enhance their position. A move in the wrong direction can spell disaster for the active trader. Despite the higher degree of risk involved, serious active traders are not gamblers. The actions they take are calculated to maximize return and minimize risk.

Defining Active Trading

Active trading is best known by its holding periods, which can range from seconds to weeks. There are several types of active traders, but they all have one thing in common: they attempt to profit from price changes (sometimes very small price changes) in the securities they trade. While investors measure their holding in years, some active traders consider anything beyond 8 to 12 weeks way too long to be in one position. On the other end of the active trader spectrum are those who will not conclude a trading day without liquidating all of their accounts and starting fresh each morning.

def•i•ni•tion

The **intraday price** is the price quote of a security during active trading. It is neither the opening nor closing price and will change many times in the course of the trading day.

Traditional investors are not concerned with the *intraday price* movement of a stock. In fact, they are little concerned with daily changes unless the stock is trending down as a reflection of a change in the fundamentals or key financial ratios that measure the company's economic health. The buy-and-hold investor knows that over time great companies produce superior results as measured against the market and other companies in the same industry.

Active traders, on the other hand, focus on price changes over short time periods. They use tools to help them predict when a stock's price movement will start or stop or reverse direction. These changes in intraday prices may be just fractions of a dollar, but short-term active traders (such as day traders) can capitalize on those movements if they are clever and quick. Other active traders look for securities to make a move (either up or down) and ride that wave for as long as they can earn profits, which may be hours, days, or weeks.

Investor or Active Trader?

It is important to clearly distinguish between investors and traders. The actions of active traders are often contrary to what investors consider sound practices. Consider a marathon runner and a sprinter. Both runners' goals are the same—to win—but the races are different, requiring different skills and tools to succeed.

Investors typically focus on long-term goals and make their investment choices to match these needs. One of the main goals investors work toward is a financially secure retirement. To achieve this goal, they hope to pick investments that will give them above-average returns year after year, in all types of market conditions. The ideal investment will grow in value at a rate greater than inflation and better than the market to provide a real rate of return. Investors measure their holding periods in years.

Active traders, on the other hand, are more concerned with a very short holding period. While investors are seldom concerned with how a security is doing on any particular day, active traders are very interested in price and price velocity. The direction and velocity of price changes tells traders it's time to buy or sell. Active traders try to capture short-term profits by recognizing when the market has temporarily mispriced a security.

Active traders who focus on very short-term price changes are also known as day traders. The term "day trading" simply means all trades originate and conclude within the same trading day. Day traders were the superstars of the dot.com boom in the late 1990s. The practice skyrocketed on the back of a super bull market and advances in trading technology that reduced the time and expense of turning around quick trades. When the dot.com bubble popped, many of the day traders of that time discovered that making a living in a declining market took more skill than they possessed.

Since then, many in the industry have moved away from the term and embraced the broader descriptive name of active trader. Active traders include day traders, but also several other types of traders who deal in slightly longer holding periods. We will explore more differences between investors and traders in Chapter 2 because understanding the different motivations and strategies is central to understanding the science and art of active trading.

Going Against the Grain

Active traders seemingly go against the grain of conventional investing wisdom. Many knowledgeable investment professionals strongly urge investors to avoid frequent trades because of the increased transactions costs and the tax implications. Commissions paid to stockbrokers, even the deep-discount online brokers, add up. You pay a commission when you buy and again when you sell. Those dollars come out of any profit you make in a winning investment and increase your losses when you bail out of a losing position.

If you take a profit before holding the security a full year, your gain is taxed at ordinary income tax rates rather than the preferable long-term capital gain for securities held more than one year. You can offset some gains with losses; however, it is generally better to hold a security longer than one year and qualify for the long-term capital gains treatment. You should always consult a tax professional before making decisions that have tax consequences. We'll explore tax issues in more detail in Chapter 21.

Conventional wisdom also cautions that money needed any sooner than five years does not belong in the stock market because of the volatility. While a chart tracking a stock over a lengthy period might appear to be on a steady path, a closer look at intraday prices might reveal a different story. Hotly traded securities can experience wide swings during a trading day. Likewise, securities may suffer prolonged periods of decline before beginning a long climb to record highs.

Investors who need their money when a security is stuck in a low point are in trouble. That's why it's important to begin converting a substantial portion of your portfolio out of equities and into fixed-income securities as you approach retirement. You don't want to be caught with all your cash tied up in stocks during a bear market. Active traders will get out of a losing position quickly; however, they risk dumping a stock that suffers a temporary decline but rebounds sharply. Unlike investors, active traders look for profits now. An active trader is not trying to build wealth by holding investments over lengthy periods, so they are not caught in the same dilemma as investors. However, active traders can use conventional investing strategies to build a retirement account, for example.

> **Margin Call**
>
> The stock market experiences a bear, or down, market about every four to five years on average. However, it can suffer major retreats that don't qualify as full bear markets at any time. Active traders get in and out of the market quickly, so the volatility helps them, but it can be deadly to investors.

Active Traders Are Investors, Too

Many active traders are also buy-and-hold investors. Active trading is how they earn a living, just like the job you go to every workday. However, they invest for long-term goals like everyone else, because they know that active trading is a means to build your investment portfolio. Smart active traders will move some of the profits from trading into an investment account and keep it there to preserve it.

Active traders who have been in the business for some years know how hard it is to make money in a market. They don't take extra chances just to generate income, because taking chances is a short road to ruin. Tough markets come and go and active traders adjust. The ones who survive are disciplined in their trades and in their money management. Active traders work hard to minimize risk and maximize return, which is a strategy that can't succeed without discipline.

Many professional active traders view their trading as a supplement to investing, not a substitute. The fact that both activities involve the buying and selling of securities is not coincidental, but the approaches are completely different. Active traders who set thresholds in terms of what their trading capital is have a better chance at succeeding.

Active Traders Begin as Investors

Many active traders are experienced investors. This was, and remains, a problem for novices who view active trading as an easy road to quick riches. Novice traders were drawn to the lure of easy money during the dot.com boom. Thanks to a wild market, some of them did very well, at least for a short time.

It is possible to learn to be an active trader with no previous investment experience, but your odds of succeeding are low. Many investors view active trading as a way to take advantage of very short-term price movements that are otherwise wasted on traditional investors. They also see the opportunity to use a small portion of their investment capital in a higher risk strategy that has the opportunity to significantly beat the market.

> ### Market Place
>
> Although active trading and investing have different approaches, most active traders begin as investors. Understanding securities and what moves the markets can be very helpful to active traders.

For these investors, active trading is another tool, but not an exclusive tool. They remain primarily traditional investors in terms of the amount of capital they allocate between traditional investing and active trading.

Investors Can Learn From Traders

While it may be helpful to have some background in investing before beginning active trading in earnest, the traditional investor can learn from the active trader as well. Traditional investors normally don't have much use for the tools employed by active traders except at two important points in any investment: buying and selling. One of the keys to successful investing is buying at a good price and knowing when to sell.

Many traditional investors try to determine a company's intrinsic value through fundamental analysis (see "Fundamental vs. Technical Analysis"). If they can buy at or below this price, they have entered at a good point. Obviously, investors would like to sell when the stock is peaking. However, because traditional investors usually hold a good stock for years, they are not too concerned about pinpointing an entry and exit price down to the penny. They set a target entry and exit and are happy to get both.

Active traders focus on short-term and very short-term price changes. They look for technical signs that indicate a price movement in one direction or the other and move to take advantage of the change. They aren't always right because the time frame they work in is so short and much is happening that can change the environment rapidly. However, they aren't guessing either.

Where the two investment strategies meet is forecasting the correct time to buy or sell. If traditional investors wanted to convert a security to cash and use some of the tools available to active traders, that knowledge might influence when they actually sold. If the stock looks like it is in danger of a reversal, investors may want to accelerate the sale, for example.

Market Place

Investors may approach the problem differently, but finding the right entry point—that is, buying a security at the right price—sets up potential profits. Both investors and active traders put a great deal of effort into this one decision.

When buying a security, traditional investors have an entry point in mind. If active trading tools indicated the stock could be had at a lower price, traditional investors would be interested in lowering their entry point and possibly increasing the profit potential.

The tools used by active traders are available to anyone, including traditional investors willing to learn how to use them. As we'll see in later chapters, the tools are guides, not absolute predictors of price changes. Investors still need to use good judgment and common sense when making investments.

Fundamental vs. Technical Analysis

Traditional investors tend to rely on fundamental analysis, which is a detailed examination of companies to identify those that will be market leaders and provide above-average returns. Fundamental analysis focuses on what a company does and how efficiently it converts assets into earnings.

Technical analysis, a process of identifying price changes and movement of stocks, is the primary tool of active traders. Technical analysis is concerned with short-term price changes. It assumes a stock's price is reflective of everything that is known about the company—in other words, there is nothing hidden in the price that is known only by a few investors. Technical analysis also assumes that price changes follow trends and that these trends can often be seen and predicted. It is expressed primarily through charts that are easy to read for the experienced eye.

Technical analysis is part science and part art. In rapid intraday trading, no tool will tell you what a stock's price will be in the next few minutes or hours. However, if you are a practiced active trader, you will gain a confidence in reading the indicators and making quick and frequent trades to take advantage of the price changes. Successful active traders will count it a good day's work if more trades are profitable than not.

We'll examine technical analysis in more detail throughout this book and see how active traders use it in their decision-making. You'll also see that serious active traders don't guess or "have a feel" for the market. They base their trades on solid evidence and judgment honed by experience.

> **Margin Call**
>
> Many investors and certainly very short-term active investors live by technical analysis and the charts it produces. On the other hand, there are investors who look at technical analysis as a step above voodoo. It is not an exact science, but it is not smoke and mirrors either.

Using Leverage

Most active traders, especially those who make a living at it, are serious users of leverage to enhance their trading potential. Leverage is simply short-term borrowing to give you more investment capital. Some traditional investors also use leverage, but active traders frequently use it in every trade they make, whereas traditional investors typically use it less frequently.

Leverage in the investment world is also known as *margin*. In its simplest form, you borrow up to 50 percent of the price of a stock purchase from your stockbroker. For example, if you have $10,000 in capital, your stockbroker might lend you another $10,000 so you could buy $20,000 of a stock. If the stock goes up 20 percent to $24,000, you sell and pay back the $10,000 to your stockbroker and pocket $14,000.

def•i•ni•tion

Margin is the ability to borrow against the value of a security to extend your investment capital. Margin accounts with brokerage firms usually let you borrow up to 50 percent of the account value for a reasonable interest rate.

You earned 40 percent on your $10,000 investment. Had you only invested your $10,000, your profit would have been $2,000 or 20 percent. Leverage doubled your profit (obviously, I'm ignoring interest on the loan from the stockbroker, commissions, and taxes for the purpose of this illustration).

Leverage can help active traders achieve spectacular returns. However, it cuts both ways. If the trade goes sour, leverage works as hard against you as it did for you. Using the same numbers as above, suppose your $20,000 investment suffers a 20 percent loss instead of a profit. Now your account is worth $16,000. Your stockbroker requires you to maintain a certain account balance, which means you must either put cash into your account to raise the equity or sell out and pay off the note to the stockbroker.

If you sell at $16,000, you pay back the stockbroker and are left with $6,000, which is a 40 percent loss of your original $10,000 investment. Had you not used margin, you would have suffered a $2,000 loss on your $10,000 of original capital, or 20 percent. Leverage doubled your loss and, because of the stockbroker's margin requirements, you may have been forced to sell when you would have preferred not to.

The Price of Risk

Whether you are a conservative "buy and hold" investor or an active trader, risk is part of the investment equation. Even though active trading typically carries a higher degree of risk than traditional investing, serious traders take calculated risks—meaning they understand what the risks of a trade are before making it.

Beginning active traders typically have more losing trades than winners, in part because of the high-risk nature of the trades and in part because of inexperience. This is where an education can become expensive. Frequent trades mean more commissions paid to brokerage accounts and potentially higher fees. You can mitigate this expensive learning process by trading with practice accounts or paper trading that most brokerage firms provide. These accounts let you trade using real market data, but you aren't actually risking real money. This will give you a feel for the market and help you learn the trading platform or direct access broker system you choose.

Direct access brokers offer trading services to active traders that include sophisticated trading software, often called a trading platform. Trades through this platform go directly to the market, which means almost immediate execution of your buy or sell order. Conventional online or discount brokers take your order and then pass it through their trading system, which creates a delay in the actual execution. As we'll see in later chapters, quick execution is what gives active traders an advantage. Direct access brokers also offer sophisticated trading tools and information such as Level II Nasdaq quotes, which are essential for active traders to succeed. Chapter 12 discusses direct access trading in detail.

However, paper trading is no substitute for trading real money. When you invest real rather than play money, your emotions become a factor. If you can't handle losing some of your own money, active trading is not for you. Almost everyone who starts off in active trading loses money in the beginning. Managing risk is a top priority in learning how to actively trade.

Trading Tip

Practice or paper trading at most stockbrokers or trading platforms is just like the real thing. You may, or may not, see live data, but the experience is as close to real trading as possible. It is a safe way to get familiar with the trading software and comfortable with the markets.

Important Considerations for the Active Trader

To many people, active trading means buying and selling stocks, but the market is awash with securities that lend themselves to active trading—and some that don't work so well. Because active traders have a short-term perspective, their requirements for a *security* to trade are different from traditional investors' concerns.

def•i•ni•tion

A **security** is any type of investment product such as stocks, bonds, options, future contracts, and so on that is traded in an open market such as a stock exchange. These products are called securities because they are all registered with regulatory authorities that govern how the security is created, bought, and sold.

A primary concern of active traders is liquidity of the security, which means the security trades frequently on a readily accessible market. Liquidity gives the trader the ability to buy and sell the security with ease, knowing there will be a market.

Some securities trade infrequently or only seasonally (some commodities, for example crops that are only harvested during certain seasons). Active traders need securities that trade frequently so their trade won't upset the market price levels. Active traders want to move into and out of a security that is moving up (or down) and change that direction with their transaction.

Volume is another important factor for active traders. Traders want a high volume of transactions in the security because it allows the opportunity for quick profits without disturbing the market price. Volume is also an important technical indicator, especially when paired with price changes. This relationship will give you strong hints about which direction the security's price is likely to continue to go. We'll examine these indicators in more detail in Chapter 16.

The best securities for active traders also let them employ leverage—in some cases a lot of leverage. Not all securities readily allow you to leverage them. For example, some common stocks are not allowed to be leveraged. You can actively trade these securities, but you lose the advantage that leverage gives you.

Market Place

With so many securities to choose from, you may find it hard to focus on one type, but you will have better success if you identify one type of security and stick with that one until you are comfortable with how it trades.

Another important characteristic that active traders look for in a security is volatility. Volatility is how much the security's price changes over a given period of time. A security that trades in a very narrow range—$24 to $26, for example—does not provide as much opportunity as the security that trades between $18 and $28. These two securities could have the same average price of $25, but the one that varies from that average is more likely to produce profit opportunities.

Traders measure this variation from the average with a formula that calculates the standard deviation. The standard deviation is a mathematical way to measure volatility and risk. The trading platform you use will show this value, but in short the higher the number (meaning the greater the variance) the higher the volatility. Higher volatility translates into more opportunities for active traders to capture profits.

What Active Traders Trade

Many active traders focus on stocks, but thanks to the growth in technology that delivers prices and markets for other products, traders can also specialize in bonds, options, futures, commodities, and currencies.

Stocks may be the most popular choice of active traders, especially novices, because they are the easiest to understand and most familiar. There is a wealth of technical analysis and charting software covering stocks. Stocks have all the qualities active traders look for in a security (ready market, liquidity, marginability, volatility, and so on). The most popular trading platforms all cover stocks with the tools and information you'll need to be successful.

Many active traders focus on one type of security until they feel proficient and then add another security type to their skill set. This gives them the flexibility to find profitable trades in two or more different areas, so if stocks are flat, for example, they can switch to another security type to look for opportunities. While many of the skills in one market translate to another, each market has its own characteristics and patterns. The difference in the securities dictate different trading strategies in some cases.

We will explore the individual products in more detail in Chapter 8.

Types of Active Traders

This book focuses on four generally recognized types of active traders: short-term active traders, also known as day traders (including scalpers), momentum traders, swing traders, and position or trend traders. The length of holding period is one, but not the only, difference that marks the four different active trading styles from each other.

The form of active trading with the shortest holding period of all is called, ungraciously, scalping, which will be a familiar term to those with a history in day trading. Scalpers grab very small profits on dozens of trades each day. These traders must have swift reflexes and move quickly to take advantage of small changes in price. Really aggressive scalpers may make 100-plus trades a day. Scalpers make the most use of information from trading platforms. They may follow a particular security that is consistently volatile. Scalpers close out their positions at the end of each day.

Momentum traders also hold positions for a very short period. However, unlike the scalper who may be in and out of a position in a matter of minutes or seconds, momentum traders may ride a trade for several hours. Momentum traders spot price trends, either rising or falling, and

> **Trading Tip**
>
> Scalping and momentum trading are the two most intense and risky forms of active trading. They are the classic forms of day trading with traders huddled around multiple computer monitors staring at rivers of data looking for opportunities.

ride them until signs indicate a reversal. The idea is that once a trend is established it wants to keep going. These price trends are short-term intraday changes, not the long-term growth or decline traditional investors watch. Like scalpers, most momentum traders close out their positions each day.

Swing traders look for securities with short-term price trends and may hold it for one to four days or until the trend slows or stops. Swing traders look for one thing: a trending price change that they can identify through technical analysis.

The last type of active trader, position or trend traders, may hold a position for months (usually holding an asset for a year or more would qualify as investing as opposed to trading). Both look to establish a position in an asset as it begins a trend up (or down) and hold on until the security reverses course, which could be months.

We will examine each type of trading in more detail and look at how active traders put this information to use in actual trades.

A Final Word of Caution

Active trading is risky. Don't invest your retirement fund (and certainly not your mortgage). Active trading is not a get-rich-quick scheme, and it is not gambling. Some estimates indicate that up to 80 percent of the people who try very short-term active trading lose money. If you are serious about this as a career, be prepared to lose money while you learn.

The Least You Need to Know

- ◆ Active trading is riskier than traditional investing.
- ◆ Active traders follow short-term strategies including scalping or day trading, momentum, swing, and position trading.
- ◆ Active traders rely on technical analysis, not instinct, to guide trades.
- ◆ Active traders may hold a position from a few seconds to months.
- ◆ Most beginning active traders lose money.

Chapter 2

Characteristics of the Active Trader

In This Chapter

- ◆ Personal and professional characteristics of active traders
- ◆ Risks of active trading
- ◆ Active trading as a career choice
- ◆ Emotional and intellectual challenges

Active trading may seem like the investing equivalent of the National Football League, where aggressiveness, supreme self-confidence, and a no-excuse attitude are rewarded. While those characteristics come into play, they alone won't make you a winner as an active trader. In fact, most active traders work very hard to keep their emotions out of their business. Emotions cloud judgment and, when you are doing very short-term trading, can trick you into following one bad trade with another. People who trade on emotion or gut instinct usually don't last long.

Most active investors do it as a full-time career. Like any other complicated profession, it requires dedication and practice to master. The capital, equipment, and services needed for active trading make a part-time effort inefficient. The extremely fast-paced action of active trading would be difficult to adjust to on an infrequent basis.

What Makes an Active Trader Tick

Active traders come in all ages and genders. The market doesn't care if you're a man or woman, young or old. The traders you compete against don't give anyone a break and, in that sense, trading is one of the most egalitarian businesses you can enter.

Most active traders focus on very short-term trading patterns—still called day trading in many circles. This is the most intense and complicated form of active trading. It is the one that requires the greatest commitment if you have any hope for success.

> ### Market Place
>
> Like most endeavors that are worth doing, active trading requires a commitment of time, energy, and money. The idea that anyone can be successful with little effort on his or her part is not true.

Despite what you might see on late-night television ads, this form of active trading is not something that most people can do an hour or two each day and be successful. Day trading requires all the skills and personality traits that make a full-time trader successful.

Most successful active traders seem to have a combination of personality characteristics that increase the odds of success.

Most Active Traders Are Quick Learners

Short-term active trading (such as day trading and momentum trading), where you make dozens of trades each day in a market that changes with every tick, requires a mental agility to adapt to new conditions instantly. You have to see the market by looking at rows of numbers and charts. This learning process takes time, but if you take too much time, you'll run through your investment capital before grasping some notion of what the market is telling you. This is one of the main reasons (along with poor money management) that many beginning active traders fail. As we look into the actual mechanics of active trading, you will see how important it is to always be a learner.

> ### Trading Tip
>
> Practice trading is a must for beginners, but it can only take you so far. You can learn the trading platform and how the markets work, but you won't really know if you're cut out for active trading until you risk real money.

Not only do you need to learn the market, there is usually the fairly complicated software used by the trading platform of your direct access broker. Both are complicated and you shouldn't plan to pick up all you need to know in 20 minutes of tinkering around. A caution that will reappear repeatedly throughout this book is to use the practice accounts offered by direct access providers to learn the software and get familiar with the market in which you choose to work. It's a free and painless way to get the basics down.

Active Traders Process Lots of Information

If you choose to try active trading, be prepared for data overload. The amount of information you must process is staggering. Trading platforms are marvels at assembling information, and most will let you customize the presentation of onscreen information. Still, many short-term active traders use more than one computer monitor to have access to all the information they want at one time. You must develop the ability to look over those areas of the screens that are the most urgent and evaluate what you see quickly. When we look at trading platforms in Chapter 16 and at screen shots throughout this book, you will notice the large number of areas competing for your attention.

Active Traders Make Quick Decisions

Very short-term active trading requires split-second decisions, especially if you are scalping profits. If you are hesitant to make a decision where money is involved, active trading is probably not for you—at least, very short-term active trading. Not only do you need to "pull the trigger," but you need to move on quickly if the trade doesn't work. Beating yourself up over a bad trade or mistake in the middle of trading action leads to more mistakes or missed opportunities. Quick decisions should not be confused with guessing. Active traders make a trade because it fits their plan and the technical signs are right.

Most Active Traders Review Their Work

We just noted that traders do not tarry over a bad trade or mistake. However, at the end of the day, active traders take the time to review what happened and why. Going over the day's trades, both the winners and losers, gives traders an opportunity to check their performance. Traders are self-critical in a positive way to determine how they can improve their performance in future trading.

Margin Call

Active traders, beginners and even veterans, make dumb trades on occasion. It is important to learn from mistakes, but if you harp on failures, it will hold you back and taint future decisions.

Traders review their trading plan and question whether they need to make adjustments or simply improve execution.

Most Active Traders Work Alone

Thanks to high-speed Internet connections available almost everywhere and high-performance trading platforms offered by direct access providers, most active traders work from their homes or private offices. There are still a few day trading centers where traders gather and access the markets through workstations often provided by a stock brokerage company. However, most traders work alone, and that can be daunting for people who thrive on contact with others. Active traders are very focused and many would find others distracting. If you enjoy the camaraderie of a traditional office or work environment, you probably won't enjoy sitting in front of multiple monitors by yourself for hours.

The Emotional Challenges

The market doesn't care about you or your personal problems. That may sound harsh, but anyone who enters active trading with the hope that newcomers get any kind of break is in for a rude awakening. Active trading is not like investing. When you buy a stock for an investment, you are not trying to beat someone else out of a profit; your intent is to hold the asset for at least one year or more. Active traders compete against other traders for a profit.

> **Trading Tip**
>
> Most active traders set a schedule around when the securities they specialize in trade. They stick to this schedule as a way to avoid becoming compulsive about trading and to give themselves time to recharge emotionally and intellectually.

As we'll see in Chapter 18, day trading and momentum trading involve a highly charged atmosphere where traders use a variety of tricks and feints to manipulate prices or the appearance of price change in order to grab a profit when others fall for the bait. This is not a gentle way to make a living.

Emotionally, active trading can be devastating if you aren't prepared for the stress and able to suffer resounding defeat and come back the next day as if nothing happened. Many active traders find the isolation of working alone too emotionally vacant.

Successful traders find ways to cope with the stress and are passionate about what they do. The danger on the other end of the emotional scale is that the active trader will become consumed by trading. With markets open 24 hours a day somewhere, it is possible for active traders to become virtually addicted to trading. This, of course, is not healthy and can only lead to deterioration in proficiency.

Active Trading as a Substitute for Gambling

Active trading is not gambling. It is a serious and thoughtful way to make money on price changes of securities. However, thanks to infomercials and misguided stories in the media, there is a perception among some that active trading is easy money. Unfortunately, the facts are that over 80 percent of the people who take up active trading lose money.

Still, the image of quick and easy money attracts people who are inclined to have problems with gambling. They believe active trading will give their gambling problem an air of social acceptance. It certainly sounds better to say you are an active trader than it does to say you are a gambler.

Some people may make money in active trading by guessing (gambling), but they won't last long. You can be lucky for only so long before it turns on you. People who gamble tend to be poor money managers also, so early luck is soon consumed by later bad luck. If you have a problem with gambling, active trading is not a substitute that will make your problem go away. You will lose money just as quickly (probably quicker) in the market as you will in a casino.

Full- and Part-Time Active Trading

Many active traders, especially those engaged in scalping and momentum trading, do it as their full-time occupation. These two forms of active trading are the most intense and require the longest learning curve. The trading platforms are complicated. The markets are challenging and the pace of trading is unbelievably fast. Learning all there is to know about these two forms of active trading is usually best done by immersion. Active traders are driven to know all they can know about their business, while realizing there is something new to learn every day they trade.

We'll dig deeper into these forms of short-term trading in Chapter 3 and then look at what it is like to actually be an active trader in Chapter 17 and beyond. You'll see more clearly why day traders have a passion for what they do. Without some internal drive to do this type of work, most people don't stick with it for long. It is a difficult way to make a living, but if you have the right skills and personality, you may find you love it.

It is possible to be a part-time active trader. However, you will still need most of the same equipment and services a full-time trader needs. This means your overhead costs are not spread over as much trading activity and become a bigger percentage of your costs.

Trading Tip

Active traders spend more time with their investment capital than typical investors do because they are interested in exploiting current profit opportunities, not building for the future.

If you have a job that starts later in the day or you can adjust your work schedule, you may decide to trade only half a day. Some markets trade 24 hours a day. Another option is to only trade two or three days a week. If you work on weekends, you may want to trade on your days off.

If you opt for one of the longer-hold active trading systems, such as swing trading or position trading, you have much more flexibility. Many people do this without leaving their present job. When we look at these two opportunities in Part 4, you will see that they lend themselves to a much less intense level of activity. However, they also lack the hard competition and chances to score well that the short trading strategies offer. You can, however, employ them on your lunch hour, something not really practical or advisable with day trading or momentum trading.

Understanding Risk and Return

You can define risk several ways, but for long-term investors and active traders it usually means the chance that you won't earn the return you expected. Investors may go to great lengths to avoid losing money, which is not a bad thing. However, in doing so they rob themselves of the opportunity to earn returns that will beat inflation and truly increase their wealth.

Connecting Risk and Return

The problem for many investors and traders is they don't connect risk and return properly. This is one of the most important concepts for both investors and traders, since it is directly related to your success in either endeavor. The rule of the investing/trading jungle is this: the higher the risk, the higher the potential return.

The risk/return rule has several stumbling blocks for investors and active traders.

◆ **People don't understand the risk.** One of the most serious problems facing investors and traders is understanding the risk of a particular investment. Investors have a big edge here because they typically hold for long periods. Temporary setbacks can be recovered over time if you have invested in a good company. Active traders face a much more challenging task since they must usually decide quickly and hold only for a very short period.

◆ **People don't understand the return.** Too many novice investors and traders enter the game with unrealistic ideas about the return they can earn. They may remember the dot.com days and hope to become rich overnight. An equally serious and more common problem is investors and traders taking too much risk for too little potential return. Why take a big risk for a potential 9 percent return, when you can take very little risk for an 8 percent return?

◆ **It is a *potential* return.** Taking the risk doesn't mean you will earn the return—if it did, then it wouldn't be a risk. Yet, some investors and traders are incredulous when they take a risk and it doesn't work out. One secret of successful investing and trading is finding a level of risk you can tolerate and adjusting your financial goals to that expected return.

> **Market Place**
>
> It is important to understand your personal risk tolerance. You cannot be successful with a trading strategy that pushes you outside your comfort zone.

The Risks of Active Trading

Since active traders hold for such short periods, the risks can be higher in some areas than for long-term investors. Depending on the security being traded, intraday prices can change rapidly and swing widely. This may create opportunities for day and momentum traders, but it also is challenging to determine if a downtick is the start of a general downward price trend or just a bump before prices rally. Active traders can make money if prices go either way, but they must be right in the direction—taking a position that prices are moving one way only to have them reverse is a big risk.

Active traders follow price trends (which we'll discuss in more detail in subsequent chapters). Those traders shoot for the biggest profit trade at the extremes—that is, they attempt to buy at the bottom just before the price begins an upward trend and sell just before that climb stops or reverses. Identifying those points is not an exact science. Using charts and factors from technical analysis, traders combine science and art into their own trading system. Many traders don't shoot for the highest possible profit, but aim for a certain return and exit when they hit that mark, knowing that a fast-moving market can take away their profit in a heartbeat if they are not careful.

On the other hand, short-term traders close out their positions at the end of the trading day. They won't suffer any losses because of bad news that happens after the markets close. Investors and active traders holding shorter-term positions risk the effect news events or corporate announcements (a change in earnings estimates, for example) have on prices of securities they hold.

Time and Money Management

One of the important skills active traders need is the ability to manage their time and money. Time management is important because traders cannot afford to waste time on nonproductive efforts during trading hours. Money management is important because traders will lose money, especially those just beginning. Managing those losses requires discipline and a plan.

The Importance of Time Management

Active traders are bombarded with data—some of it useful, a lot of it noise. Some of the noise may be interesting, as in news items or new trading technology. There is a time for exploring those items, but it is not during the active trading day. Many successful active traders have a set routine they follow every trading day. This schedule helps keep them focused on what is important for success during trading that day.

The Importance of Money Management

Successful active traders have a trading plan that covers how much of their investment capital they will risk at any one time. They stick to this plan and don't change it without careful consideration. Most traders set a percentage of their investment capital as the maximum they will trade at any one time. This limits their risk somewhat, should things go badly.

It is a good idea to have a plan and limits in place so you will not have to think about what is right during the heat of trading. If you set daily limits and hit those during a trading session, close out your positions and take the rest of the day off. It is better to take a small loss so you can come back another day than to stubbornly hang on and watch a small loss turn into a big loss.

We'll discuss time and money management in greater detail in Chapter 23.

Margin Call _____

Failure to manage investment capital is one of the main reasons active investors fail. If you do not have a plan for risking your capital and sticking to it, you may let emotions interfere with trading decisions.

Active Trading as a Business

Earlier we talked about active trading as a career choice. Another way to look at it that people find helpful is as a business. There may be some tax consequences for actually setting yourself up as a one-person business. We'll look at those in more detail in Chapter 21.

As a business, active traders put their capital at risk, the same as other business people who start an enterprise. Your trading plan is how you will run the business and manage your money. For many people, it is important to think of their active trading in these terms because it helps keep emotion out of decisions. The failure rate for small businesses is high, and the business of active trading is no different. If you remain focused on your strategy and learn from your mistakes, like other small business people, you'll improve your odds for success.

The Least You Need to Know

- Active traders are quick learners who keep their emotions in check, are able to process lots of information, and are comfortable working alone.

- Active traders usually work at it full-time as a career.

- Active trading has its own set of risks that can be managed.

- Active traders are concerned with managing their time and money.

Chapter 3

Short-Term Trading: Day and Momentum Trading

In This Chapter

- ◆ Day traders dominate short-term trading
- ◆ The role of momentum traders
- ◆ Risks and opportunities of short-term trading
- ◆ Technological changes in short-term trading

Short-term trading, for the purposes of this book, refers to day traders and momentum traders. These two types of traders use essentially the same strategies. Many people who practice short-term trading still consider themselves day traders. Others (momentum traders) have expanded their view of short-term trading to include some longer holding periods of securities than day traders traditionally employ. Yet, most of what short-term traders do is day trading in every sense of the word.

Not Your Father's Day Trading

The business of day trading suffered an unfortunate association with a number of get-rich-quick schemes during the wild bull market of the late 1990s. The Internet was still in its infancy and broadband connections

Trading Tip _____

Day traders used to be shackled to the market by connections through workstations in the offices of brokers that specialized in this type of trading. Thanks to high-speed Internet access, short-term traders are now free to trade almost anywhere.

were the rare exception. Companies sprang up all over the country offering training in day trading and work stations at their offices for traders to use (for a fee). Many of these companies often known as trading arcades were legitimate businesses, but some were not. They promised (or strongly hinted) that after completing their high-priced seminars and workshops, you would be ready to make millions day trading.

Although some day traders made a lot of money during the dot.com bull market, many did not. Day trading was not the easy money some providers advertised (it still isn't today). For awhile, a loophole in trading regulation gave an advantage to small traders with orders of 1,000 shares or less. This slight advantage in the priority in which orders were executed allowed day traders to make a small profit off their orders at the expense of larger traders. That advantage was eliminated in 2000.

Many of the day traders of that era chased high-tech companies and looked for much bigger profits than they were garnering with their small advantage. Unfortunately, many day traders that hooked up with the less reputable providers of market services found that fees took such a big bite from their gross that not much was left for them. Traders were encouraged to use excessive margin and to borrow against their homes or other assets if they needed to raise more cash.

Margin Call _____

When the market was hot with technology stocks, it was also hot with urban legends of people quitting their jobs and becoming rich in three months by day trading. You don't hear those stories anymore, and there's a reason.

It's hard to know how many day traders from that era lost all their investment capital (and perhaps more) or simply quit before losing it all. The ranks of day traders thinned considerably after the markets crashed in 2000 and have never regained those numbers. However, the numbers began growing, thanks to a bull market beginning in 2003. Fortunately, the short-term traders who survived and the new ones coming into the business have a more reasonable attitude about what to expect.

How Short-Term Trading Works

Short-term trading is a strategy of taking small profits on multiple trades during a single day of trading. When the short-term traders have a good day, they may make 80 to 100 trades. Many of the trades may only be open for minutes or seconds. Some trades may lose money or close out with no profit. However, short-term traders aim for more profitable trades than losing trades. The profit from good trades is very small, which is why short-term traders make so many in a single day. It is a difficult way to make a living; however, with a good trading plan and careful money management, short-term traders can do very well. Some days, there may not be many trades for short-term traders. Disciplined short-term traders will not force trades and will sit out a trading session rather than make bad trades.

The Bid-Ask Spread

Short-term traders look for certain signs that may indicate the price of a stock is going to change. It is important to understand that we are talking about live transaction prices scrolling across a screen, not conclusions drawn from hours of research. Short-term traders who want to profit from scalping are looking at the bid-ask spread of the stock they are following for small profits. These profits usually amount to pennies per share, which is why scalpers trade so often. To understand how short-term traders make money from such small profits, you first have to understand the bid-ask spread—what it is and how it informs the trader.

The bid-ask spread is the difference between what you can sell shares for and the price you pay when buying them. The bid price is what a broker will pay for a stock; the ask price is what she will sell for. The ask price is always higher. How much higher (the difference between the bid and ask prices) is the bid-ask spread. On wide-held and actively traded stocks, the bid-ask spread may be only one or two pennies. For other stocks, the spread may widen.

Market Place
In 2001, stock prices switched from fractions to decimals. This changed the smallest price difference from $1/16$ or $0.0625 to $0.01. This made it harder for short-term traders to make a profitable trade.

Traders watch the bid-ask spread (among other things) for a supply imbalance— a widening spread may indicate that the balance between buyers and sellers is shifting. Real-time market order data available through a direct access provider shows the trader all the pending orders. When an imbalance begins developing, traders may find an opportunity for a profit. We'll dig into this deeper in Chapter 18.

Short-term traders make many trades and trade large blocks (1,000 plus) of stock if they are able. This way, very small profits per share can add up over the day. For example, a 1,000-share trade with a two-cent per share gross profit is only $20. Out of that must come brokerage fees and other transaction costs. If the trader is left with a $10 net profit, she will be lucky. This is why short-term traders may execute 100 or more trades per day. Not all will be profitable, so the trader must have a strategy to strictly limit losses on bad trades and to exit even on profitable trades.

Momentum Trading

A variation of day trading is momentum trading. Most momentum traders close out their positions at the end of each trading day, although there are some who do not. The idea with momentum trading is that once a stock price begins a trend in one direction (up or down) it tends to continue that way until it reaches a point of reversal. Momentum traders work to spot the beginning and end of trends. By riding the trend as long as possible, momentum traders earn the largest profit. Short-term traders should avoid stretching momentum positions over more than one trading day. However, those traders willing to take more risk for a larger profit may hold a momentum trade longer. The risk is that the price trend will reverse and any profit in the trade may be lost.

Margin Call

Spotting the beginning and end of very short trends is complicated and requires judgment and patience. The momentum trader relies on excellent timing to make a profit or avoid a loss.

In practice, many momentum trades last only a few hours before the trend ends or reverses. Traders look for technical signals and order activity that indicates a trend is beginning. The trick is to know when you are truly seeing a trend and not a quick blip that will bounce one way and then the other with no discernable direction. There are technical signals to watch for, but they aren't foolproof. Momentum traders must be quick to jump on a trend, but even quicker to get out of a position if the trend proves false. It's a risky way to make a living, but the rewards can be substantial for the patient and disciplined trader. We'll look at momentum trading in more detail in Chapter 18.

A Typical Day of Short-Term Trading

The workday for short-term traders can be intense, exciting, boring, challenging, and/or dull—and you can experience all of that in the first hour. The pulse of the market drives the day for short-term traders. However, most successful short-term traders don't let the market control their businesses. Traders can't control how the market is running, but they can establish a trading strategy or plan that they test and update. By sticking to a plan, traders remain in control of their trading and avoid emotional decisions.

Short-term traders will likely spend most of their day in a home office connected to one or more direct access providers. The office has multiple ways to connect to the Internet, but the primary connection is a high-speed DSL or cable connection. The computer has a large amount of memory and is hooked to two (or more) large flat panel monitors. There may also be a television tuned to a financial news channel. From this nerve center, short-term traders can research and execute trades on multiple markets and multiple products—although most short-term traders follow one or two primary products.

Trading Tip

Short-term traders find ways to combat the isolation and intensity of their business. Exercise, yoga, or other physical and mental routines help reduce stress and clear the mind for a new day of trading.

The Risk Factor

Short-term trading can be risky—after all, you trade on price movements that are measured in minutes and seconds. This is one of the reasons many trades executed by short-term traders lose money—the high risk of predicting very short-term price movements. Finding a good strategy and gaining the experience to read technical signs and the markets takes time and can be expensive lessons. Many short-term traders never get beyond the learning stage because they run through all their investing capital before they gain enough knowledge to execute more winning than losing trades.

On the other hand, short-term traders close out their positions before the end of each trading day. There are no loose ends and no open positions that can turn into big losers overnight on some bit of bad news—and no big winners that will add to their gains, either. It takes discipline to close out all your positions each night, especially if you have a winning position that looks like it will continue to grow when the market opens tomorrow. But most short-term traders know the key to their survival is to start each day with a clean slate.

Margin Call

The market may appear to react emotionally to news, but it is the participants who are reacting. The market has no emotion or compassion for you or anyone else. It owes you nothing, so don't expect anything from the market or you have quit trading and begun gambling.

Short-Term Trading Expectations

Short-term traders in today's market frequently do it as a full-time business. The traders who are successful spend a lot of time learning their profession and try to add to that knowledge every day. The comparison to a business is appropriate because most small businesses don't survive many years. Depending on the type of business, the failure rate can be as high as 90 percent in the first five years. It usually doesn't take that long for short-term traders to either fail or admit this is not the business for them and give up before their capital does.

> **Market Place**
>
> Plan to spend as much (or more) time learning the short-term trading business as you would learning any other business. This is not something you can master with a brief amount of reading or practice.

The short-term traders who are successful find emotional and intellectual satisfaction in the business as well as financial rewards. Short-term trading is difficult to do well day after day unless you develop a passion for the business. Fortunately, it can be very addictive in a positive way. Every day the market is different and the challenges change with the blink of an eye.

Role of Short-Term Traders

Short-term trading is not the same as speculating in the sense that speculators often hope to influence the price of a security through their actions. Short-term traders try to capture profits from short-term price changes. They would rather their activities did not cause the price of the security to change, since that would tip their action to other short-term traders.

Short-term trading does provide liquidity and capital to the markets. The securities they buy and sell may or may not be from other traders. An investor entering a market order to sell a stock could be on the other side of a transaction from a short-term trader who wanted the stock at that price. There must always be a buyer and seller, so short-term traders add another level of liquidity to the market since their motives aren't the same as buy-and-hold investors.

This is important because a factor that might cause a buy-and-hold investor to sell a stock may have no interest to a short-term trader who sees an opportunity to pick up the security on a price change that could be sold back in the same trading day for a small profit.

Short-Term Trading Regulations

Because of past excesses, the regulatory agencies that oversee the securities industry have some strict rules about who can be a short-term active trader and who can't. The securities industry is highly regulated and is self-regulated in many areas. The primary agency charged with overseeing the securities industry is the Securities and Exchange Commission (SEC). The SEC has tremendous authority, but not complete authority, over the markets and industry professionals. Several self-regulatory organizations also monitor industry professionals. In addition, product-specific regulatory agencies and state agencies are involved.

Brokerage firms, securities exchanges, and other organizations belong to self-regulatory groups that monitor and mediate client disputes and license professionals. Although the consumer is the least represented in all the regulatory organizations, the customer needs the most protection.

For short-term traders, the regulations are designed to determine if you meet "suitability" standards. The rules require brokerages and others providing market access to determine if you are engaging in appropriate trading activities for your financial situation and understanding of the market. What that means is before you can open an account, you must sign a bunch of forms declaring that the money in your short-term account is risk capital, meaning you can lose it and not lose your house.

Trading Tip

Regulators and your broker will monitor trading patterns, and if you qualify, will put you in special class for regulatory consideration.

If you are deemed a "pattern day trader," you must have at least $25,000 in your account. This is not something the broker can waive, but the rules. You can't open an account with $5,000 and try to sneak in short-term trading. If you buy and sell the same security on the same day within a margin account, you are day trading as far as the regulators are concerned. Perform four or more of those trades within a week or five market days and you are a pattern day trader.

Be Prepared for Paperwork

Short-term trading accounts, by definition, involve at least $25,000 of cash to get started, more in some cases. Thanks to a number of rules to prevent money laundering, you will be required to prove you are not a member of organized crime or a known terrorist. Criminals have used legitimate businesses and investment accounts to launder ill-gotten cash for years. New rules that affect banks, investment companies, and other financial service organizations require them to report suspicious cash transactions (such as depositing large sums of cash in $100 bills).

Margin Call

Various laws enacted after the 9/11 attacks coupled with efforts to thwart organized drug trafficking make any major financial transaction complicated, often requiring multiple forms of identification.

It was discovered that the terrorists who carried out the attacks on September 11, 2001, were able to obtain large sums of cash from sources without triggering any alarms. As a result, most financial transactions or accounts require positive identification of various sorts before the firm will accept your business. This will include the usual identification information such as name, address, Social Security number, and additional identification, such as a passport and driver's license.

For pattern day traders, you will be asked to provide financial statements to prove the money you are depositing is truly risk capital and not your kid's college fund.

The Tax Bite

Short-term trading can be a tax nightmare if you don't keep good records. Your broker will report your earnings to the IRS and you will get Form 1099 at the end of year. There is a special reporting consideration for full-time traders, but your records must be in order. We'll cover the details in Chapter 21, but plan on setting up your trading business with tax reporting in mind.

Technology Helps, Hurts

Technology has made short-term trading possible from almost anywhere a high-speed Internet connection is available. Direct access providers and other vendors provide web-based applications that give traders access to domestic and international markets for just about any type of security you want to trade. Most short-term traders set up in their homes or an office to conduct their business full-time. However, with properly equipped laptop computers, short-term traders could take their businesses on the road. High-speed Internet access is available in many locations such as hotels, airports, and other locations. Trading from an airplane is just around the corner.

All this access and technology has put powerful tools in the hands of traders. While that has made the business of short-term trading more accessible, it is no substitute for experience and judgment. Technology will help you be a better trader, but it can't be a substitute for market knowledge. You can tell technology to execute certain trades if conditions are met (the stock hits a certain price, for example). However, you must still tell the program what price point will activate the action and that requires your judgment. Too often traders confuse technology with judgment and rely too heavily on programs and charts for absolute answers.

The Least You Need to Know

- ◆ Short-term trading is the most aggressive of all active trading strategies.
- ◆ Scalpers take many small profits to make a profitable day.
- ◆ Momentum traders look for larger profits by riding price trends.
- ◆ Short-term trading is highly regulated.

Swinging Trades

In This Chapter

◆ Swing trading may be an entry point for beginning active traders

◆ How swing trading fits into the active trader's strategy

◆ Swing trading in action

◆ Risk and reward in swing trading

Swing trading is a strategy that capitalizes on price tendencies of some stocks to move in a certain direction for short periods before reversing. This "swinging price," from up to down, gives active traders a window of opportunity to make some money. It is not easy money (nothing about active trading is easy), but it can be lucrative.

Swing traders look for profits they can ride for one to four days or even a week or more. This requires discipline because it is impossible to know when a stock will hit a top or bottom price. Swing traders look for stocks that will move on news, but not necessarily by huge amounts. They look for larger profits than the short-term traders we met in Chapter 3, but they know that greed could cause them to hold a stock until the price goes down.

Traders use technical analysis to identify when certain conditions are right for a stock to start moving either up or down. However, swing traders also rely on fundamental data to inform their decisions, especially when identifying potential trading candidates. Because the holding time is longer than the holding time for short-term traders, the swing trader is at some risk of economic or company news derailing the trade. But there are also some higher-risk trades the swing trader can enter (with eyes open) that offer the potential for a bigger payoff.

Swing Trading Is Not So Fast

Swing trading may be a good alternative or addition to short-term trading. It requires some more work on the front end to identify the right type of stock. You will also want to become familiar with the best market conditions for swing trading.

The swing trader identifies a stock that is beginning a one- to four-day upswing in price, which is usually followed by a corresponding retreat. In most cases, these swings occur when the overall market is not blowing hot or cold but trudging along "sideways." Major stock indexes may not move up or down much from week to week, and stocks, especially stocks of larger companies, fall into a price oscillation above and below a *baseline* price.

The Good Old Swing Days

When the market was crazy with tech and Internet stocks, swing trading became very popular. There was so much new (and undisciplined) money rushing into the market, big swings of 10 to 20 to 30 points were available for professional traders. Big run-ups of stocks and corresponding crashes were common, and swing traders made money going both ways.

After that market imploded in 2000, the swings became much more tame and realistic. It is not likely we'll see that kind of over-the-top market again, but swing traders are well-positioned to take advantage of stock runs of any size if they know how to use the tools available to them.

What Swing Trading Looks Like

The idea behind swing trading is that stock prices will rise in steps or swings, each lifting the price up to a new high or lowering it to a new low. The ideal candidate steps up in price from one level to the next with regularity. A chart will show how this works as swings push the price to new highs. A swing trader can find the entry point by observing a historical chart and seeing a pattern in how much the stock retreats after an upward swing. The chart will show highs and lows for the day and, when included over a long period, you can see the previous swings that elevated the stock to its current price.

> **Market Place**
>
> The go-go days of the 1990s tech boom are gone and not likely to come back soon. There are still many opportunities for traders to make good money in markets that are saner.

Not all swings come neatly wrapped and easy to identify. By their nature, most swings are in small increments and last for short periods. Frequently, traders look for days when the market is not going up or down with any strength. During these market days, some stocks can be identified as good swing candidates. Large-cap stocks work well for many traders. These stocks of larger companies that are not moving on any particular news often swing up or down over a period of several days.

Many swing traders work with strictly technical analysis. However, a number also use elements of fundamental analysis to spot longer swings or stocks that may be moving up due to strong earnings or other corporate news. The best swing traders use a combination of both to find the best candidates. Fundamental analysis looks at key financial components that change and create news (earnings, SEC filings, insider trading, and so on). These often signal a stock that may be a good swing trading candidate.

Using daily charts, swing traders can catch one of the swings and ride it for a nice profit. How does the trader know when to get in and get out? We'll discuss that in greater detail in Chapter 19 when we look at actual swing trades. But for now, consider that the swing trader is using the stock's baseline price as a reference point. The techniques for profitable swing trading involve technical analysis of the stock's price relative to this baseline.

> **Margin Call**
>
> Swing traders should use caution when relying heavily on technical analysis. Holding positions over several days leaves you open to bad news that can't be predicted with a chart.

The Basics

Tools for fundamental analysis may help you identify a potential candidate for swing trading, but most traders rely on technical analysis to help them identify entry and exit points. Once you find a good candidate for swing trading and the market is right, you can use technical analysis research tools offered by your direct access provider, broker, or third-party vendor (you don't necessarily need a direct access provider, although many part-timers use one) to calculate a price baseline for the stock. The baseline will be a moving average—a 20-day moving average is common—that is your reference point (more about moving averages next). When the stock price moves above this baseline, you buy, and when it dips below the baseline, you sell or short. It's somewhat more complicated than that, and we'll see how it works with several variations in Chapter 19.

The key to successful swing trading is no different from any other type of trading or investing. You must be disciplined about when you buy and sell. You can't control the price of any security you buy, but you can control your entry and exit. Swing trading is good training for the discipline all traders and investors need to be successful.

Just About Average

Technical analysis uses moving averages to establish baselines and for other measurements because they give you a picture of what a stock's price or sales volume is doing over time. Moving averages (MA) eliminate the fluctuations that can be confusing by smoothing out peaks and valleys of price changes. Charts developed from MAs give you a sense of momentum (or lack of momentum) in price or volume changes. They are used for other aspects of technical analysis, but we'll leave that discussion for Chapter 16. An MA can look at any period, and two periods or more are often combined on the same chart to contrast changes and spot trends.

An MA is easy to calculate, although most charting software or direct access provider platforms will do the work for you. Here's how to calculate a simple moving average (SMA) of these hypothetical stock prices:

15 12 14 19 13 16 11 15 19 18

15 + 12 + 14 + 19 + 13 + 16 + 11 + 15 + 19 + 18 = 152/100 = 15.20

This is the average. To calculate the MA, we add a new price (17) on the end and drop the oldest price (15):

~~15~~ 12 14 19 13 16 11 15 19 18 17

12 + 14 + 19 + 13 + 16 + 11 + 15 + 19 + 18 + 17 = 154/100 = 15.40

Each day, the oldest price drops off, the newest price is added, and the average is recalculated to give you a moving average.

A simple moving average is helpful for a number of trading and investing strategies, but many swing traders want something that is more responsive to current price changes. For this information, they turn to exponential moving averages, or EMAs. These tools take simple moving averages and give more weight to recent price changes. This is important to swing traders since timely changes mean more than historical ones. The calculation is more complicated and it's best to rely on your software to make the calculation.

The benefit of using EMAs is that they respond more quickly to price changes than SMAs do. This is important for swing traders because a stock price increase will raise the EMA sooner (and a price drop will lower the EMA sooner) than using the SMA. When you are using very short-term EMAs, this is important. As the EMA is plotted against the baseline, you will see a buy or sell (short) signal developing. The sooner that signal makes itself apparent, the sooner you are in a position to make a trade decision.

Since swing traders are most interested in what's happening now, they may focus on EMAs of some length for establishing a baseline for a stock. This is where the stock will trade during a good (fairly flat) market for swing traders. The market will drift up and down with little permanent movement in either direction. In this type of market, the swing trader can follow a stock up for several days as it rides the market and

Trading Tip

Exponential moving averages can be plotted on a chart to see how prices have moved over time. One of the strengths of technical analysis is converting data to charts that make it easy to grasp conclusions quickly.

reverse his position and ride the stock back down, taking profits both ways. This is somewhat of an oversimplification, but the process is the same for swing traders: riding a very short trend in either direction.

Channel Surfing

In many cases, a stock will trade between a high and low value rather consistently. These barriers are called support on the low side and resistance on the high side. The area between these two levels is called a *channel*. When a stock breaks through resistance on the high side, it is considered a signal to buy. If a stock drops below its support level on the low side, that's a signal to sell or short. We'll explore these terms and their significance in detail in Chapter 16 when we look at technical analysis.

def•i•ni•tion

Channel is the price zone between resistance and support that a stock will trade in. Depending on the stock, that zone can be wide or narrow. If a stock breaks above the channel, that's a bull signal (moving up), and if it falls below the channel, it's a bear signal (turning down).

This sounds simple, but the trick is identifying the right market conditions and stock for this type of swing trading. While you can plot a strategy that watches short-term averages cross the baseline to determine your entry point, there is no guarantee the stock will follow the swing for you. It could briefly rise and then abruptly reverse course, shattering your strategy.

While swing traders don't usually need to watch every tick of the market like day traders do, it is important to pay attention. Most traders of all varieties use special instructions to their brokers to protect themselves from significant losses. We'll discuss those stock orders and strategies in Chapter 13 and see how they apply in several other chapters.

Full-Time or Part-Time?

Swing trading is not easy, but it may be the best place to start for people just beginning in active trading. It is possible to do swing trading part-time until you get the hang of it. You are not required to watch intraday prices like short-term traders must,

Trading Tip

Swing trading may not sound like a way to make a full-time living, but once you become familiar with the strategy, you'll see its potential and why it is so popular with active traders.

so your level of detailed information doesn't have to be as deep as that of day and momentum traders. You can subscribe to charting services if that information isn't available through your discount broker. In other words, it is possible to part-time swing trade on the cheap.

However, if you are interested in making real money, you must do your trading full-time. Part-time swing traders will only have time to follow a few trades.

While full-time swing traders don't do the dozens or more trades a day that short-term traders manage, they are prepared to take on multiple trades as the market provides opportunities.

What It Is Like to Be a Swing Trader

Professional swing traders, like most other traders, follow a routine in the trading day that prepares them before the market opens, keeps them informed while stocks are trading, and provides a period of reflection and evaluation at the end of the day. The two primary tasks each day are gauging the market sentiment (bull or bear or flat) and finding possible trade candidates. Although markets don't generally reverse their long-term direction quickly, they will bounce back and forth depending on economic and corporate (earnings) news. A market that has been in a general decline can be lifted by good news, and a climbing market can stumble over bad news. String enough good news or bad news together and the market can begin a long-term reversal.

Swing traders are not really concerned with where the market is going to be in six months; they are concerned with what will move the market today or tomorrow. That's the type of news they can make money on because it will lift or depress stocks. When there is not much happening in the market and there is little in the way of economic or corporate news to shake things up, swing traders can use a strategy of riding the rise and fall of stocks within their channel to keep making money if they are clever. Short-term traders may be yawning and wondering where they stored their golf clubs in this type of market.

Market Place
Swing traders don't need to watch every tick of their open trades—standing orders protect against losses. Traders do need to be aware of what's happening in economic and market news for possible trade opportunities.

The other difficult task is identifying good candidates for swing trading. There are a number of strategies—using news of fundamental changes is one—to spot good candidates. Then it's a question of choosing the right stock for the current market conditions. Traders may have a favorite group of stocks that have exhibited in the past a predictable swing pattern. They may also look for new opportunities in sectors that are hot, using exchange-traded funds (see Chapter 8) to work the sector for profits.

As noted previously, some swing traders will stay glued to their charts looking for the right patterns to tell them a swing is underway or about to begin. Without considering what is happening in the world about them, technical analysts run the risk of being blindsided by news that will wreck the swing pattern for better or worse.

Relying solely on fundamental news or technical analysis is fraught with peril. Keeping up on financial and economic news tells traders if the market sentiment is bear or bull. This knowledge is helpful to swing traders because it tells them what to expect in intraday trading. Likewise, ignoring what charts can tell you, especially on days when there is no market push in either direction, means you will miss opportunities.

Weighing the Risks

Although swing traders usually hold a position for one to four days, the truth is they will hold it until in hits the point where the traders believe the potential for reversal is too high and it's time to take a profit—in other words, when the risks outweigh potential future gains. That may come quickly if the price stalls or reverses itself or it can stretch out for several days. Traders will often decide before entering the trade where that point is and plan to exit when the stock hits the target price. This means you'll leave some money on the table when some stocks go up after you exit. However, it also means you will avoid a loss or a much-reduced profit if the stock suddenly does an about-face.

Swing traders, like short-term traders, aren't trying to wring every penny of profit out of every trade. They know that is the riskiest strategy of all. It is better to set a profit goal and capture that and set a maximum loss and exit at or before that profit. This strategy is money management, and it will keep you trading long after high-rollers have lost everything and entered a career in the food service industry.

Margin Call

Greed is the great profit killer. Traders who try to squeeze every penny of profit out of trades will eventually lose more money than they make by having stocks reverse on them when they should have taken an earlier profit and moved on to the next trade.

Greed and fear are the two primary motivating emotions that cause traders to lose all their investing capital. Greed keeps them in trades long after they should have exited, trying to squeeze more profit. Fear makes traders stay with losing trades, hoping they will turn around. Fear makes traders timid when they should be bold and greed makes traders aggressive when they should be cautious. Don't let either of these emotions get in the way of your trading success.

Making an Exit

Many novice traders spend most of their time identifying and buying stocks and don't give enough thought to an exit strategy. In short-term trading, prices can change so quickly traders often set a target profit and when that price is hit, they sell. They absolutely have a maximum loss in mind when they make the trade. If the stock dips to this price, it is automatically sold, thus limiting their loss to a pre-determined amount. Swing traders must have the same discipline with some variations.

Before they enter into the trade, swing traders must determine how much risk they are willing to take. Ask yourself, "How much of a dip in price will I tolerate before closing (selling) my position?" Once you determine this level of risk, don't back off of it. Don't take on more risk in hopes a bad situation will get better—that's how you lose money. You must learn, as the short-term trader must every day, that it is better to take a small loss and move on than to take more risk and lose big.

Trading Tip _____

Many swing traders come up with their own system of ranking trades based on risk and reward. They are willing to take a certain amount of risk for a potential reward; and if the trade doesn't appear to meet that standard, they skip it.

When it comes to a winning trade, the swing trader sometimes has an advantage over the short-term trader. You should have an exit price in mind. However, if the stock keeps rising and is not showing technical signs of slowing down, you can move your exit price up so that profits are locked in. When the stock does show signs of resistance, you can exit. This is a distinct advantage for swing traders: the latitude to let winners run, but keeping an exit price under them to protect their profit. Traders should also stay on top of news that might create a fundamental reason for a price change. Technical analysis is a wonderful tool, but it can't predict the CEO of the company being charged with cooking the books.

The Importance of Research

Short-term traders have little need for research. They don't care what company they are trading or what it does. Swing traders, however, do benefit from research. Their research is focused on identifying potential trade candidates, which means finding stocks that may be ripe for an upturn or downturn in price due to an economic or fundamental trigger. They are not attempting to calculate what the stock's price will be in a year or six months or even six weeks. Swing traders are interested in stocks that look like they could move today or tomorrow.

Market Place

Every three months, companies report quarterly earnings. This is a time when stocks can rise, but more likely a time they can get hammered if the market is not happy with their earnings report.

For example, when large bellwether stocks like Microsoft or Intel report earnings, other technology stocks may rise or fall based on how well or poorly the news is received by the market. Swing traders may know that a certain stock or group of stocks reacts to news of certain industry leaders, so they trade these stocks rather than the industry leaders. In other cases, news of mergers, buyouts, initial public offerings, and other major market news may create opportunities.

Playing It Risky

Most traders try to find opportunities for the most reward with the least risk; however, there is always some risk. Traders calculate the amount of risk relative to the potential reward to determine if a trade is in their best interest (this is true of investors also). Taking a risk is not a bad strategy if the trader knows the risks and believes the potential reward is large enough to justify the trade. Novices and traders who succumb to greed and fear will take wild risks that are often disproportionate to the potential reward. Worse yet, they will enter trades with no understanding of the risk or a misunderstanding of what the potential reward is.

Margin Call

Going against the market is always risky, but it can be rewarding. The market is not always right, and it doesn't always react appropriately. However, your trade can't change the market. Even when the market is wrong, it is still the market and you must live by its direction.

Swing traders can take calculated risks when the opportunity presents itself in hopes of capturing a much larger profit than they might normally expect. One of the popular calculated risks is taking a contrarian position, or going against the market: you buy when everyone else is selling and sell when everyone else is buying. Experienced traders will employ this strategy around a fundamental news trigger with the idea that the market often overreacts. Some fundamental news triggers include mergers, acquisitions, initial public offerings, restructurings, and so on.

For example, an announcement of a merger of two leading companies in an industry can create a quick price bubble for some stocks in the same industry, which can deflate when the excitement cools. A clever swing trader might notice that the market is bidding up several stocks (thinking they might be acquisition candidates in an industry consolidation) beyond what was reasonable. Whether the stocks are candidates or not, it is likely that it will be some time before any other announcements are made.

If swing traders believe the potential reward is significant, they can short one or more of the overpriced stocks and wait for the air to come out of the price. If their strategy is correct, traders and others who rode the price up will sell and the price will fall. The further it falls, the more money swing traders make. Of course, if the swing traders are wrong and the price holds or continues to rise, they will have to cover their position for a loss.

This discussion has focused on stocks to keep the explanations simple and to emphasize the tools and techniques. Swing traders can use other types of securities, too, such as exchange-traded funds. We'll go over those in Chapter 7.

The Least You Need to Know

- ◆ Swing traders may hold a position for up to several days.
- ◆ Swing traders use both fundamental and technical analysis.
- ◆ Entry and exit points are extremely important to a swing trader's success.
- ◆ Swing traders can control risk by choosing trades that fit their risk profile.

Chapter **5**

Position and Trend Trading

In This Chapter

- ◆ Position trading as a form of active trading
- ◆ Benefits and drawbacks of position trading
- ◆ Riding the trend
- ◆ All about arbitrage

Position trading and trend trading are extensions of the active trading philosophy of grabbing profits, then exiting the trade. The only difference is the time period. Some call position and trend trading short-term investing. True investors will generally stick with a good company as long as nothing has fundamentally changed, even if the stock price has dropped due to market conditions. Position traders won't wait for companies to have a better price in the market. They are focused on stock price alone. Price trends that may annoy buy-and-hold investors can be profit machines for position and trend traders.

Another form of active trading that is less well known outside the industry is arbitrage trading. Arbitrage trading can be relatively risk-free or quite edgy, depending on which form you try. The varieties of arbitrage trading allow for holding strategies that range from a very short duration to much longer.

Position Trading Defined

Position trading is the most laid-back form of active trading. If you think of day trading as a frantic grab for profits during the market day, position trading is capturing a stock at the beginning of an upward (or downward) price trend and riding it up as far as it will go. As long as the stock's price continues to rise and shows no signs of halting, position traders sit tight. When traders see signs of weakening momentum, they take steps to protect existing profits and prepare to exit.

> **Market Place**
>
> Position trading is another tool that active traders have in their arsenal. Traders should not ignore it just because the longer holding periods seem dangerous and unnecessary.

Obviously, the longer the price trend continues, the more profit position traders make. Position traders have no predetermined hold period. The price of the security controls the hold. If traders are clever, they will take their profits just before the trend collapses or runs out of momentum. It is difficult to know exactly when this will happen, so position traders watch weekly technical analysis charts for specific events that suggest it is time to throw in the towel.

The trend may last a week, a month, or many months. Technical indicators play a big role in keeping the trader informed about pending trouble or price changes. Moving averages (see Chapter 4) play an important role in position trading as reference points. Major securities' indexes also are used to spot changes in price trends.

Like swing traders, position traders expose themselves to the risk of time. The longer you hold a security, the greater risk there is that a company or an economic event will overtake the stock and destroy your trading strategy. That is why position traders need to keep current on events that may have an impact on their positions.

 Trading Tip _____

Position trading is definitely something you can do on a part-time basis. It is much less intense and requires fewer technical resources. Some research is involved in the front end and that can be done after your day job. There are few trades to enter and you can start with just one or two positions.

The Opportunities

The point of active trading is to take profits and exit trades before price changes take profits back from you. Position trading is no different from other forms of active trading in its goal. It simply is another tool that allows active traders to "let profits run" when a security is on a price-changing trend. While many people think only in terms of buying low and selling high, traders always consider the other side of trading, which is selling high and buying low. *Short selling* is an effective tool for the position trader since downward price trends are as profitable as upward price trends.

Position traders look for securities that can move over longer periods. Stocks are good candidates, although other securities also work. Stocks are preferred by many active

def•i•ni•tion

Short selling is a trading strategy that seeks to profit when the price of a stock falls. Traders "borrow" shares from their broker and sell them. When the price drops, the trader buys the shares back at the lower price and returns them to his broker. The difference between selling high and buying low is profit.

traders for all the same reasons other traders prefer them: liquidity, ready markets, abundance of information, and so on. Stocks can also be linked or paired with major indexes in charting programs, which is an important strategy in identifying candidates for position trading. More about this later.

Because there is no product life to stocks—as there is on many derivatives, such as options and futures—position traders could keep a trade open as long as they wanted. To be faithful to the position-trading strategy, you would close out your trade as soon as the profits show signs of evaporating, but that could be days, weeks, or months.

The Risks on the Upside

Position trading opens you to the risks of time. While short-term trading has its own set of risks, it avoids the risk of time by closing out all trades at the end of each day. This prevents any bad company or economic news from hurting the traders after the market closes. Swing traders have some exposure to the risks of time, but it is usually limited to a few days at most. The longer traders hold a trade open, the greater the risk that something will happen to destroy their strategies.

Position traders typically monitor daily and weekly charts to watch for potential price trend reversals. When the technical analysis signals a possible reversal, clever position traders take their profits and move on to the next trade. However, technical analysis

Margin Call

Active traders should practice trade with their brokerage account using a variety of buy and sell orders until becoming familiar with how these work. Knowing when and how to use these market orders is mandatory.

charts won't predict all the bad things that can happen to a company. A major product recall, unfavorable court rulings, allegations of fraud, poor earnings, and so on can wreak havoc on a company's finances and stock.

When stock prices change on bad news, they can change dramatically and move suddenly. Even with standing stock orders, you may find yourself selling in a market that can't fill your order at the price you want, so you sell for much less than you hoped to get.

The Risks on the Downside

Short selling is one way position traders make money in a bearish market or by playing a bearish stock sector. Traders are counting on the downward price trend continuing to make profits. Position traders will sell stocks they have borrowed from their brokers that appear to be heading downhill. As long as the stock continues to go down, position traders are in a good spot to make money. When it looks like the stock is about to bottom out, traders buy the stock at the reduced price and replace the shares they borrowed from their brokers.

While it sounds like an easy way to make money (in a bearish market, there are many opportunities), short selling as a position trader has its risks. Like all short sellers, position traders must be aware of the risks should the stock reverse direction and begin to rise in price. You suddenly might have to buy the stock at a much higher price than you sold it. To replace the stock that you borrowed from your broker and then sold short, you must buy shares on the open market. If the stock is rising rapidly in price, you might find it difficult to buy replacement shares at a good price.

Market Place
When choosing the stocks you are going to trade, keep in mind how difficult or easy it will be to get in or out of your position. There may be some attractive opportunities in small-cap stocks, but the risks may outweigh the potential rewards.

Position traders must be careful about the stocks they pick for shorting. In most cases, you are better off shorting a large-cap, widely traded stock. The reason is that if the price reverses and begins to rise, you'll want the stock to be widely traded so you won't have trouble buying replacement shares. When stock prices begin to rise and short sellers can't find enough replacement shares—as would be the case with small-cap stocks (stocks of small companies)—they bid the price even higher. This is known as a short squeeze, and it can result in a disaster for the short position trader.

Why Position Trading Is Not Investing

The distinction between position trading and investing may seem tenuous at best. Many would say that any holding beyond a year is investing and it is possible for position traders to hold a trade that long. However, beyond the holding period, there is a difference between position trading and investing.

Investors are not concerned with daily or weekly price changes. They look for companies that are building future value through their business model. Investors believe that a company's stock price is a reflection of its ability to generate earnings and dividends for shareholders. As the company gains market share and grows new product lines, the revenue will rise and earnings will increase. This will ultimately lead to a higher stock price, if not now, then at some point in the future.

> **Trading Tip**
>
> Short-term trading relies exclusively, and swing trading almost exclusively, on technical indicators for trade signals. Position trading, however, blends both technical and fundamental analysis to compensate for the long hold time.

Traders don't care about earnings or dividends except as they might affect immediate stock prices. Poor earnings can mean a lower stock price, so position traders keep an eye on fundamental news. However, traders have no interest in a future payoff. Current profit is the goal, and only those actions that affect today's stock prices are of concern. Position traders want to see the stock continue to rise, but aren't willing to sit through a slump in price, while investors will if they still believe in the company. As soon as traders receive any indication that the stock's price is about to reverse direction (from technical analysis or fundamental news), they will exit the trade.

The Trend Is Your Friend

Position trading is often called trend trading. The idea behind trend trading is that once prices establish a movement in one direction they tend to continue in that direction until they meet resistance or a fundamental factor changes. This acknowledges the psychology of market prices and proves correct more often than not. Traders say the trend is your friend because you want to go with the movement of prices, not work against it.

Trends can be short, medium, or long in duration. Position trading falls in the medium and long range. It doesn't matter which direction prices are going; the important work of the trader is to identify the trend and jump on as soon as the trend is confirmed. When the trend begins to falter, traders should exit with their profits.

The trend is your friend until the end, when you want to abandon it quickly to prevent prices from reversing course and eroding your profits.

Unlike short-term traders who have a profit target, position or trend traders are willing to let their profits run. However, they protect their profits with automatic sell orders that follow the price of the stock as it rises. (More about these protective orders in Chapter 13.) Because a stock may reverse its price run for a variety of reasons that can't be seen, it is wise to stay tuned in to technical and fundamental indicators that may signal a reversal.

> **Margin Call**
>
> While the strongest proponents follow technical analysis almost like a religion, it is not an exact science. Technical analysis can show you what has happened in the past and make assumptions about the future. Any look into the future is a sophisticated projection of the past, no more.

Arbitrage Trading Explained

If there were a way you could make profits without risk, you would probably want to know about it, wouldn't you? That sounds like a pitch from a late-night infomercial. However, it describes an actual form of trading known as pure or true arbitrage. Arbitrage trading is a form of trend or swing trading that is distinctive in its strategy.

True arbitrage involves trading assets that concurrently trade at different prices on different markets. You buy the asset on the market where it is at the lower price and sell it on the market where it is selling at the higher price. Assuming the spread between the two prices is sufficient to cover your trading costs, you have a profit with no risk.

> **def•i•ni•tion**
>
> **Market makers** are broker dealer firms that make a market for a particular stock by holding a certain number of shares in inventory. They display bid and ask quotes—offering to buy or sell the stock. The Nasdaq (see Chapter 6) has more than 500 market maker firms that keep the exchange working.

Do such trades exist in the real world? Yes, they do. However (you knew there would be a catch, didn't you?), the reality is that most active traders have little chance of capturing pure arbitrage trades. The reason is when these inequities pop up in the market, they last a very short time. Major institution investors and *market makers* with sophisticated software are usually the first to spot them. Many employ specialized software that trolls the markets looking for arbitrage opportunities. Programmed trading executes orders without human intervention when the trade meets certain qualifications.

The differences in prices are often very small, so huge orders using a large amount of leverage are employed to turn the opportunity into a money maker. Most active traders lack the technical and financial resources to compete in pure arbitrage trading situations. That doesn't mean there aren't other arbitrage opportunities for them to explore.

Other Arbitrage Opportunities

Since pure arbitrage opportunities are rare for active traders, they must look to other types of trades. The most common type of arbitrage employed by active traders is generally called risk arbitrage. Risk arbitrage takes several forms, but it always involves trading securities with a price inequality. The difference is the securities are not the same as they are in pure arbitrage. You still buy one and sell the other—the key is understanding the relationship between the two securities and how the price inequity works.

Trading two securities that are similar or related in some way is not the same as trading the same security at two different prices. That's, in part, where the risk comes into the trade. The securities are related but not the same and will react in ways that may not be expected. However, if you understand the dynamic of the relationship—more about that next—you can profitably engage in risk arbitrage.

Margin Call

The longer it takes arbitrage trades to settle or reach profitability, the more risky they become. Time exposes the trades to the possibility of something going wrong that will ruin the trade.

Another significant difference between pure and risk arbitrage is that while pure arbitrage usually settles out quickly, risk arbitrage can take days or weeks to balance the price of the two securities. Because the securities are different, the market dynamics to bring them into balance may not be as strong. This is not extra time to study the trade, but time for the trade to mature. In many risk arbitrage trades, you will still need to act with some speed to get in before prices of the securities narrow the gap.

Merger and Acquisition Arbitrage

This is the most common form of arbitrage and one that active traders can cash in on if they are looking for the opportunities and are willing to move quickly. Typically, a company will announce that it plans to buy another for a price that is some premium over where the stock is currently trading. Two things happen: the acquiring company's stock often drops because of the risk the deal won't go through, and the acquired company's stock will rise, but not all the way to the offered level. Investors will hold back because of the risk that the deal won't happen.

> **Market Place**
>
> Mergers seem to come in bunches. Active traders who follow this type of arbitrage stay on top of financial news and watch for other opportunities if an industry is going through a consolidation.

The active trader will immediately short the acquiring company and buy the acquired company. If things happen as they should, the acquiring company's stock will drop and the trader can profit from shorting it. In addition, the acquired company's stock will rise when investors realize the deal will go through and the trader profits there, too.

Using Options and Other Derivatives

Options on stocks form the basis for dozens of strategies for active traders interested in arbitrage trading. Here you are trading a derivative and a stock in tandem to accomplish your goal. Stock options, for example, are tied to the underlying securities. As the price of the stock moves, so should the option. When there is a discrepancy, active traders can step in and profit.

If the stock is trading on the market lower than its options seem to indicate (meaning the options market believes a higher price is warranted), the active trader can buy shares of the stock and execute an options strategy that effectively sells the shares at the higher price. (The options market is beyond the scope of this book. You should have an understanding of it before attempting this type of trade.)

Pairs Trading

Pairs trading is a type of arbitrage that exploits the relationship between two securities that tend to move together most of the time. Active traders are looking for securities that are highly correlated—that is, they move in tandem to the same influences most of the time. A common example is Ford and General Motors. However, you can also use market indexes, options, futures, and other securities. What is important is the relationship. The opportunity for profit comes in when these highly correlated securities diverge in price.

When that happens, the active trader can short the security that is overpriced and buy the security that is underpriced relative to the pair's historical relationship. The active trader is counting on a correction that will bring the two securities back into track with one another. This will mean the overpriced security will fall in price and the trader will profit on the short trade. It will also mean the underpriced security will rise in price and the trader can sell for a profit. The risk is that the two will either not converge or converge at a new level that makes the trades unprofitable.

Index Arbitrage Trading

Market indexes such as the S&P 500, the Dow, the Nasdaq Composite, and many others are also the basis for popular trading vehicles (see Chapter 6). All of the major and some of the minor indexes are covered by mutual funds and exchange-traded funds. In addition, you can buy options and futures contracts based on the indexes. With each index represented by multiple securities there is plenty of opportunity for arbitrage players to find pricing inequities. These differences may not always be large enough to make a profit, but this is fertile ground for arbitrage traders.

Create Your Own Arbitrage

Traders with a keen understanding of derivatives (options and futures) and their pricing relationship with the underlying asset can create an artificial arbitrage opportunity. By utilizing the product characteristics of options and futures, traders can construct arbitrage (buying at one price and selling at another) when the pricing relationship with the underlying asset is not as it should be.

Up until recently, such trades were only available to hedge fund managers, institutional investors, and other traders with deep pockets and access to the information and technology to make them happen. The Internet has opened the door for many active investors to execute complicated trades based on the same information previously available only to a certain class of investors and traders.

> **Trading Tip**
>
> Once you have mastered the relationships between assets and derivatives, you are on your way to building you own trading model. Test it first before risking your money to see if it works under market conditions.

Live price information and sophisticated trading models combined with high-powered personal computers have made this sophisticated form of trading possible. Traders with extensive knowledge of derivatives can put that knowledge to use constructing buy and sell models that effectively give them a low-risk arbitrage trade.

That level of trading is beyond the scope of an introductory book to active trading. However, if you are interested in a career as an active trader you should know that you are not limited to simple transactions that make up the bulk of the examples in this book.

Don't Try This at Home

Arbitrage trading is a form of active trading that experienced traders should investigate. You can make a good living without it, but arbitrage is another tool for making money as an active trader and one you should consider if you plan to make a career of trading. However, it is not the place to start your active trading career. Arbitrage trading is for more advanced traders who have some experience in the markets and are comfortable with complex securities and complicated trades.

The Least You Need to Know

- ◆ Position traders may ride a trade for weeks or months, depending on how long the profit continues to grow.

- ◆ Position trading has the potential for large profits, but it can also tie up a traders' capital for lengthy periods.

- ◆ Position trading exposes you to the risks of time, in that unforeseen events may destroy profits.

- ◆ Arbitrage trading is a complex but powerful tool that involves an intimate knowledge of securities and pricing.

Part 2

Markets and Products for Active Trading

Active traders have traditionally mined the equities markets for profit opportunities and many still prefer stocks as their favored security. However, the trading world has expanded in both size and product choice. Today's active traders have global markets at their disposal thanks to trading opportunities in foreign exchanges.

In addition, the financial markets have exploded with a wide variety of products that lend themselves to active trading. Product originators have recognized the importance of the active trading market and created securities that offer the liquidity and leverage that active traders demand.

Chapter 6

Today's Stock Markets

In This Chapter

- ◆ Major U.S. stock exchanges expanding to meet global competition
- ◆ Foreign exchanges threaten U.S. dominance of financial markets
- ◆ After-hours trading no longer a marginal activity
- ◆ Merging of markets may mean some form of continuous trading

The stock markets have come a long way from the days when stockbrokers had a lock on commissions and dictated terms of doing business. Beginning with deregulation in 1975, the financial services industry has exploded with new products, new services, lower prices, and technology that puts vast amounts of information in investors' hands. While the service providers such as stockbrokers and financial planners evolved, the stock exchanges themselves trailed in innovation. However, when these bastions of American capitalism began reinventing themselves they did it in a big way. The Nasdaq, the first purely electronic market, led the way with an innovative trading platform that attracted investors interested in young, high-tech companies at just the right time.

The high-tech, Internet stock market explosion of the late 1990s propelled the Nasdaq into the financial big leagues. The venerable New York Stock Exchange has reached across the Atlantic seeking European partners to expand its reach, while the American Stock Exchange is home to the hot new exchange-traded funds. These are but a few of the examples of innovation in the face of consumer demand and global competition facing U.S. exchanges.

The Major Stock Exchanges

The New York Stock Exchange (NYSE), Nasdaq, and the American Stock Exchange (ASE) are the major national stock and bond exchanges. The exchanges have their own regulations and listing requirements. The regulations cover trading activities and financial reporting of listed companies. The exchanges monitor trading patterns to look for stock manipulation.

The NYSE

The New York Stock Exchange is the most prestigious securities trading center in the world. Its roots go back to 1792. The exchange is synonymous with the stock market and it is often referred to as "the Big Boar." Although it was in danger of falling behind technologically, the exchange has made major moves in the past decade to upgrade its trading system to state of the art.

Trading Tip _____

Like the Nasdaq, the NYSE is moving toward more electronic matching of orders and less reliance on human interaction to complete trades. Let's face facts—humans are just too slow and prone to error. Electronic markets don't become distracted, get the flu, or take vacations.

The Nasdaq

The Nasdaq (the name was formerly an acronym, but now is the official name of the exchange) is an electronic market where buyers and sellers are matched through a complex computer network. Designated brokers act as market makers for individual stocks to ensure that the system functions smoothly and fairly. Many of the stocks listed on the Nasdaq are younger, high-tech companies.

The American Stock Exchange

The American Stock Exchange was in danger of being lost in the race between the Nasdaq and the NYSE, but in recent years has experienced a rebirth through the issue of new types of securities such as exchange-traded funds.

Major Exchanges Expanded

The major U.S. stock exchanges were long regarded as the financial centers of the world. Indeed, a bull market that ran from 1990 to 2000, the longest in history, corresponded to a period of economic prosperity that made that decade one of the most profitable for investors in the stock market's history. Political and economic instability around the world only highlighted how attractive investing in America was. Foreign investors also began to push innovations in their markets. Stock markets in the Far East from Japan to China experienced rapid growth, as did European markets, thanks in part to the adoption of the euro by a number of the European Union countries as a common currency.

However, U.S. exchanges began to see that like the companies that traded on their floors, globalization was in their future also. Thanks to technology, geographic barriers to trading in foreign financial markets disappeared. As foreign markets opened their exchanges to U.S. companies and investors, U.S. exchanges saw a major challenge to their dominance as the financial leaders of the world.

> **Market Place**
>
> The financial markets of the United States may feel threatened, but it is doubtful that many other major exchanges around the world could have survived the recession of 2000 to 2003 and the tragedy of September 11, 2001, and come back with one of the strongest bull markets on record.

U.S. Exchanges Moving Abroad

Many of the largest U.S. companies count most of their sales from foreign operations (for example, Coca Cola takes in about 70 percent of its sales from places other than its U.S. operations). The companies have expanded around the world and those operations are much larger than the original domestic business. In every sense of the word, these companies are global or multinational companies that happened to be headquartered in the United States. In the same manner, U.S. stock exchanges have gone through a period of domestic consolidation and global outreach to expand their reach and resources.

Nasdaq attempted to buy the London Stock Exchange, but failed to win shareholder support. In the meantime, the exchange has merged with the Boston Stock Exchange and acquired other companies that provide a variety of services and products to the investment community. It is reasonable to expect Nasdaq will continue pursuing a global stock exchange. Nasdaq owns a piece of OMX, which is a holding group operating stock exchanges in several Scandinavian countries. It has opened an office in Beijing, China—a country with a growing investing class and a volatile stock market.

Margin Call

As global markets expand, so do stock scams. Traders should be doubly cautious following recommendations about foreign securities from sources they don't know. Checking on foreign stocks is difficult and some exchanges in less mature markets are little more than organized gambling.

The New York Stock Exchange has managed to, in their words, form the largest, most liquid exchange group. Known as NYSE Euronext, the group was introduced in spring of 2007 and combines the NYSE with Euronext. According to their website: "NYSE Euronext, which brings together six cash equities [Paris, Lisbon, Brussels, Amsterdam, NYSE, NYSE Arca] exchanges in five countries and six derivatives exchanges [Paris, London, Brussels, Amsterdam, Lisbon, NYSE Arca], is a world leader for listings, trading in cash equities, equity and interest rate derivatives, bonds and the distribution of market data."

The NYSE Euronext has strategic relationships with the Tokyo Stock Exchange and the National Stock Exchange of India, both enormously important financial centers in the global market. With this global expansion, the NYSE has joined the major U.S. companies listed on its exchange. It is now realizing a significant contribution to its gross revenues and operating income from the Euronext operations.

Growing Due to Competition

While neither major U.S. exchange owns a large stake or is in partnership with a stock exchange from an Asian or Pacific Rim country, it seems just a matter of time before such a deal is cemented. NYSE's span now covers more time zones than any exchange. It offers a wide variety of financial products both domestic and foreign, which allows investors to diversify across geo-political boundaries—an important feature in today's volatile world. Investing in foreign markets was once considered a high-risk bet. However, with well-established and regulated international markets in many countries, this doesn't need to be the case.

It may still be difficult to find the level of disclosure investors are accustomed to in the U.S. market; however, investing in developed and many developing countries can be a reasonably sound move. There are still risks that investing in domestic equities do not have, such as currency fluctuations and the potential of political instability in some countries.

Currency risk is the danger that you will lose money in exchanging dollars for the currency of a foreign stock. For example, if you buy a stock in one of the European Union countries that uses the euro, the U.S. dollar is converted to euros at the time of the purchase. When you sell the stock, it is quoted in euros, which must be converted to U.S. dollars. If between the time of purchase and sale of the stock, the euro has gained value against the dollar, you will get fewer dollars per euro. The loss in currency exchange could consume a significant portion of your profit.

When these factors are reflected as risk premium in foreign stocks, it makes an investment potentially more profitable (and correspondingly, more risky).

> **Market Place**
>
> Currency risk has become apparent even to supermodels. The news media was quick to pick up a story of a Brazilian super model who insisted on being paid in euros by a U.S. agency because the U.S. dollar was so weak.

One of the other benefits for all investors, but in particular active traders, is that the trading day is extended. After-hours trading in U.S. markets (discussed in more detail later in this chapter) does not yet provide the volume or liquidity that open-market trading does. However, thanks to multiple time zones and technology, active traders can participate in open-market trading that is not confined to what is convenient for U.S. exchanges. Active trading in foreign markets is not for beginners, but it illustrates the benefits (and pitfalls) globalization of financial markets offers to those who are willing to extend their trading horizons. We'll look at foreign markets and the risks and opportunities in more detail in Chapter 9.

Global Markets

Not too many years ago, if the U.S. stock market sneezed, the foreign markets got a cold. The dominance and wealth concentrated in the U.S. market set the tempo for other markets around the world. That has changed. As foreign markets and economies have grown at rates much faster than our own, events overseas begin to affect the U.S. market. This is particularly true of the Nikkei, Japan's stock market; the

Singapore Stock Exchange; Hong Kong Stock Exchange; and China's stock markets. These exchanges aren't necessarily open to U.S. investors, but major movement, especially negative news, can ripple through U.S. markets.

One of the prices of globalization is financial markets that may become more sensitive to events in other countries. This is not always a bad thing because it gives investors the opportunity to diversify geographically in ways that have not been possible in the past. It also allows active investors to capitalize on the relationship among markets for sophisticated trades. The other benefit to U.S. consumers is that this competition has pushed the major exchanges to become more user oriented. The exchanges are working harder to introduce products and services to retain their existing customer base. The exchanges also understand that many foreign investors still look to the United States as the most financially and politically stable country in the world. Attracting those investors becomes easier with a global footprint.

> **Trading Tip** _____
>
> Globalization has not always been a good thing for U.S. workers as hundreds of thousands of jobs have moved overseas to cheaper labor markets. Just as the Industrial Revolution drew the population out of rural America and threatened agriculture, the shift from manufacturing to information processing is threatening the manufacturing heartland of America.

Foreign Markets Seen as Threat

Active traders and regular investors are seeing global markets open to them in increasing numbers. Several online brokerage firms offer direct access to foreign exchanges through their trading systems. Despite the additional risks, trading in foreign stocks is often a good idea if you are an experienced hand. Beginning active traders would do well to stick to domestic stock markets until they have some solid experience.

> **Market Place**
>
> The extent to which active traders can use foreign markets depends on how much market information is readily available and how reliable that information is.

However, trading on foreign markets opens some interesting possibilities given time zone differences and how the markets react to news. As those foreign markets become more open, they will add enhancements to attract American and other investors and traders. Traders create volume and liquidity for markets, although they are often called speculators. For some foreign markets, that volume and liquidity is just what is needed to provide a better trading environment for all customers. In other markets such as China's rapidly growing exchanges, the explosive volatility can be a killer. Whether those markets will mature into less of a high-rolling speculator's guessing game remains to be seen.

It is important to remember that active traders will succeed when they can predict stock or market movements, whether it is ultra-short up or downticks or longer swings. Active traders don't guess. Trades are made on information and an understanding of how stocks or markets move and why. Wildly volatile stocks or markets that move irrationally because of an undisciplined market or economic/political upheaval make it difficult for traders to see where the movement is going.

Pacific Markets Growing

The Pacific markets, stock exchanges on the other side of the Pacific Ocean, have exhibited the fastest growth in recent years. Japan's Nikkei is the equivalent of the NYSE on that side of the world. It has grown up following World War II to be a major financial consideration in the global economy. Its daily results (the Nikkei 225 Index) are reported along with the Dow, Nasdaq 100, and S&P 500 as another major market. When Japan's economy was in trouble, the Nikkei suffered losses and those ripples were felt in the U.S. market. A number of Japanese firms do significant business in the United States (think electronics and cars, for example) and difficulties in that economy and stock market can have repercussions in the United States. Active traders who make buy-sell decisions on economic news need to understand how important these relationships are and learn to exploit them.

The stock exchanges in China are growing at a tremendous rate, just like the rest of the economy. U.S. markets have already felt the backlash of problems in Chinese markets. The idea of investing is still relatively new, as is the idea of a middle class with income to invest. Their market is highly volatile and at one point became a huge bubble that popped. Values plunged as Chinese investors learned a lesson that speculative markets rise and fall. The huge sell off caused a precipitous drop in U.S. markets on fears that the sell off fever would spread or Chinese investors would sell some of the huge cache of U.S. Treasury bonds they hold.

European Stock Exchanges Important

As witnessed by the NYSE's partnership with Euronext and Nasdaq's ownership of OMX, European stock exchanges also play an important role in the global financial markets. The European exchanges are gaining strength thanks to the adoption of the euro as a common currency among 13 countries on the European Union. The adoption of a common currency helps eliminate the currency exchange risk of trading in foreign stocks for residents in those 13 countries, as well as U.S. traders because there is only one currency conversion to be concerned with when trading stocks from these 13 countries instead of 13 currencies. Because the value of the euro is tied to the economies of multiple countries, it tends to be more stable. Even though the exchange rate between the U.S. dollar and the euro fluctuates, it is less volatile than the currency of some individual countries. This relative stability helps U.S. traders by reducing the currency risk and giving traders a single value (the euro) to follow.

The Importance of Global Markets

There is a theory that capital seeks out the best return and will go where that return is available. Think of it as a natural selection process for money. When a sector of the stock market is hot, that's where people sometimes irrationally put their money. For active traders, opening global financial markets means more places to find opportunities that may not be over-bought or oversold. If domestic markets are flat, foreign markets may be where traders can find the activity they need. Opening global markets is a two-way street. As countries grow their economies to the point where there is a significant investing class (people with more than enough income to meet basic needs), those people will be looking for places to put their money.

> **Trading Tip**
>
> Because active traders range from those making almost instant trades to others with longer holding periods, opening global markets opens the challenges up to foreign traders. Competition will make products and services more responsive to traders' needs.

Electronic Communication Networks Change Everything

When trading stocks was controlled exclusively by humans, many of the markets now opening to U.S. traders were not viable for short-term transactions. Short-term trading has changed dramatically in U.S. markets also thanks to Congress-mandated Electronic Communication Networks, or ECNs. Authorized in 1998, these networks allow investors to bypass traditional stock exchanges and enter trades directly. ECNs match orders (buyers and sellers) and post orders for others who subscribe to the network to see.

The ECNs reduce expenses and offer a faster way to trade since there is no middle-man. The Nasdaq computerized ordering system could be thought of as the first ECN. As the industry has evolved, traders who need access to live price information and virtually instant execution have pushed ECNs to offer more services to individual investors. Active investors who trade on very short-term cycles should use a trading platform that operates with an ECN. Routing trades through any type of structure before execution is too time consuming, even if it can be done in less than a minute.

ECNs offer price transparency to a degree not previously available to individual investors. This price transparency allows short-term traders to see what orders are pending and where other traders believe the security is headed. For example, if the short-term trader sees sell orders building, that is a strong signal which direction the price is likely to head. Customers of traditional stock brokerage accounts seldom have access to this level of detail.

Advanced trading platforms take advantage of ECNs' execution speed, price trans-parency, and other information to help short-term customers see the whole market for a particular stock or stock sector. This vision along with other tools allows short-term traders to make quick decisions based on price movement and the direction of perceived demand.

Active traders interested in foreign markets will find that ECNs and advanced trading platforms give them access to many oppor-

> **Margin Call**
>
> When selecting a broker for your active trading account, be sure you understand how it works with the ECN. If you are doing very short-term trading, you must have direct access to the ECN through your account. Otherwise, you are e-mailing orders to your broker and that's too slow.

tunities. One area of active trading on a global scale is in the foreign currency markets, or forex. This market operates 24 hours a day, six days a week. Price transparency and rapid execution bring global and after-hours trading to anyone's computer. More about the forex market in Chapter 9.

After-Hours Trading

For a number of years, institutional investors and some high–net worth investors had been able to trade stocks after the close of the U.S. stock markets. Thanks to technol-ogy and pressure from individual investors, the exchanges now allow individuals to trade stocks after the markets have officially closed for the day. Known as after-hours trading, the practice has been growing in recent years, but is still a tiny fraction of the volume transacted during regular business hours. While opportunities exist for active traders in the after-hours market, it is also instructive in what may be coming in the near future—markets open on an expanded schedule. There are many reasons U.S. exchanges should stay open longer, including the competition from foreign exchanges. Expanded live hours would better accommodate American investors and traders not shackled to a stockbroker's office to manage their accounts.

After-Hours Trading Explained

Before advanced trading platforms and online investing, traders were stuck with relying on stockbrokers to enter trades for them. Traders are now in control of the process and can enter trades and manage their account directly thanks to the technology of trading platforms. With this access and the ability to settle accounts electronically, there was not much reason to keep individuals out of the after-hours trading market that institutional investors used.

After-hours trading begins at the close of the live markets at 4 P.M. EST and runs until 6:30 P.M. There is also a pre-market trading session that runs from 8 to 9:30 A.M. before the live market opens. During these trading sessions, you can trade any stock listed on the appropriate exchange. Note: you can enter an order to buy or sell at the opening of the next live session any time, but this is not the same as after-hours trading.

> **Market Place**
>
> If you are interested in after-hours trading, it will pay you to shop for a broker that supports that market. Some brokerage houses offer special services for active brokers and include after-hours trading services in the package. Commissions, fees, and other considerations may be different from live market trading, so be sure you understand the terms.

It is smart to stick with limit orders (see Chapter 13) in most cases (many trading platforms won't accept any other kind during after-hours trading). Realize that if your order is not filled during after-hours trading, either after the close of the market or before the market opens, it may or may not carry over to the next session of live trading. Check with your broker for their policy.

After-Hours Trading Challenges

The after-hours market can be a very volatile environment because major news stories are often released after the market closes for the day or before it opens. For example, earnings reports, especially if they are a surprise, may come out after the market closes. Likewise, news of mergers or other significant events that could move individual stocks or the whole market is often released after the market is closed. This illustrates an important fact: after-hours market trading is frequently news driven.

Like the live stock market, after-hours trading is dominated by large institutional investors, but more so. There are fewer "amateur" investors trading, so your competitors are professional mutual fund, pension, and insurance account traders. These traders move large amounts of stock and can have a dramatic impact on an individual stock's price. These professionals may also have access to information you may not possess. When they move for or against a stock, things happen in a hurry.

With most advanced trading platforms, short-term traders can see what is happening as it unfolds and react. That is not always the case with after-hours trading. When only institutional investors could trade after hours, they enjoyed anonymity. That secrecy is still there since many companies won't let you see any quotes except from the ECN it uses. Even if you can see quotes from other ECNs, you may not be able to trade on them or with other investors using competing systems. This means you may not get the best price for your order.

Part of this problem is related to a larger problem in the after-hours market and that is the lack of liquidity. In this sense, lack of liquidity means finding a willing buyer or seller for a particular stock. Unlike live market trading, where almost any stock can be easily bought or sold, the after-hours market does not have the volume to assure that will be the case. Many stocks may not trade at all during the after hours. You could be in a situation where you wanted to act quickly on a stock, but could find no buyers or sellers in the after-hours market. Another manifestation of the liquidity issue is larger spreads between the bid and ask prices. This can make it hard to get your order filled at your price.

Margin Call

Liquidity, or lack thereof, is a serious problem for active traders. Active traders are usually responsible for liquidity, but only when there are sufficient numbers of buyers and sellers. Insufficient liquidity in markets where there are only a few buyers and sellers results in poor pricing of securities.

Is the After-Hours Market for You?

Active traders look at the after-hours market with caution. One of the major concerns is the possibility of low liquidity in a stock. Traders rely on being able to get into and out of a stock when they choose. If the market for a particular stock suddenly loses its liquidity because the few interested traders have exited, other traders may be stuck in a bad position or be forced to exit at a price that is not to their liking. During active trading, short-term traders in particular must have a completely liquid market in the stock they are trading.

The after-hours market is particularly ill-suited for quick profit taking except in circumstances of a very active stock. Even then, other factors (potentially wide spreads and unexplained volatility) put short-term traders at a disadvantage over the position they normally hold during a live market. The volume of after-hours trading has never reached more than 1 percent of the daily live market volume of the NYSE, and many brokers report similar numbers for their customers trading after hours.

Some experienced active traders will take positions in the after-hours market; however, beginners should stick to the live market until they have some experience. Most of the activity will happen in the first hour after the live market closes. This is when quarterly earnings are announced and it can make for some interesting activity.

Trading Tip

You can't know a stock's opening price based on the previous close. It will usually be close, but many factors could result in a higher or lower opening price.

Active traders should keep an eye on the after-hours market for a different reason. Trading activity in the after-hours market may give you a clue about what to expect when the market opens for live trading. The operative word here is "may." For many of the reasons listed previously (lack of liquidity, domination of institutional investors, high volatility, and so on), you can't count on an after-hours price carrying over to the opening price for the next live market session.

This is where your observation skills and understanding of the market will work to your advantage. Big movements in a stock during after-hours trading may be a sign that can be read several different ways. Often inexperienced investors will see a big jump in a stock as a sign that they need to get on board, when an experienced trader knows this is the right time to short the stock. Regardless of what happens in the after-hours market, the stock does not have to open at that closing level anymore than it has to open at the closing level from the previous live trading session.

Trading Possible 24/7?

Some market watchers thought that the opening of after-hours trading to individuals combined with the advanced technology of trading platforms and trading networks meant that 24/7 trading was just around the corner. There is no real technology barrier to offering 24/7 or at least 24/5 trading. Before the Internet and electronic networks, trades had to clear within three business days, which was to allow time to process the order, collect money from the customer, and so on. With electronic processing of orders directly to the trading floor and more sophisticated means of settling trades, there is no reason to trade on "banker's hours." However, the lack of interest in after-market trading suggests that it may be a "chicken or the egg" problem.

The volume won't come until more traders are involved, and more traders won't become involved until there is more volume. There may be other equally valid reasons. For traders seeking activity in live markets, foreign markets are trading when U.S. markets are closed. There are 7 to 10 hours' difference between U.S. markets and European markets—they are ahead of us. The Pacific and Asian markets are a day ahead of U.S. markets and many hours' difference.

However, this is just the very short-term outlook. A reality not readily accepted by many of the old hands on Wall Street is that the global financial markets are growing at a tremendous pace and may soon be more of an influence on the financial services industry than in the past. The financial press is full of excited stories from India, Singapore, and other growing economies of the growth of their stock markets. As young people earn more money in those markets, they are learning to invest it, which creates opportunities for active investors in the United States.

The Least You Need to Know

- U.S. markets are pushing technology and geographical borders to win and retain customers.
- Foreign markets threaten U.S. dominance of financial services.
- Foreign markets bring new opportunities and challenges to U.S. traders.
- After-hours trading hasn't gained popular support.

Chapter 7

What Active Traders Trade

In This Chapter

♦ Active traders not limited to stocks

♦ Securities must meet certain requirements

♦ Options and futures: important tools for traders

♦ Currency trading as the last frontier

The outsider perception of active traders, particularly those labeled day traders, is that they play the stock market. That is partly true—stocks are the security of choice for many active traders. However, depending on the traders' expertise, experience, and interests, they may specialize in trading many different types of securities to fit market conditions and opportunities. The different types of securities have unique characteristics that create opportunities and impose limits on the active trader.

Active traders also trade derivatives, such as options and futures. Derivatives are so named because they derive their value from the underlying security.

You'll need a thorough knowledge of how a security or a derivative relates to market influences before including it in your tool kit.

A Whole Range of Securities

A security is another word for any financial instrument that conveys ownership of an asset. For example, a share of common stock gives the holder partial ownership in a corporation. However, securities can also control all or parts of other assets. A bond, an option, and a futures contract are all securities.

Trading Tip

Beginning active traders should master one type of security, usually stocks, before moving on to more complex trading strategies.

The other characteristic of securities is that they can be bought and sold. This is an important point because it is what makes the security a product that can produce a profit for the active trader if used correctly.

The Liquidity Factor

Liquidity is the ability to convert an asset into cash or, in the case of the active trader, the ability to quickly buy or sell a security. One of the reasons active traders prefer stocks is their liquidity. If traders stick with mid- and large-cap stocks, there will almost always be a ready market to buy or sell shares. This assurance makes trading stocks safer in some ways than other securities that may not have the same level of liquidity.

Swing and position traders may be fine with this definition of liquidity for the stocks they trade. In most cases, they only need the ability to get to a position when they want and to exit at the appropriate time. That degree of liquidity is not enough for short-term and momentum traders. Short-term and momentum traders need an extra measure of liquidity that allows them to move into and out of a stock without affecting the price. If a stock is not widely traded (illiquid), short-term traders may change the price with their trades. Short-term traders will make more money if they can get in and out of a stock without affecting the price.

Market Place

Short-term traders may find that market makers working for large firms will attempt to trick novice traders with phony orders in an attempt to move the price in a certain direction.

Traders working Microsoft, for example, will probably not affect the price because the stock is widely held and actively traded. One trader's order isn't going to change the price by itself. However, if you trade lesser-known or not as widely held stocks, your trade may change the price, which could reduce your profit potential. Short-term traders may trade the same stock many times during the day if it presents opportunities, taking small profits each time. This won't work if every trade you enter changes the price, up or down. It will alert other traders of your activity and they will counter with trades of their own. It is often easier to make multiple trades if you can do so without attracting attention to yourself and your trades.

Traders who use other types of securities must be aware of any special rules regarding buying and selling that may be of concern. For example, options' contracts have an expiration date. As that date approaches, the volume of trades in the option may rise or fall depending on whether the option is profitable or not. If you want to trade futures contracts, there are certain rules regarding how much the contract can change in value in one trading day. When the futures' contract moves the maximum amount, trading in that security is halted for the day. This can be a problem for traders caught in a position that requires them to exit. Some futures products avoid this rule, which we'll discuss in more detail in Chapter 9.

The Role of Margin

Margin lets active traders multiply their investment capital with funds borrowed from their brokers. By increasing the amount invested, active traders multiply their profit potential—and their potential loss. The use of margin is not required, but it is a powerful tool that can extend your investment capital and add to your profits. However, it is borrowing and, like any debt, you must use it wisely. Because of the implications of irresponsible margin use, the Federal Reserve Board sets the maximum amount you can borrow.

Irresponsible borrowing in the stock market and an economic downturn combined to help bring on the stock market crash in 1929. By the time the market hit bottom in 1932, it had lost 89 percent of its value from its 1929 peak. It would not regain that lost ground until 1954.

Margin Call

Can we have another market crash like the one in 1929? The stock exchanges have put in place "circuit breakers" and other trading rules including the use of margin that should prevent another total meltdown.

Many of the investors during the pre-1929 market frenzy were buying with borrowed money. As prices fell, brokers called those loans. When investors couldn't come up with cash, shares were sold at rapidly declining prices, which only fueled the collapse. To prevent that type of financial panic, Regulation T sets limits on how much a trader can initially borrow and how much must be maintained in the account.

Initially, traders can borrow up to 50 percent of the purchase price—that's called initial margin. For example, if you want to buy $10,000 worth of stock, you could borrow $5,000 from your broker and add $5,000 from your account. This assumes you are not a pattern day trader like we discussed in Chapter 3. Those traders can borrow up to 75 percent of the purchase price because they close their trades out at the end of each day. For swing and position traders, you will only get to borrow 50 percent by law. The rule doesn't stop there, however. Your account must maintain at least 25 percent equity or you will be required to bring it up to that level. That's called maintenance margin.

Here's how it works for active traders who hold a position overnight. Continuing our preceeding example, you want to buy $10,000 worth of stock. You borrow $5,000 from your broker and put in your initial margin of $5,000 from your account. (Most brokers require at least $2,000 equity in your account to open a margin account.) The most you can borrow is 50 percent, but you don't have to borrow that much. You now have extended your buying power from $5,000 to $10,000 if you so choose.

Of course, like all borrowed money you must pay interest on your margin loan, although the rate is usually not onerous. It will add up over time, so margin works best for trades that are going to be completed in a short period. The longer you hold a margin trade open, the more interest charges build up and the harder it will be to make a profit on the trade. When you close your trade, the broker will take the proceeds and pay off the margin loan and any interest due first. What remains, after commissions, of course, is your profit or loss. You'll face the tax consequences later. We'll look at more tax implications in Chapter 21.

When things go well, margin can increase the return on your investment. We'll see what happens when trades go bad after this example. You borrow $5,000 to buy $10,000 worth of stock. It rises 15 percent and you sell. What is your return on this trade?

Initial margin:	$5,000
Borrowed from broker:	$5,000
Total invested:	$10,000
Stock rises 15%	$11,500
Pay off margin loan:	−$5,000
Your equity:	−$5,000
Profit:	$1,500
Return on investment:	30 percent

Your return is 30 percent or twice what the stock rose because you borrowed money to make the purchase. Of course, it's not quite this rosy, as I've ignored interest, taxes, and commissions. However, you still come out way ahead with the margin loan.

What happens if you did not choose wisely and the trade is a bust? Let's look at the same setup and see what happens when you have used margin on a losing trade.

Initial margin:	$5,000
Borrowed from broker:	$5,000
Total invested:	$10,000
Stock drops –15%	$8,500
Pay off margin loan:	–$5,000
Your equity:	–$5,000
Loss:	–$1,500
Return on investment:	–30 percent

If you guessed the mirror image of the profitable trade, you were correct. Not only will margin trading magnify profits, it will also magnify losses. A 30 percent loss is bad, but it can get much worse. Margin can result in losing more money than you have invested, which is impossible in straight cash investment. Here's every trader's worst nightmare. The stock not only drops, it plunges on some horrible, unexpected news.

Initial margin:	$5,000
Borrowed from broker:	$5,000
Total invested:	$10,000
Stock plunges –55%	$4,500
Pay off margin loan:	–$5,000
Your equity:	–$5,000
Loss:	–$5,500
Return on investment:	–110 percent

The $4,500 goes to the broker and you will have to come up with another $500 to cover the full $5,000 loan. Your $5,000 equity is gone. If you didn't close out the account immediately, your broker would because you have fallen below the margin maintenance level required by law and the broker. Your equity (the initial $5,000) is gone and by law, it cannot drop below 25 percent of the initial margin deposit.

Trading Tip

If you practice the proper use of market order as discussed in Chapter 13, you can usually prevent these types of disasters.

In this example, your account equity (assuming it was $5,000 to start) dropped to negative before you closed the account. By law, as long as you have a margin loan outstanding, it cannot drop below 25 percent of the $5,000 (initial margin) or $1,250. This number would include cash and the value of securities held in your account. If your account drops below this amount, you will get a margin call, which is a communication from your broker telling you to increase the equity in your account to the minimum. If you can't or fail to do so within the time they give you, your broker can sell the securities in your account to pay off your loan. Some brokers don't bother with a call, they will simply sell your securities when the equity hits their minimum mark.

Your initial margin is the basis for the percentage of margin maintenance that is required. The law requires at least 25 percent, but some brokers set the limit higher. Be sure to check this limit with brokers so that you understand their requirements.

Eligible Securities for Margin Loans

Stocks and bonds are generally eligible for margin trading, but not all stocks. Stocks of companies that have just gone public, so-called *penny stocks*, and other over-the-counter stocks are not eligible. Individual brokers may have their own restrictions on certain types of stocks. The type of stocks that active traders favor generally fall into the acceptable group that most brokers will allow for margin trades.

def•i•ni•tion

Penny stocks are generally stocks of very small companies that trade outside established exchanges. They may sell for several dollars per share and are considered very speculative.

Brokers will have a list of marginable securities and their initial margin requirements. Bonds, both U.S. and corporate, can be margined, but may have different requirements. Options and short selling margin requirements differ among brokers. Certain option trades may have their own set of margin requirements. If you are interested in trading derivatives or plan on selling short frequently, you should discover what a broker's policy is regarding these types of trades before signing on.

The Role of Volatility in Active Trading

Volatility refers to the range of price changes for a security over a short period. Two securities can have an average price of $10 per share. One security can fluctuate between $6 and $14 per share in price, while the other security trades between $9 and $11 per share. The first security is said to be highly volatile because the price swing is extreme. The second security is not volatile because it trades in a tight range. Short-term traders have a better chance at making a profit on the volatile stock, although the risk is greater.

One way traders talk about a security's volatility is to measure its standard deviation. Calculating the standard deviation is a statistical measure of how much the security price will vary from its average price. The math for calculating standard deviations is complicated, but your direct access provider or broker probably provides it through research software.

The higher the number, the higher the security's volatility. This means the price will change in a given range. This creates opportunities for traders to capitalize on those price movements. This benefits short-term traders the most since they seek to capture small profits in quick trades. A higher standard deviation and higher volatility increases the risk also. It means prices are less predictable and can be harder for swing traders to work with over multiple trading days. However, it also means the potential is there for very profitable trades. As with all trades, the more risk, the higher the potential return should be.

> **Trading Tip**
>
> Higher risk should mean higher potential return. If there is not a higher potential return, avoid taking extra risk. High volatility can help or hurt you.

Other Securities for Trading

Stocks, in particular, and bonds are the most common securities traded by active traders, but they are not the only tools you can use to make a living as an active trader. The financial markets are extremely innovative at producing new securities that open opportunities for active traders. We have also noted that clever traders can use combinations of securities and derivatives to create unique arbitrage trading opportunities—in effect, creating new securities for trading purposes.

Margin Call

Novice active traders are often lured into trying exotic trading strategies by the promise of extraordinary profits. Ask yourself, if a system really worked as well as they claim all the time, wouldn't everyone be using it?

There are very sophisticated ways to trade securities, especially derivatives that are beyond the scope of this book. However, even using the basic features of exchange-traded funds, options, and futures will allow active traders to put together attractive opportunities in the right market conditions. That is a key factor for active traders—the ability to match tools (securities) to market conditions for the best chance at profits.

Exchange-Traded Funds Explode

One of the newest securities available to active traders is exchange-traded funds (ETFs). These securities are still "newbies" by market standards, but they have exploded in number and coverage in the market.

ETFs are very much like mutual funds in that they track a basket of assets that mimics an index, stock sector, commodity, or some other logical grouping of assets. The first ETF tracked the S&P 500 index. Unlike mutual funds, ETFs trade on stock exchanges as stocks do with continual pricing. Traders can use the same trading strategies with ETFs that they use with stocks—selling short, buying on margin, and so on.

Because of their structure, ETFs are often more efficient than mutual funds. You get the diversification of mutual funds with greater efficiency and the ease of trading stocks. Many of the ETFs cover broad sections of the market via indexes. Almost every stock index is covered by an ETF.

While active traders may not find broad index coverage especially beneficial, ETFs are also available for a variety of industry sectors. These sector ETFs can be used with individual stocks to structure arbitrage trades and for swing and position traders who want to follow hot (or cold) sectors. There are even ETFs that cover segments of foreign markets. The importance of opportunities in the global economy should not be overlooked. You have hundreds of ETFs available to you.

Trading Tip

Exchange-traded funds are worth getting to know because you can find one to buy (or short) an industry sector or foreign market, for example.

Although you will see lower expense ratios with ETFs compared to most mutual funds, you buy and sell them as you would stocks, so be prepared to pay a commission both ways. See Chapter 8 for more on ETFs.

Options for Active Traders

Options offer active traders several opportunities depending on whether you are a short-term trader or take a longer view as swing and position traders do. It is the same security, but used in different ways for different trading goals. Before you attempt to trade options or use them in your trading strategy, you should become very familiar with their characteristics and features. We'll go into more detail in Chapter 9 on how they work and how active traders use them.

Options are contracts that give the owner the right, but not the obligation, to buy or sell a security at a set price within a defined time frame. The value of the option is tied to the underlying asset and the amount of time left before it expires. Breaking down the key points of options, there are several important considerations.

Rights of Ownership

The owner of an option has the right, but not the obligation, to buy or sell (depending on the type of option) the underlying asset. The owner doesn't have to do anything. If the option reaches its expiration date and the owner has not done anything, it simply goes away and the owner is out the premium he paid.

Beginning and End

Unlike stocks, which have no end date, options have an expiration date. If the owner has not exercised her rights or sold the option by that date, the option ceases to exist. All options expire on the third Friday of the month.

Set Price of Underlying Asset

The option gives the owner the right to buy or sell (depending on the type of option) the asset at a fixed price or strike price. Regardless of what happens to the price of the underlying asset, the option price of the asset remains the same. If you have an option to buy a stock at $10 per share and the stock rises to $15 per share before the option expires, you have a built-in profit of $5 per share.

Market Place

How do you know an option is fairly priced? This is a complicated question that must include consideration of the underlying asset, time left on the option, and other considerations. Several models will help you decide if the price is right.

Value of the Option

Most option contracts are sold for a profit rather than exercising them and then selling the stock for a profit (you pay tax on two profits). The value of the option depends on the underlying asset. If the value of the underlying asset is such that your option is profitable, the value (price) of your option increases. You can sell the option at a profit. Pricing options is complicated by the amount of time remaining before expiration.

Types of Options

Options come in two varieties: call options give you the right to buy an underlying option; put options give you the right to sell an underlying option. It is easy to see that if you believe the asset is going to increase in value, you would buy a call option. If you believe the asset is going to decline in value, you would buy a put option.

Why not buy the asset or sell it short rather than use options? One of the main reasons is margin. Options have tremendous margin built into them because you can control a large block of stock for a fraction of the cost of buying it outright. Option contracts are sold in 100-share lots. You can buy an option on 100 shares of stock for a few dollars per share, called an option premium. For example, you might be able to buy a call option contract for 100 shares of a stock selling at $15 per share for $200, depending on the option characteristics. Rather than buy the stock for $1,500 or even $750, if you margined the trade, you are in for $200.

Margin Call

Selling options is a different strategy than buying options. If you don't own the underlying asset, you can face serious losses if you have to sell what you do not own.

Options trade on exchanges just as stocks and bonds do and most brokerages will let you trade them through your account, although you may have to fill out extra paperwork. Options are considered risky because they have expiration dates and you can lose all of your money.

You Can Sell Options, Too

So far, our discussion of options has been about buyers, but you can also be a seller of options. Under these circumstances, you receive the option premium when the option is bought (less fees). However, unlike the buyer, you are obligated to fulfill the terms of the option contract. For example, if you sell a call option for a stock with a strike price of $15 per share, you are obligated to sell 100 shares of the stock at $15 per share to the holder of the call option. Likewise, if you sell a put option at $15 per share, you are obligated to buy the stock at $15 per share. We'll discuss these obligations and trading strategies in more detail in Chapter 9.

Trading Futures Contracts

A futures contract is another derivative that active traders can use to great advantage—although at some risk. A futures contract, unlike the option contract, obligates you to buy a commodity or financial instrument at a future date for a specific price. Active traders can use futures contracts and variations to help them react to different market and currency conditions. Like options, futures are not for beginners. They are even more risky than options because the amount of leverage is huge and it is possible to lose more money than your initial investment.

Not everyone who uses futures contracts is a trader. The securities were created as a way to hedge risk for producers and consumers of commodities such as wheat, beef, and precious metals. Producers can use futures contracts to lock in a price for their products before they are produced (a future grain crop, for example). Consumers, such as food processors, can also use futures to lock in prices so they will know future costs of raw material (grain, for example).

Trading futures can be very profitable because of the huge leverage involved. Most exchanges require a 5 to 10 percent deposit to control a futures contract. A few thousand dollars deposit can control $75,000 of an asset. Because of this huge leverage, a small change in price up or down means a big gain or loss for the investor.

The real danger for traders is that the exchanges where futures contracts trade set daily limits on price changes. These limits prevent the price from rising or falling too rapidly. If a futures contract hits an upper or lower limit during the trading day, the exchange halts trading for the day. When trading resumes the next day, new limits are in place. What this means for traders is that it may be difficult to get out of a position quickly if the market is falling rapidly, for example. We'll look at more features of futures trading in Chapter 9.

> **Market Place**
>
> Trading futures may require a separate agreement or even a separate broker. It is a specialized transaction that not all brokers are licensed to handle.

Trading Currency

The last wide-open frontier of trading is on the foreign exchange or forex where trillions of dollars in world currencies trade every day in an unregulated market. You can't go on any financial website without seeing ads for brokers wanting your forex business. The market for trading currency (U.S. dollars for Japanese yen, for example) is open six days a week, 24 hours a day.

Like other forms of trading, you look for bargains by buying one currency while selling another. Contracts are settled in cash with profits and losses on each trade going into your account. The leverage is huge with deposits of 10 percent per contract typical. This has allowed average traders to participate in this fast-moving but very risky market. The factors that change currency relationships are complex and not always transparent. We'll look at forex trading in detail in Chapter 9.

The Least You Need to Know

- ◆ Active traders are not limited to stocks, but can also trade in a variety of securities such as futures contracts and options.

- ◆ Securities must meet certain characteristics, such as a high degree of liquidity and volatility in price to be good active trading candidates.

- ◆ Derivatives like options and futures are good tools for active traders.

- ◆ Complex securities and trading techniques associated with options, futures, and the forex market require in-depth knowledge.

Chapter 8

The Scoop on Stocks and Other Equities

In This Chapter

♦ Stocks are very popular with active traders

♦ Developing or purchasing your trading system

♦ Options allow sophisticated, highly leveraged trades

♦ Exchange-traded funds open new opportunities

Stocks are the weapon of choice for many active traders. They have all the characteristics that active traders need whether for short-term, swing, or position trading. Options on stocks allow traders to use huge amounts of leverage to control blocks of stock that the trader has the right, but not the obligation, to buy or sell. Exchange-traded funds (ETFs) let traders buy or sell market indexes, industry segments, or market segments. In this chapter, we'll examine stocks, options, and ETFs.

Stocks Still Tops with Traders

Beginning traders usually start with stocks for a variety of reasons, not the least of which is that stocks require less of a learning curve to get started. Many active traders have some investment experience, so stocks aren't a complete mystery.

Stocks of companies listed on major exchanges are transparent—that is, traders can know all they want to know about the company behind the stock. The information is public and available at no cost from many sources. Although short-term traders don't rely on this information, swing and position traders need to have some knowledge of fundamental information about the company to protect themselves from news-driven price changes.

Shares of stock are an asset with a value that rises and falls, in part based on how well the company performs. While buy-and-hold investors are concerned with the long-term value-generating capacity of the corporation, active traders know that in the short run, it is supply and demand that drives stock prices. Traders, especially over shorter periods, look for the ratio of buyers to sellers to see whether the price is likely headed up or down.

Market Place
Investors who try their hand at trading may be frustrated by the heavy emphasis on technical analysis and the light consideration of fundamental analysis. However, there is ample evidence that, in the short run, technical analysis is a helpful and necessary tool of successful traders.

Traders are more likely to employ technical analysis tools in their decision-making than investors are. Technical analysis focuses on price, volume, momentum, and a host of other indicators to give traders signs about when to buy or sell a security. It is not an exact science and trying to interpret the hundreds of charts and graphs available to traders can lead to "analysis paralysis." However, over short periods, these tools correctly applied and interpreted can help traders anticipate changes in the price and direction of stocks.

Your Trading System

Most successful traders use a system of some type to add discipline and consistency to their trades. The system can be one the trader develops over time, one of the common systems, or a commercial system she buys or subscribes to. Regardless of which system you use, it must work most of the time, and you must stick to it. Otherwise, you will run out of money soon.

Trading systems, whether simple or complex, are a set of rules that traders use to help them make consistent trading decisions. If you are familiar with math or simple computer-coding techniques, the systems will make sense. A trading-system rule might look like this:

> If X happens and Y happens, then buy.

Or

> If Y happens and X happens, then sell.

A true system is usually more complex than one or two rules. Since it relies on technical indicators, the system is limited by the effectiveness of those rules.

It takes time and a thorough understanding of technical analysis to develop a trading system that works for you. However, there are real benefits to developing a trading system. They include:

♦ **Consistency.** Systems help you become a consistent trader, which is good if your system works most of the time. The discipline of a system helps keep you focused on what's important.

♦ **Emotions.** This goes with consistency. A trading system will help keep your emotions out of trading. Fear and greed are the two emotions that lead to most bad trading decisions. A trading system takes the emotion out—if you stick to it.

♦ **Automation.** Trading systems can be built into many of the advanced trading platforms. After you have built, tested, and optimized your system, it can generate buy or sell signals for you to act on or it can execute trades automatically.

You don't even have to develop your own system. There are vendors that will sell you signals or a complete system you can run on your own. Many of these systems are from reputable companies that use reasonable premises and that don't promise you will earn 1,000 percent each year. However, there are less reputable companies that make incredible claims about the effectiveness of their trading system ("I turned a $1,000 investment into $336,457.35 in just

Margin Call

Trading systems don't take the place of good judgment. What they will do is automate some of the more routine trading tasks. If you rely heavily on an automated trading system you don't completely understand, you are setting yourself up for a disaster.

six months!"). You should ask yourself: If their system is so good, why are they selling it instead of using it to get rich?

Using even legitimate trading systems—yours or one you buy—has its disadvantages. Here are some:

- **It takes time.** Developing a trading system or learning to use one you buy takes time. Sometimes the lessons are expensive as you gain experience with the system, particularly as you develop your own. Practice trading the system and *back testing* it against historical data can help. However, there is no substitute for live trading as the best test ground.

def•i•ni•tion

> **Back testing** is a process of running a trading system through sets of historical market data to see how the system would perform. It can be helpful when used objectively, but it can also be manipulated by commercial providers to elicit the results they want.

- **The complexities.** Trading systems can be complex. The more complex a system, the more prone to error and failure it is. To develop such a system requires a thorough knowledge of technical analysis and how the indicators work. If you buy a system, you still need to know how it works to spot errors that may occur.

- **Assumptions and expectations.** To develop a trading system that you can use, you must have an accurate grasp of what your cost (transaction fees, commissions, and so on) will be and you need reasonable expectations for success. This requires real-world information and experience—something you will acquire in your career as a trader.

Testing Your System

Whether you have developed your own system or have bought one, it is critical to test it under a variety of market conditions before you put it into use with real money. This is where you discover flaws and weak spots. You will also discover that one system that works very well in one type of market may not do well in another market. This testing will point out those areas to correct and improve.

The best way to rapidly test your system is through a process called back testing. Back testing allows you to test your system under a variety of market conditions without risking any money. Some advanced trading platforms have this feature included that will let you run the tests.

Once you have spent extensive time back testing and refining your system, the next step is to paper trade your system to see how it functions with live data under current market conditions. This process also lets you see how you are going to react to the system and how much of the process you are comfortable putting on automatic pilot. If you have constructed the system correctly and it meets your provider's guidelines, you can automate your trading. The system will take over all or most of the duties. Other traders are more comfortable with a system that simply presents them with possible trades.

In either case, you must be comfortable with the results of the system. Systems that work only work when traders stick with them. Of course, even the best systems don't return winning trades every time. The systems are built on technical indicators, which are not foolproof, and a myriad of other factors can sabotage the best technical indicators.

A detailed discussion of building trading systems is beyond the scope of this book. However, systems are important tools that many active traders use once they gain some experience. As you gather trading experience, you will see where a system might be advantageous.

Trading Systems for Other Securities

This brief look at trading systems focused on stocks because that is the topic of this chapter. You can, however, use trading systems on almost all securities that active traders might trade. Some markets, such as the forex market, lend themselves to trading systems more easily than others do. Institutional investors, hedge funds, and large professional investment operations use trading systems for most if not all of their trading.

Options on Stocks

The concept of options is simple: traders can buy a security that gives them the right to buy or sell (two different options) that security for a fixed price (or strike price) within a certain period. But while the concept is simple, options are extremely complex.

Option contracts convey the right, but not the obligation, to buy or sell 100 shares of a stock at a fixed price before the option expires. You pay a premium per share for the option. There are two types of options: call options and put options. A call option gives you the right to buy; a put option gives you the right to sell.

Suppose you buy a call option on a stock at $50 per share with a premium of $3 per share. If the underlying stock rose to $60 per share before the option expired, you could sell it and pocket the difference between the premium you paid originally and the current price that reflects the profit in the option. Your break-even price would be the strike price ($50) plus the premium ($3) or $53 per share. The difference is $7 per share. (This and other examples ignore commissions, fees, and taxes, which will affect your profits or losses.)

Margin Call

Despite what you may read in your e-mail or see on infomercials, trading options is not the easy road to riches. Most investment professionals warn against it. Active traders who are successful at options trading spend a great deal of time learning on paper before risking real money.

But suppose the stock is trading at $46 per share when the option expires. In that case, your option to buy is said to be "out of the money." You lose the entire premium and commissions you paid for the contract.

Put options are the same strategy as shorting a stock. You believe the price will fall and want to profit when it does. The difference is that with a put option to profit, you simply sell it in the marketplace. If the stock rises instead of falling, your put option is worthless, and you lose your premium and commissions paid.

For example, you believe a stock currently selling for $40 per share is overpriced and will decline to a reasonable level when investors begin selling to take their profits. You could buy a put option at $40 if you feel the price will drop during the period the option is in force. If the price of the stock does decline from $40 per share, the value of your put option rises because it gives you the right to sell shares at $40 regardless of what the actual market price is. As the price of the stock falls, the value of the put option rises. When you are ready (but before the put option expires), you can sell the option for a profit.

In addition to buying options on stocks, you can buy options on stock indexes (such as the S&P 500 or the Dow). These options may have a few different attributes than stock options, but for the most part, they are the same.

Equity options are physical delivery contracts, meaning you can take possession of the stock if you own a stock option that is in the money. Options on stock indexes are cash settlement contracts, which mean they must be paid up in cash because there is nothing physical to deliver.

Part of the value of an option is tied to the price of the underlying stock. Actively traded stocks with strong price swings will make for a volatile option. Active traders are attracted to options, in part, as another way to play active stocks.

Options have another attribute that active traders like: leverage. Traders can control large blocks of stock or stock indexes with a relatively small investment. Depending on the features of the option, you could control a stock selling on the market for $25 per share for a $2 per share option premium. Traders can make (or lose) money by buying and selling call and put options.

Trading Tip

Check with your broker about the margin requirements for option accounts. Some firms are fairly strict about the account size and level of sophistication of traders they will take.

A Riskier Strategy

Traders can also make (or lose) money by being on the other side of the transaction. Traders can sell, or write (in option terminology), call and put options. Writing options can be a more risky strategy. If you write a call option, you receive the premium, which is yours to keep. However, if your option is in the money it may be exercised and you will be required to sell your stock at the strike price of the option, which will be lower than the current market price. Many traders write what are called "naked options," meaning they do not own the underlying stock. Thus, if traders write a call option and it is exercised, they will have to buy the stock on the open market to provide delivery of the commodity.

The writer of a put option is obligated to purchase the stock at the strike price, no matter what the market price of the stock is. If the strike price of the put option is $50 per share, and the stock falls to $25 per share, the owner of the put option could buy the stock on the market at $25 and exercise her put, forcing the writer to buy the stock at $50 per share. A more likely outcome would see the writer of the put buying the same put option at the same strike price, which would offset the option he wrote. His loss would be the premium paid for the put option (which would be substantial in this case) minus the premium he received for the option he wrote.

This shows the order-entry screen for options from the Interactive Brokers' Trader Workstation. Notice the buttons that allow one-click configuring and addition of information.

(Photo courtesy of Interactive Brokers.)

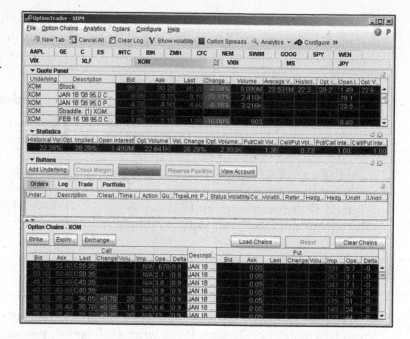

LEAPS for the Long Shot

Traders who want a longer hold on a stock or index can buy Long-Term Equity Anticipation Securities, or LEAPS. LEAPS are equity options with expiration dates of up to two years. Traders are usually too impatient for this long of a hold on a security, but LEAPS offer a way to hang on to a position in a stock or index without tying up a lot of investment capital.

Market Place

Holding a position for a long period makes most traders nervous—they fear what can happen to the company and the economy. LEAPS offer a way to hold stock or an index without tying up a lot of investment capital.

LEAPS have a higher premium than typical options because of the longer period they have for the stock to rise (or fall in the case of puts). These securities may be a good alternative for traders who want a longer hold but not the capital commitment. Some find it a good way to play the market long-term, rather than individual stocks. The closer the strike price is to the current stock price or index, the higher the premium. Of course, time can work against you, which is one of the reasons traders usually are reluctant to hold positions for long periods.

How Traders Use Options

This brief overview of options only scratches the surface. The Chicago Board Options Exchange, the major exchange for options, has tremendous educational resources for further information, and you will find other references in Appendix A.

Active traders can use options on stocks and other equities including exchange-traded funds (see the following) in a variety of strategies. Many active traders make a career out of trading options. There is plenty of action and a host of strategies for everyone from aggressive traders to cautious investors in the options market. It is a testament to their versatility that options are branded as highly risky and you must be qualified by your broker to trade them, yet many investors use them as insurance to protect positions.

We saw in Chapter 5 that arbitrage traders can use options when there is a difference between the price of the underlying stock or security and the premium of the option. This is highly technical work, because determining whether a particular option contract is overpriced, underpriced, or fairly priced can be complicated. Options also let traders take a position in a stock for a longer period than they may feel comfortable actually holding the security itself (less capital is committed).

As with all securities, the more you understand about options and all their variations and strategies, the more ways you will see how they can fit into your trading plans. However, these are definitely securities you want to be very familiar with before you begin trading or you will not understand why you are losing all your money.

Trading Tip

Some active traders do nothing but trade options. However, many combine options with other securities to take advantage of opportunities as they find them in the market.

Exchange-Traded Funds

Most active traders don't have much use for mutual funds. Mutual funds are almost impossible to trade (trading is discouraged and penalized by some funds). However, the ability to trade market segments or the market itself has a lot of appeal when traders can do it in real time like they trade equities. This is exactly what exchange-traded funds (ETFs) do for active traders.

ETFs are a basket of stocks much like mutual funds, but different in several important ways. First, they trade on exchanges just as stocks do, which means traders can get in and out the same day. Traders can use all the same market orders with ETFs they use with stocks and pay a commission just as they do with stocks. This familiarity and flexibility gives traders just the freedom they need to move quickly on trades.

ETFs are very much like index mutual funds; in fact, the very first ones started in the 1990s tracked the major equity indexes such as the Dow, the S&P 500, the Nasdaq Composite, and so on. Since then, hundreds of new ETFs have been added to the market and they track dozens of widely known indexes and many obscure ones. You can find an ETF on many very narrow industry segments, commodities, and technologies, as well as foreign investments.

> **Market Place**
>
> Exchange-traded funds have grown at a tremendous rate, and the industry continues to look for new products. If you don't see an ETF for a particular situation that interests you, it will probably be just a matter of time before one is created.

ETFs are generally less expensive than mutual funds and usually tax friendly—since they trade on the market, there is no buying and selling shares and no capital gains to report each year.

Investors like ETFs for their diversification and ease of holding. Traders are drawn to ETFs when they want to play bigger sections of the market in connection with economic news or changes in industry. It may not always be easy to pick the right stocks in some industries, but ETFs let you play the whole sector if that's what you want. You can short ETFs as well, so a sense of impending doom can pay off if you have researched an industry sector.

ETFs Come in a Wide Variety

Traders enjoy the way they can pinpoint their trades by choosing one of the ETFs that covers a narrow section of the market. Other traders want a way to play the whole market and use one of the broad index ETFs to cover movement (up or down). ETFs are known by some colorful names. Here are the most widely known:

◆ **SPDRs**   These ETFs, known as spiders, track the benchmark S&P 500 index. SPDRs allow traders to own the index's stocks in a security they can trade like a stock. SPDRs also divide various sectors of the S&P 500 stocks and sell them as separate ETFs. The technology select sector index, for example, contains over 85 stocks covering products developed by companies such as defense manufacturers, telecommunications equipment, microcomputer components, and integrated computer circuits.

◆ **DIAMONDs (DIA)**   The Diamonds Trust Series I tracks the Dow Jones Industrial Average and is structured as a unit investment trust.

- **Nasdaq-100 Index Tracking Stock (QQQQ)** The ETF representing the Nasdaq-100 Index, which consists of the 100 largest and most actively traded nonfinancial stocks on the Nasdaq, is one of the most actively traded ETFs.

- **iShares** iShares is Barclay's (Barclay's Global Investors "BGI") brand of ETFs. The company has more than 120 iShares trading on more than 10 different stock exchanges. Barclay has put out a number of technology-oriented iShares that follow Goldman Sachs's technology indexes.

- **VIPERs** VIPERs are Vanguard's brand of the financial instrument. VIPERs, or Vanguard Index Participation Receipts, are structured as share classes of open-end funds. Vanguard also offers dozens of ETFs for many different areas of the market.

> **Margin Call**
>
> Providers have rushed many ETFs to market and, in some cases, have not given enough thought to the securities. Check out ETFs the same as you would any securities because they are not all equally created.

The ETF market has grown to more than 650 offerings in a little over a decade, attesting to the popularity of the securities with investors and traders alike.

How Traders Use ETFs

Active traders can trade ETFs just the same as they trade equities, including short-term, momentum, swing, and position strategies. Rather than pick a single stock, ETFs let traders pick up the whole market or market segments. The QQQQ (the Nasdaq-100 ETF), for example, is one of the most actively traded securities on any exchange.

Traders can use margin to buy ETFs, which gives them leverage over markets or sectors of markets. Some of these ETFs can be very volatile, especially those that slice out high-tech companies. Traders can also short ETFs, which makes them a good play when the market or market segments appear headed for the dumps.

Not all the ETFs enjoy the activity of the QQQQ or the SPDRs, so be careful when trading some of the ETFs that have been formed around very narrow and specific market segments. They may not have the trading volume to support an active trader.

The Least You Need to Know

- ◆ Stocks remain the active trader's product of choice.

- ◆ Stocks have all the attributes that active traders need to trade successfully.

- ◆ You should refine your stock trading system through back testing and practice trading before implementing it.

- ◆ Options on stocks are an attractive, although risky, security for active traders.

- ◆ Exchange-traded funds give active traders a way to trade market indexes or industry segments without using a mutual fund.

Chapter 9

Trading Futures and Currency

In This Chapter

- ◆ The futures market offers opportunities for big gains and losses
- ◆ Cash and commodities present challenges and potential for active traders
- ◆ The forex market is an unregulated trading frontier
- ◆ The risks and opportunities of extreme leverage

Active traders are attracted to more exotic financial products because they offer the opportunity for extraordinary gains. With this opportunity comes a corresponding amount of risk. This brief introduction to futures contracts and currency trading is also a warning that you should have some experience as an active trader of equities before attempting these securities.

Futures Contracts

Futures contracts are binding legal agreements that commit the owner to deliver or fill the terms of the contract at a future date. Unlike options, which convey a right, but not an obligation, future's contracts obligate you to deliver the goods. Most people are familiar with the commodities markets in beef, orange juice, precious metals, and so on. If you have a future's contract to deliver thousands of pounds of beef on a certain day, you are legally obligated to deliver. Of course, most futures contracts are offset or closed before the settlement date.

The purpose of the futures market is to provide a way for producers and consumers to hedge future price changes. For example, a farmer might be concerned about the price of wheat, but it will be months before he is ready to harvest his crop. He can sell (short) a futures contract of wheat for delivery at about the time his crop is to come in, thus locking in a price. When it is time to harvest his wheat, he has a price already fixed through the futures contract. If market prices are lower, he can close the futures contract for a profit to help offset the lower market price. If the market price is higher, he can offset his position and be out only the premium he paid for the future's contract.

> **Market Place**
>
> For the commodity producer and the commodity user, the futures market is more of an insurance pool where future prices of raw materials can be hedged. It is quite different for traders.

Food processors who need wheat can use the same strategy, but in reverse. Food producers want to lock in a low price for wheat now by buying a futures contract. If the price rises above the futures contract, producers profit and offset the higher price they are paying in the market for wheat. If the price falls below the futures price, producers would close out the contract and are only out the premium. This is a somewhat oversimplification of how the process works, but it is the basic idea of hedging future prices.

Traders are also players in the futures markets. Unlike producers and consumers who want to protect against future price uncertainty, traders hope to profit in a market of changing prices. Traders play an important role in the market by providing liquidity (in buying and selling contracts). Market rules help prevent traders from manipulating the price of the commodity.

Types of Futures Contracts

What began as a way to stabilize prices of commodities has grown into a much larger securities market that includes a variety of financial securities as well as physical commodities. As a result, there are two types of future contracts: physical delivery contracts and cash settlement contracts. Physical delivery contracts are what you might expect: agricultural products, precious metals, and so on. Cash settlement contracts are for financial securities such as futures on stock indexes, Treasury notes and bonds, and other financial instruments. Active traders don't plan on taking delivery of pork bellies (you must stay focused on contract dates or face awkward settlements). Financial and securities' futures always settle in cash, meaning they are usually "marked to market" (their value is adjusted up or down) on their settlement day and your account credited or debited accordingly.

How Futures Contracts Work

Active traders like futures contracts because a small deposit controls a large asset. The initial deposit you are required to make is called a performance bond (sometimes called a good-faith deposit). At the end of each day's trading, all contracts are marked to market. If your contract gained value, your account is credited, and if it lost money, your account is debited. If the amount falls below the minimum required by the exchanges to keep the futures contract open, you will get a performance bond call from your broker requiring you to bring up the balance or face liquidation of the position. You will be required to make up any loss in your account even if it is more than your initial deposit.

The amount of this performance bond can equal 5 to 20 percent of the value of the contract. When you liquidate the contract, you receive the funds in the account as your profit or loss. The amount of the initial deposit depends on the future contract and market conditions. However, even at 20 percent you are experiencing a tremendous amount of leverage that can produce stunning gains or disastrous losses.

Margin Call

Trading full futures contracts is an expensive way to trade. Some contracts have performance bonds in excess of $25,000 with values of $300,000 or more. Small movements in the value of the contract are multiplied by the huge leverage to your advantage or detriment.

Futures contracts have time limits. They begin and end as stock options become due on certain cycles. Some are on a quarterly cycle, which gives the contracts a three-month life. You are responsible for closing out or extending your positions—or expect delivery and a bill for a lot of something you really don't want.

This shows the futures' quote screen from Interactive Brokers' Trader Workstation. The tabs across the top give you more information and options.

(Photo courtesy of Interactive Brokers.)

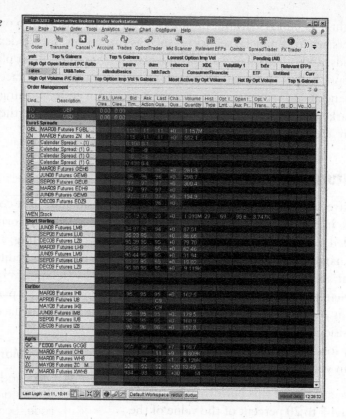

The Long and Short of It

Two terms you will hear in a variety of investment settings, but in particular in futures trading, are long and short. To be long in a futures contract means you have bought the contract and expect it to rise in value. If you are short in a contract, you have sold it and expect the commodity or financial instrument to fall in price.

Either position is closed by offsetting it with the opposite transaction. You can also roll your position into the next period through a transaction that lets you close out one position and open the exact same position in the new contract period. *E-Mini contracts* (more about these contracts next) have a three-month life and expire in March, June, September, and December, usually on the third Friday.

def•i•ni•tion

E-Mini Stock Index Futures or E-Minis are an electronically traded futures contract. The E-Minis are a smaller size than normal future contracts and are issued on stock indexes such as the S&P 500, Dow, and so on.

Ticks

Ticks are the minimum units by which a future's contract can change. The amount is set for each contract by the exchange. For example, the E-Mini S&P 500 futures contract (more about them below) has a tick of 0.25 of an index point or $12.50. Some E-Mini contracts trade in ticks worth one-tenth of a point. The purpose of fractional ticks is to allow traders to set precise buy and sell orders. To understand ticks, you also must understand the "multiplier" for the futures contract.

In the case of the E-Mini S&P 500, the multiplier is $50 per index point. The multiplier tells you two things. First, it tells you the value of the contract. If the S&P 500 Index is at 1250, the value of the contract is $62,500 (1250 × $50). Second, you get the value of the tick ($50 × 0.25 = $12.50).

As the E-Mini S&P 500 contract is traded, its value will rise and fall in ticks. If the index rises from 1250 to 1250.50, it has gone up two ticks or $25 dollars. If you are long (you have bought) the contract, your account is credited with two ticks or $25 dollars ($12.50 × 2 = $25).

All futures contracts, whether for commodities or financial instruments, have multipliers and ticks of varying sizes. Some of the futures contracts control huge dollar amounts with multipliers in the hundreds of dollars. A futures contract such as the full S&P 500 index has a multiplier of $250, giving it a value of several hundred thousand dollars. This becomes especially important when we discuss the advantages and dangers of the vast leverage built into contracts.

Trading Tip

Each futures contract has its own multiplier and tick value. Be sure you understand the numbers before venturing into futures trading.

Market Limits

Most futures contracts have limits on how much they can move up or down in a single day's trading. The amount is calculated differently for each contract. For example, a contract may have a $15.50 daily limit. If the price of the contract rises or falls by that much, the exchange halts all trading for the day. The next trading day, the limits are reintroduced around the closing price from the day before. Financial futures are measured in percentages rather than a specific dollar amount for limits, and the formulas can be complicated. Be sure you understand how they work before you begin trading. The Chicago Mercantile Exchange and the other exchanges that trade financial futures set the rules and provide that information for all the futures traded on their exchange. A list of those exchanges is found in Appendix A.

These trading limits prevent a free-fall or runaway market by shutting down trading. However, it also may make it difficult for you to get out of a bad situation. If something dreadful happens, and the market begins dropping rapidly, it may be hard to exit your position because trading will be halted as soon at the price limit is hit. As the equity in your account drains each day you can't exit the position, you will get a performance bond call from your broker demanding more money in your account. As we'll see in our discussions on leverage, it is possible to not only lose your performance bond deposit, but a whole lot more. Futures are one of the few trades you can make where it is possible to lose a lot more than you invested—that should be sufficient warning to anyone who thinks trading futures is the easy road to wealth.

The exchanges also prevent individuals and groups acting together from controlling large blocks of futures contracts. People have tried to "corner the market" in the past by buying huge quantities of contracts and manipulating prices. Controls are in place to prevent that from happening any longer.

Trading Futures Contracts

Futures contracts are well suited for active, experienced traders. They cover a wide variety of commodities, precious metals, financial indexes, bonds, and foreign currency. There is something for every trading taste. However, many traders stick with the financial indexes, precious metals, bonds, and foreign currency. These tend to be the most volatile and, as we have discovered, that presents more possibilities for active traders.

The stock indexes in particular are very active and can be traded on an intraday basis or held for swing trading opportunities. Because it is just as easy to go short as it is to go long, you can play the market both ways in the same trading day. As volatile as indexes can be, they present some exciting short-term opportunities.

The exchanges also offer options on many futures contracts; however, those products are best addressed after you have mastered futures contracts.

> **Market Place**
>
> The futures market offers a wide variety of opportunities to trade everything from agricultural products to precious metals, to petroleum products, to financial securities, and even the weather (you can buy or sell futures contracts based on weather patterns, which have a direct impact on many agricultural commodities).

A Futures Trading Account

Trading futures is not the same as opening an online brokerage account and buying a few shares of stock. The broker must be licensed to trade futures, and you'll want a direct access service if you plan short-term trading.

Because of the high-risk nature of futures trading, you will be required to sign several documents including the performance bond, which obligates you to cover your loss even if they exceed the equity in your account—in other words, you are on the hook. If your account falls below the performance margin, expect a performance bond call and a polite insistence you bring the equity up immediately.

E-Mini Contracts

One of the most popular trading vehicles with active traders is the E-Mini futures contracts on stock indexes. These contracts use major stock indexes for their underlying target. The contracts are smaller (thus the "mini") than regular futures contracts and that offers some advantages for active traders. The E-Mini contracts generally require a smaller performance bond and have a smaller multiplier. The contract still allows ample room for profits, but the potential for losses is much lower than with regular futures contracts. However, you can still suffer substantial losses if you are not careful.

E-Mini contracts are available on several exchanges and cover every major stock index and some not so major indexes. You can also trade E-Mini contracts on foreign stock indexes. Each contract has its own specifications, so you will want to familiarize yourself with the details before you begin trading. Contracts trade from Sunday afternoon though Friday afternoon, giving traders the opportunity to react to news events even when the stock market is closed.

E-Mini S&P 500 Futures Contract

One of the most popular of the E-Mini series is the E-Mini S&P 500 futures contract. We'll look at it in some detail as a representative of the other E-Mini contracts and futures contracts in general.

The E-Mini S&P 500 contract is a more manageable version of a futures contract on the S&P 500 stock index. This is the most widely quoted index in the financial community and is often used as a proxy for the whole stock market.

As noted previously, one index point is worth $50 (as opposed to $250 for the full-size S&P 500 futures contract). When the S&P 500 index is at 1400, the contract is worth $70,000 ($50 × 1400 = $70,000). The performance bond set by CME is $4,000, although brokers are free to set a higher bond. The performance bond is subject to change by the exchange, so check with your broker. Each tick is 0.25 of a point, or $12.50.

The S&P 500 index is less volatile than the Dow or the Nasdaq 100. You can see how that is represented in the respective E-Mini contracts. The E-Mini contract for the Dow has a multiplier of $10 per index point and the Nasdaq 100 multiplier is $20 per index point.

For example, on an unusually active day for the S&P 500 Index, it traded in the range of 1394.83 to 1419.91. If you drop the decimals for the sake of simplicity, that's a 25-point range, which means if you managed to buy at the bottom (1394) and sell at the top (1419), you made a $1,250 profit—excluding taxes, commissions, fees, and so on.

Of course, you could have bought the other way and suffered that big of a loss because on this particular day the market was in a nosedive. The savvy trader would have used the appropriate technical analysis tools and fundamental news to determine that the market was headed down this trading day and shorted the E-Mini S&P 500 futures contract.

On this same trading day, the Dow was down 265 points, for a move worth $2,650 ($10 × 265). A trader with a *short position* early in the day may have done very well.

def•i•ni•tion

Short position in futures trading means you have sold a contract anticipating its value was going to decline. Unlike shorting stocks, you don't have to borrow a contract from your broker and there are no restrictions on buying or selling short contracts.

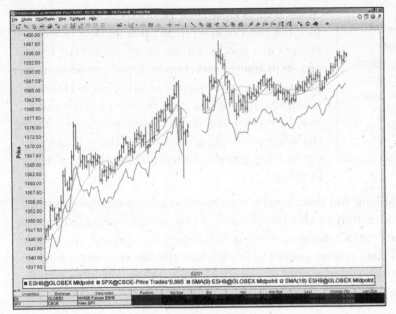

This shows a five-minute chart of E-Mini S&P futures contract. It includes the S&P 500 Index to show how it tracks with index and 9- and 18-day moving averages from Interactive Brokers' Trader Workstation.

(Photo courtesy of Interactive Brokers.)

How Traders Use E-Mini Contracts

The preceeding two examples may give the impression that it is easy to make money with E-Mini futures contracts—of course, it's always easy to identify good trades after the fact. The problem is stock indexes have a habit of reversing themselves, sometimes several times in a single trading session. For the active trader, this means you need to be able to switch directions in an instant when the market begins moving against you.

For example, if your analysis indicates the market should be heading down, you might open your trading day with a short position. At mid-morning, for whatever reason, the market reverses itself and takes a solid jump. If you have protected your position with limit orders (more about these in Chapter 13), your position will be closed out with a small profit or loss, depending on where you put the order to close the position. If you didn't put any limits on your position, your losses could mount dramatically if you aren't paying attention to the market.

If your limit order closes your position, you are out of the market and must get back in if you want to participate. So, now the stock is headed up, but is it just a bump before coming back down or will it stay or climb at this level? Maybe this isn't as easy as it seems! Careful use of moving averages and charts along with practice can help you develop a strategy for short-term trading of E-Mini contracts.

Margin Call

Because stock market indexes can be very volatile and reverse directions frequently, traders should protect their position with appropriate trading orders or face the possibility of disastrous losses.

Many traders close their positions before going to bed, but you can keep them open for days or weeks if you are in a good position. By adjusting your limits and stops (more market orders), you can protect your profits and keep a contract position open. However, if you are right on the edge between a profit and a loss, be very careful about closing your eyes without the safety of standing limit orders that will get you out of the position if things go bad while you're not looking.

In addition to straight long and short orders, traders can employ a number of other strategies ranging from mildly to very complicated. These include spreads where you buy and sell the same contract; hedging existing holdings; arbitrage; and much more complicated trades. When you are comfortable with how the futures market works and understand the risks, you may want to consider learning about the more complicated plays that are possible with futures, E-Mini futures contracts, and options on futures contracts.

Advantages and Disadvantages of Trading Futures

Trading stock index E-Mini futures offers active traders numerous advantages, which is one of the reasons they are so actively traded. Among the benefits are:

- **Extended trading hours.** You can trade 24 hours a day from Sunday afternoon through Friday afternoon.

- **Leverage.** The performance bond is a small percentage of the contract's value, giving you the potential for tremendous return on investment.

- **Long or short.** You can go long or short on the contracts with equal ease. There are no restrictions on short sales like there are with stocks.

- **Buy or sell markets.** Like exchange-traded funds, you can buy or sell an entire market with one transaction; however, you can do so with less money than ETFs.

The E-Mini stock index futures have some pitfalls you need to be aware of:

- **Leverage.** The huge leverage that worked so well to your advantage can turn against you if the market goes bad on your trade. You can suffer a huge loss— much greater than your initial deposit if you're not careful. You are legally obligated to make up these losses even if you don't have the money in your account.

◆ **Expirations.** Futures contracts expire. You are responsible for either closing the position or rolling it into the next contract period. Failure to do so can have unfortunate consequences.

Conclusion

Trading futures and E-Mini stock index contracts offer active traders an exciting and challenging avenue to profits. It is not a place to begin your trading career, but for traders with some experience and a tolerance for risk, trading E-Mini futures contracts can be a very profitable full-time business.

Trading Money

As exciting and fast-paced as the futures market in stock indexes is, the foreign exchange currency market is bigger and faster (and potentially more risky). The foreign exchange currency market, also known as the forex, is the largest financial market in the world. The daily value of trades easily exceeds the equity markets.

Trading Tip

The E-Mini contracts on stock indexes are very popular with active traders and a good place for you to start with your practice trading.

Until recently, banks and other major financial institutions were the only ones trading currencies. With the growth of electronic trading, the forex opened to retail customers. The initial efforts met with some shady dealings, but those have largely been cleaned up and traders who work with reliable brokers should not have any problems.

Like most forms of investing money, you will still find scams that promise extraordinary profits. Any company that promises you will make huge profits with any type of investment is a scam. There are no sure trading systems that will always generate huge profits in real-life market conditions. If you want to make money trading currency in the forex market, you will have to learn how to trade, why currencies fluctuate in value relative to one another, and take some risk.

Margin Call

Even though the forex is largely unregulated, it is illegal for companies to promise something they don't or can't deliver. One of the biggest complaints is companies promising trading systems and support but disappearing after taking in a lot of customer money.

The forex is a completely different kind of market, trading currency or cash, which means it offers a level of diversification for portfolios of stocks, bonds, and real estate. It is also different because there is no central market or exchange. Trading runs 24 hours a day, six days a week as banks on the other side of the world open for business while we are still asleep.

This shows an order screen for forex trading from Interactive Brokers' Trader Workstation.

(Photo courtesy of Interactive Brokers.)

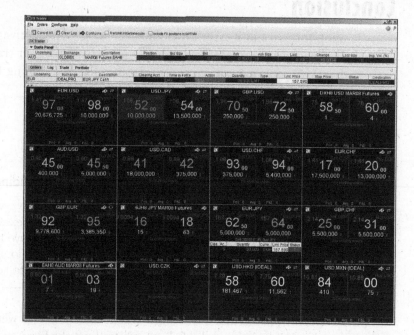

Traders like the forex for several reasons, but two of the most important are liquidity and leverage. Traders who work with the major currencies will not have liquidity problems when it comes time to trade. The leverage in the forex is almost unbelievable to many traders. It can run from 100 to 250 times your investment. At 200 times leverage, a $1,000 investment lets you trade $200,000. You can see the advantage of that power—and the danger also. We'll look at those factors in more detail later. A single unit in forex trading is $100,000, so you can see why a lot of leverage is necessary.

How the Forex Works

When you trade currencies on the forex you are hoping that one currency will appreciate in value relative to another (or you hope it will fall in value if you are short). Forex trades always involve two currencies, one you buy and the other you sell.

The currencies are quoted as pairs, with the base currency being the first one listed. For example, USD/JPY is the U.S. dollar and the Japanese yen. In this case, the quote would be for how many yen would be needed to buy a dollar. A quote might look like this:

USD/JPY = 109.06/16

The quote is showing the bid and ask price. The bid is what the market maker will buy at and the ask is what he will sell at. The ask is always the higher price. In the case of the Japanese yen, the price is quoted to two decimal places. Other currencies are quoted to four decimal places. In this case, one U.S. dollar can be bought for 109.16 yen or if you were shorting, sold for 109.06 yen. Let's look at another quote:

USD/CAD = 1.0195/05

Quotes typically only show the last two digits of the ask price. From this you would know that the ask price for Canadian dollars is 1.0205 (because the ask price is always higher). The difference between the bid and ask is the spread. In this case it equals 0.001 or 10 units of 0.0001 each (1.0205 – 1.0195 = 0.001). These units (0.0001) are called pips and they represent the minimum change in a currency quote (with the exception of the yen, which is 0.01). A pip or 0.0001 may seem like an insignificant amount of money (one one-hundredth of a cent). However, when you multiply them by many thousand thanks to the huge leverage in forex, you can see significant profits and losses.

> **Trading Tip**
>
> Pips may sound silly, but they are critical to your investing success on the forex. The spread between the bid and ask price is very important. The wider the spread, the harder it will be to make a profit because you buy at the higher price and sell at the lower one.

Currencies Traded

Most traders focus on the currencies from eight countries and the pairs they form. This makes the learning curve fairly shallow in terms of knowing the components of the market (unlike the 10,000 plus stocks or 8,000 plus mutual funds). Here are the major currencies:

- U.S. Dollar—USD
- The euro—EUR

- The Swiss franc—CHF

- The British pound—GBP

- The Canadian dollar—CAD

- The New Zealand dollar—NZD

- The Australian dollar—AUD

- The Japanese yen—JPY

Of these the major pairs are: EUR/USD, USD/JPY, GBP/USD, and USD/CHF. There are three called commodity pairs: AUD/USD, USD/CAD, and NZD/USD.

There are many other currencies, but these are the ones favored by most traders.

How to Make Money at Currency Trading

Simply stated, you make money when the currency you buy appreciates in value relative to the currency (in the pair) you sold. When that happens, you sell the other currency back to make your profit. If you believe the USD will appreciate relative to the JPY, you would buy the USD/JPY pair. When you do this, you are buying USD and selling (shorting) JPY. If you are correct and the dollar does rise relative to the JPY, you are in a profitable position. To close the trade and capture your profit, you sell dollars and buy JPY. Since the dollar now buys more JPY, your profit is the difference between what you sold the JPY for and what you can now buy with appreciated dollars. You convert the profit from yen to dollars to deposit in your account.

Here's a tangible example. You have 100:1 leverage in your account.

> USD/JPY = 109.06/16. You buy one standard unit of the pair, which means you buy USD $100,000 and sell 10,916,000 yen (ask price of 109.16 yen × 100,000).

> You are right and the dollar rises 50 pips so the quote is now: USD/JPY = 109.56/66. To close you sell one lot of USD $100,000 and receive 10,956,000 yen. Since you are short yen, your profit is the difference (10,956,000 − 10,916,000 = 40,000 yen). When you covert the yen to dollars, your profit is $365 (40,000 yen ÷ 109.56 = $365).

Your investment was $1,000 and your profit was $365 for a return of 36.5 percent. Of course, the market could have gone the other way, and you would have suffered a loss of that size or worse if you weren't careful.

Most traders use protective stops and limit orders to make sure if the market turns against them, their losses are contained to a manageable amount. The illustration above shows a trade when there is a 50-pip move. The power of leverage is the only factor that makes the trade worthwhile. Many traders find that they need much more capital than $1,000 to successfully trade in the forex.

The preceeding illustration could have been a loss and traders with only $1,000 of capital would have lost over one-third of their trading capacity in one trade. One or two more bad trades (a real possibility in the fast-moving forex) and they are wiped out. How much capital you need depends on how aggressive you plan to trade and how many trades you plan to execute on a regular basis.

This is the simplest strategy for making money. There are other more sophisticated strategies for trading on the forex that will make more sense once you are comfortable trading in the basic fashion. You can also buy forward and future contracts on forex positions, although most traders prefer the cash or spot market.

Trading Tip _____

To make money in a trade, the move has to be greater than the spread. This is why trading when there is a large spread may not be a good bet.

Forex Brokers

Many online platforms and brokers offer forex trading or you can use one of the many dedicated forex brokers. All quality forex brokers will let you practice trade using their systems so you can get a feel for how they work and spend some time trading. If you plan to do forex trading on a regular or full-time basis, sign up for as many training sessions as you can and plan to spend quite a few hours practice trading. There is no substitute for trading against live market data.

Most forex brokers don't charge a commission in the traditional sense. What they do charge are pips in the spread. It is important to know how many pips are charged and for which pairs. Most brokers either post this on their website or will provide it to you before you open an account.

Some brokers allow you to open accounts for $1,000 and sometimes less. These are for people still unsure about trading the forex. Most brokers offer a tiered service based on your initial deposit and the account balance you maintain. The higher those numbers, the more goodies in terms of tighter spreads, more research, and access to a more sophisticated platform you may receive. If you are serious about trading the forex full-time, plan on an initial stake of $25,000 to $50,000.

The Bottom Line

Forex trading is an exciting way to make a living or some extra money if you want to keep a day job and trade at night. It is easy to master the basics, but understanding the various forces that change the value of currencies around the world is much more complicated. The risks are very high due to the enormous leverage, but the corresponding rewards are equally staggering. Don't think this is easy money, despite what you may read or hear. You are trading against and with major world banks and sophisticated money managers who live and breathe currency hedging every day.

The Least You Need to Know

◆ Trading futures contracts is attractive to active traders because it offers a high degree of leverage and volatility.

◆ E-Mini futures contracts on stock indexes are among the most heavily traded securities.

◆ Trading E-Mini futures contracts utilizes tremendous leverage for possible gain with a high degree of risk.

◆ The forex market is larger and more liquid than the U.S. stock market.

◆ The forex market offers tremendous leverage, which means high profit potential, but also the possibility of suffering huge losses.

Part 3

Active Trading Tools

Active traders must have the best trading tools to succeed in a highly competitive market. That means access to the latest price information and the best order-execution systems. Specialized trading tools, including direct access brokers for short-term traders, help traders identify profit opportunities and capitalize on them.

Profiting on price changes in the fast-moving whirl of intraday trading requires discipline and practice, along with the right tools. The charts created by technical analysis are among the most important tools short-term active traders must master. Fortunately, there are many sources for this information.

Chapter 10

Information Power

In This Chapter

◆ Active traders must be right with information

◆ Information must be tailored to trading strategy

◆ Information must be easily digested and acted on

◆ Information costs cannot be excessive

Active traders, more so than buy-and-hold investors, must have good up-to-date information as a basis for their trades. Data and information are not the same thing. Data is only helpful when it is digested into actionable information that a trader can use. Finding sources of information that distill and digest streams of data into information that can be used in making a decision is not always easy. One of the strengths of technical analysis is that it presents a lot of data in a graphic form that is easy to digest quickly. It would be impossible to digest and compare columns of numbers as quickly as looking at a chart.

Trading on What You Know

Active traders need to be focused to be successful. The key is identifying what information to focus on and how to translate that information into profitable trades. Active traders who keep their trades confined to a single trading day have different information needs than position or trend traders. Successful traders learn what information is important to what they are trading today. If they switch strategies tomorrow, their information needs will change, but for today, here is what information is needed.

Data Overload

The Internet has changed the way active traders conduct their business—in fact, without the Internet, it would be hard to imaging active trading as we know it today. One of the real benefits of being connected via the Internet is the vast amount of data and research that's available, much of it free. For buy-and-hold investors who have the time, inclination, and expertise, the information on companies and stocks on the Internet is a gold mine. They can spend hours analyzing financial statements, analysts' reports, historical stock prices, and all manner of research. For many, this access is a wonderful resource. For others, to quote a well-worn cliché, it's like putting a fire hose in your mouth and turning on the hydrant—it's just too much.

> **Trading Tip**
>
> Information management is an important part of an active trader's daily tasks. The more organized and filtered it is, the more beneficial information will be to the trader.

> **Margin Call**
>
> Not only is there an overload of information on the Internet, some of it is wrong, and some of it is fraudulent. Be very careful, especially in forums and chat rooms, of people touting a particular stock or security—this is often a scheme to pump up the price and then the culprits sell a big block of shares and the price collapses.

Information by Design

Active traders soon realize that they don't need and don't have time to study the quantity of material most investors use. Depending of what they are trading, active traders will identify a small number of key indicators that serve as their primary "buy or sell" signals. Too many indicators and traders will miss an opportunity or see a trade go bad before they can check them all. Frequently, traders will use signs that lead to multistage decisions.

Short-term traders usually don't have time for multistep decision-making. Short-term traders move when they see the opportunity based on a very few indicators. In most cases, these traders want to be out in front of the market, but always headed in the same direction. Technical analysis with its easy-to-read charts suits this type of fast-paced trading well, as we'll see in several later chapters. Traders have favorite charts that they turn to for quick input.

By the Numbers

The most basic information a short-term trader needs is immediate price data as orders are entered and executed. Most direct access brokers offer price quotes as part of their package, but not all quotes are equal. Depending on the system, prices may be just a skip behind the market. For short-term traders this can be a disaster. Pricing information is so important that some traders will buy it from a vendor even if it is available as part of their direct access account. The world of scalping is measured in fractions of seconds at times. Traders who are behind the market will soon be out of the market.

As we'll see in coming chapters, comprehensive price and volume information is essential for short-term traders. It is this information that tells traders which way the market is moving and if prices are building up on the buy or sell side. *Nasdaq Level II* reporting (as opposed to *Nasdaq Level I* or summary quotes, discussed next) shows traders not only the price of the security but, equally important, the unfilled orders on both the bid and ask side. This information helps traders form a picture of where the market is going and which side they should be on to profit. You can't reasonably expect to succeed as a short-term trader without this level of detailed information.

def•i•ni•tion

Nasdaq Level I prices are the best current price in the market. These are the quotes you'll see on site offering "live quotes." They tell you the price, but that's all. Nasdaq Level II quotes show all the bid orders that are lower than the best bid price and ask orders higher than the current best ask price so that you can see orders stacking up on the bid or ask side, which may help you determine whether the market is bearish or bullish on the security.

What Do You Need to Know?

Short-term traders can be paralyzed by too much information, but position or trend traders must have much more information to establish and know how long to hold a position in a security. Your first task is to define your information needs. If you are going to do more than one type of trading, each strategy will have its own set of information requirements. In subsequent chapters, we'll go over each of the four major active trading strategies (short term, momentum, swing, and position) as we have defined them. Part of that discussion will focus on minimum information needs to be successful. However, experienced traders soon develop their own information requirements that work best for them and their trading style.

When Do You Need It?

Active traders by definition are in the market in real time. They grab small profits multiple times during a trading day or larger profits multiple times during a trading week. This type of trading strategy requires real time price and volume information. Don't confuse this requirement with the "free live quotes" you see offered through many online brokers. These quotes are "inside" quotes, meaning you are seeing the best bid and ask prices available on the market—also known as Nasdaq Level I quotes or summary quotes.

Level I quotes are fine if you simply want to know where a security is trading at a given moment. However, they do not provide enough information to traders. For that information, traders turn to Level II Nasdaq quotes. Level II quotes show all the bids and ask quotes and the order size that are *away from the market*—that is, not at the current best bid and ask price. In other words, bid orders that are lower than the best bid price and ask orders higher than the current best ask price. Here is where you will see orders stacking up on the bid or ask side (or spread evenly), which may help you determine whether the market is bearish or bullish on the security.

def•i•ni•tion

> Away from the market means the bid or the ask price on a stock is not the best order available at that moment. There are lower bids or higher asks currently available.

Your Pre-Game Preparation

Athletes prepare for a game by studying the opposition and playing field. They plan a strategy based on the strengths and weaknesses of their opponents. For active traders, this means studying the market before it opens to decide whether it will open with a positive or negative bias. You'll want to decide, based on observation and analysis, if the market looks like it will rise or fall this session, and plan your strategy around that conclusion.

Most traders develop a routine they do each morning before the market opens. This process touches the various areas they need to check before deciding if the market looks like it will open up or down. While short-term traders react to price and volume changes when the market is open, they also make themselves aware of any important news that might affect the market's direction or velocity. Traders can make money on down markets as well as up markets, although many prefer a rising market for purely psychological reasons.

Here are some news sources that traders use to gauge where the market might be headed in the coming trading session:

♦ **News broadcasts.** Early morning news from CNN or another credible news source can give you the headlines concerning any big news stories that may affect the market today. Remember, the stock market prices events in advance. If something is scheduled to happen, it is priced into the market immediately, so most of the impact is already absorbed before the event happens. What moves the market are surprises—a sudden jump in the price of oil, an unexpected ruling from a federal agency or by a court, and so on.

♦ **Stock index futures.** Your broker likely provides this, but if they don't or your want to check them before logging in, you can find them at cnnmoney.com in the "markets" section. There you'll find futures quotes for all the major stock indexes. You'll see two figures, the index and the fair value. The fair value is the relationship between the futures contract and the value of the index. If the futures contract is higher, the difference will be a positive number; if it is lower, a negative number. You will often hear early morning newscast talking about stock futures opening higher or lower. These are the figures they are looking at, and they are a good indicator of where the market will open, but not necessarily the direction it will maintain all day.

> **Market Place**
>
> Stock index futures are great indicators of where the market may open, but once the bell rings all manner of things may happen to change price direction. Count on the futures for starting guidance, but forget them after the market opens.

♦ **Economic reports.** What major economic reports are due today and will any of them hold potential surprises? The market anticipates what reports are going to say and if the reports are on target or very close, you won't see much reaction.

However, if the numbers are a surprise—good or bad—the market may have a strong reaction. Depending on the report, some sector may react more sharply than others do. If you trade in a specific industry group, learn what economic reports affect that sector the most and stay on top of that news. You can find economic report calendars on a number of websites—www.breifing.com has one of the better reports.

- ◆ **Sector reports.** Develop a short list of websites you can scan for industry and sector news. Look for headlines that may be market movers or stories that you may want to come back to after trading hours.

- ◆ **Your trading targets.** If you trade a specific group of stocks or securities, focus on any news about what has happened overnight that may move prices today. This could include upgrades or downgrades from stock analysts, regulatory news, key personnel changes, and so on. Remember, if you trade derivatives, you must follow the underlying security.

It is helpful to many traders to have a more or less set routine of information gathering before the markets open or before you begin trading. The routine gets traders in the proper mindset to do business. This can be helpful since most work out of their homes that are filled with distractions. The routine also assures you that all information bases are covered each day. The longer you work at active trading, the more refined your routine will become. You can alter it as you add new products to trade.

Short-Term Traders' Needs

In addition to the information traders gather from the sources above, short-term traders prepare for the market opening by having potential trades set up on securities they follow. The overall market information gives them an idea of whether the market will trend up or down for the day. Now they begin focusing on specific securities they plan to trade. Traders will have their charts set up and the specific indicators in place so they can focus on the action once trading begins.

Once trading begins, short-term traders focus on their charts to give them the immediate information they need. However, their initial plan for the day was established based on the information gathered before the market opened. As trading continues, things change and short-term traders must be able to adapt. Since traders will close their position before the end of the day, the only concern is how prices and volume are changing right now and what does that mean for the traders' strategies.

Beginners who jump into trading without any preparation seldom get past the beginner designation before they run out of money. Experienced traders have a trading plan of what they want to trade today and under what conditions. Experienced traders don't guess. If there are no good trades in the securities, they prepared for, they either switch to another security they are prepared for or they go play golf and try again tomorrow.

Margin Call

The market moves too quickly for short-term traders to make up a plan as they go. If your plan isn't working, close out your positions and find out why. Trying to repair your plan while trading is a recipe for disaster.

Swing Traders' Information Needs

Swing traders work at a fast pace, although not as fast as the short-term trader. Since swing traders may hold a position for several days or weeks, they are more concerned with information that can stop or reverse the upward (or downward) swings in prices. While technical indicators play a major role for the short-term traders, they play a less, although still important role, for the swing trader. Swing traders look for stocks that trade in a range or channel and may be slowly drifting up or down. This type of trading is usually difficult if the overall market is trending sharply in one direction or the other.

Swing traders need more fundamental, sector, and overall market information than short-term traders. Technical analysis traders will disagree, but many active traders find they have a large blind spot if they don't focus attention on external indicators (other than price and volume, for example). A security that works for a swing trader can become derailed by news events, economic reports, company fundamentals (earnings reports, for example) or other factors that have nothing to do with price or trading volume.

Technical analysis will tell swing traders the approximate range a stock is trading in using an exponential moving average to establish a baseline. The "swing" in swing trading is the price moving over this baseline and falling back below it, only to move up again. The high and low form the channel the stock trades in and swing traders can profit going both ways with the price. As the price moves up, swing traders

Market Place

Swing trading seems to work best when the market indexes are not going either direction with any authority. With the overall market drifting along, certain stocks will trade within a range that makes them good swing candidates.

buy or take a long position. When the price hits the top of the channel, it will typically reverse back down. Swing traders will close the long position and short the stock as it falls below the baseline. Traders will cover their short as the stock hits the bottom of the channel and begins an upward bounce.

Of course, it doesn't always work this smoothly. However, if swing traders have done their homework, they will take a long position as the security rises and if it keeps going past the top of the channel, that's more profit for them. By using protective market orders, they can cover their profits in the event the security reverses course (as many do). If swing traders have a position that breaks out of the channel and keeps going, they have become a position trader. Some swing traders set profit targets and close their position when those are reached even if it appears the security has more profit by holding longer.

The danger with holding is that traders are great at convincing themselves a security that was doing well, but is now falling in price, will reverse course again and continue upward. That may happen, but often undisciplined traders and investors watch profits evaporate while they wait for a security to reverse its slide.

Position Traders' Information Needs

Position traders who may hold a trade for months are more closely aligned with investors than traders when it comes to information needs. Fundamental analysis of a company drives the decision-making for many position traders; however, the technical analysts never stop looking at their charts for answers. What both strategies look for are securities that are beginning a sustained upward (or downward) trend. It is not necessary to buy at the first tick of the trend (and you won't know it anyway).

The position trader's goal is to identify those securities that are suited to begin a long-term movement is some direction. The trick is identifying when price movement is a trend as opposed to a bump. Jumping in too quickly can mean you may find your trend falling out from under you. However, if you wait too long and the trend is well established, most of the gain may already be gone.

The position traders' other dilemma is when to close out their positions. Experienced traders use protective market orders to cover much of their profits. Setting a rule about when you exit is a good idea. Some traders wait until the trend has backed off a certain amount before closing, while others cut their position at the first sign of a reversal. These traders tend to rely heavily on technical analysis of price and volume for buy and sell signals.

As you become more experienced, you will develop your own system for evaluating position trades and the information you need to trigger a trade. Whether you rely more on fundamental or technical analysis is less important than having a plan and following it. Traders who profess to have a "feel" for the market and base their trades on instinct alone usually are looking for another line of work soon. The instinct that some experienced traders talk about is the experience of having seen similar circumstances before and remembering the outcome.

Trading Tip

The market cliché "The trend is your friend" has a ring of truth in it. Riding a trend up or down can be very profitable, especially if the trend runs for several months.

Information Bites

Information for traders must not only be appropriate for the type of trading, but it also must be in a form that is easily digestible. Columns and columns of numbers can be difficult to understand or summarize. Even charts and graphs can be confusing and misleading if they are not constructed properly and labeled clearly. Traders need to be able to look at the information and quickly understand what it means—not just its face value, but in the broader context of how the information changes or confirms their valuation of the security.

Short-term traders are the most vulnerable to foggy information. If the data screens and charts they construct aren't clear and concise, traders will miss opportunities trying to decipher the information. A quick glance at a chart(s) should be sufficient to tell traders what they need to know about what is happening that minute in the market.

Margin Call

Agony for a short-term trader is waiting for a chart to draw while the market pushes ahead. Dynamic charts that update in real time and the Internet connection to support them are money well spent.

Swing and position traders have the luxury of more time than the short-term trader does, but that doesn't change the need for information to be clear and concise. These traders have more time to digest information, but there is no reason they should have to stumble through confusing and contradictory statements to learn the truth. The efficient market theory says that all knowledge is already priced into securities and no one has an edge on knowing something others don't know.

What that means in practical terms is that it is unlikely you will uncover some important piece of information about a company that will give you an edge that no other trader or investor has. But it also means you had better know what the market knows about why a stock is priced at a certain level. For example, if a company's stock is undervalued by the market, you should know why. Is the company in serious debt trouble? Have they lost significant market share? It may just be an overlooked company in an uninteresting industry sector, which qualifies it as a value stock. Value investors are willing to hold the right value stocks for long periods, believing the market will one day re-price them upward.

The Internet provides many sources of fundamental information for traders who want to examine companies for the inside out. You can find a great deal of free information or go to paid sources, which typically include analysis or commentary along with straight information.

> ### Market Place
>
> Full-service brokers used to earn their commissions by making recommendations to clients. That service still exists and many traders and investors use the advice. If you want someone to help you pick investments, you must have a sizable amount to invest.

Your broker or direct access provider may offer research as part of your account services. This information comes in several forms, including referrals to third-party providers, proprietary services, and a mix. Full-service brokers provide not only information but also recommendations to clients. If you are not interested or don't have the time to make your own choices, this is a viable route for position traders. We'll discuss brokers and their services and fees in Chapter 11.

Paying for Information

With all the information available free on the Internet, paying for even more may seem almost wasteful. While you must run your trading operation like a business and watch expenses, you shouldn't cut corners on services that may mean success or failure. How much and what type of information you may need to buy is determined by the type of active trading you plan to do and what is provided by your broker or direct access provider.

Price Quotes

Short-term trading demands Level II Nasdaq quotes—there is no compromise here. Simply seeing a live quote is not nearly enough information, as we'll see in Chapter 17. Many advance brokers and direct access providers offer Level II quotes as part of their package. However, some traders find that the process of the quotes passing from the exchange through the broker's system before it appears on their screens is too slow. They choose to use an outside source for quotes that specializes in providing information as their main business.

A number of vendors provide this service in some form. At the top of the line are information platforms that offer a wide and deep range of information services, including price quotes. These sophisticated platforms are dynamic, meaning they push information to the screen constantly. More importantly, you can customize the display of information to suit your needs. The combination of news, analysis, charting, price quotes, and alerts make these platforms the ultimate information centers.

Of course, you can expect to pay a hefty price for what you get. The good news is many information platforms offer a basic service for a monthly fee and then let you add on only the extras you need. The tab can still run several hundred a month, but if you are an active trader and serious about succeeding, you owe it to yourself to check out what these marvels of information reporting have to offer. Many will let you try the system or parts of it for 30 days with various money-back offers. If you are considering using an expensive information portal, try before you buy.

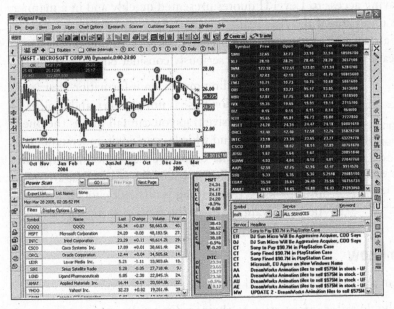

This image of an eSignal. com window shows how much information the company can place on your computer. This is just one of hundreds of configurations.

(Photo courtesy of eSignal.com.)

Basic Information

Position traders may find this level of detail too much and too pricey, although many active traders practice multiple strategies and need to cover all of their information bases. However, if you plan a slower approach to trading, Level II quotes are probably not necessary. Whether you buy a stock at $25.23 or $25.24 per share will not make much difference six months from now.

You do need access to fundamental information, including all the appropriate financial ratios and comparisons to sector and market averages. Much of this information is free or can be purchased with a subscription to one of several premium services. MorningStar.com offers a premium service for a small monthly subscription that includes a stock screener and analysts' comments on many stocks. Other similar services are sufficient for the position trader who can take time to study companies before trading.

The Cost of Information

What you pay for information is relative to its benefit to you. If you are a very active short-term trader, having access to Level II quotes presented quickly and in a manner that is clear to you is invaluable. Likewise, real-time charting software can present buy or sell signals at a glance. If these services help you make money and don't cost more than they increase your profits, you should seriously consider employing them.

Trading Tip

Almost all information and price quote services offer some type of free trial. Take advantage of these offers to see which services fit your needs the best.

Of course, spending money on information that you don't need and don't use is unnecessary and foolish. The most expensive trap you can fall into is the one of buying bells and whistles you don't understand, use, or need. The other expensive trap is not investing in the tools that will help you make trades that are more profitable. Active trading is difficult enough without taking advantage of all the tools at your disposal.

The Least You Need to Know

- Information is an active trader's tool and is necessary for success.
- Active traders should tailor information to their trading style.
- Information should be formatted for quick delivery and retention.
- Traders should avoid paying for information they don't need and invest in the information that will help them succeed.

Chapter **11**

Stockbrokers and Advisers

In This Chapter

◆ Swing and position traders can use retail brokerage firms

◆ Minimum expectations of an online broker

◆ Examine all costs, not just commissions

◆ Should you use an investment manager or financial planner?

Not all active traders require Nasdaq Level II price quotes and live streaming news feeds. You can still practice some forms of active trading using a regular online retail broker. These firms execute trades for all types of securities with proper licensing. Traders can find firms that offer rapid execution of orders and low commissions. Full-service brokerage firms have morphed into a type of investment management service that works for some investors who want a professional looking after their assets. Many active investors would rather manage their own accounts, but for those who don't or who want some extra help, there are investment management firms or services that offer assistance and/or guidance.

Retail Stockbrokers

Retail stockbrokers are familiar to anyone who has been involved in investing—and many of the names will likely ring a bell with others because of the advertising they do. First and foremost, these firms execute your trade orders—buy, sell, and so on. You cannot trade securities except through a firm that is licensed to do so for you. Brokers are required by regulation to act in your best interest, although with online order entry it is often hard for a brokerage to know what is right for you.

def•i•ni•tion

Retail stockbrokers provide general brokerage services to non-professional investors and traders. Retail brokers can adequately serve the majority of people who invest or trade.

Stockbrokers are strictly regulated because they handle your money and, in some accounts, have the authority to enter trades without the owner's approval. All of the principal employees of a broker are licensed to handle certain types of transactions and/or to supervise others who do. Later in this chapter, we'll look at the regulatory agencies involved and what recourse customers have if there is a problem.

A Brief History

The stockbrokerage industry was once dominated by a handful of powerful firms with offices in many cities around the country. During this period, you had to establish a personal relationship with a stockbroker, which usually meant going into his office and opening an account. From there, you could call in your orders to buy or sell. The broker would frequently present you with ideas or opportunities he thought were attractive. Some people turned over their assets to the broker and gave him the authority to invest on their behalf—these are known as discretionary accounts. Commissions were outrageous, often several hundred dollars for a 100-share transaction.

Market Place

An industry once noted for its snob appeal as much as its investment advice, the brokerage community is now highly competitive and market driven.

In May of 1975, the Securities and Exchange Commission abolished the fixed commissions and let the market set rates. Charles Schwab was the first to see the potential of discounted commissions and founded the first discount stockbrokerage. His company is still one of the industry leaders. Others soon followed and the stuffy Wall Street firms either adapted to the new world or disappeared. Commissions went from the hundreds per trade to the low teens and less.

However, when commissions dropped so did much of the "service" that had been part of the full-service brokerage. This included access to research, a person to help you with investment decisions, and so on. While many investors and traders embraced the no-frills discounted commissions approach, others wanted some assistance in investment and trading decisions. This led to brokerage firms forming investment management practices.

This service operates under different trade names and may offer different services by vendor, but it is a step back to more personal contact with the customer. As we'll see below, it also offers a different method of compensation.

Basic Brokerages

Many active traders (swing and position) simply need a way to execute stock orders. They don't necessarily need intraday prices and use protective orders to make sure their losses are minimal if the trade goes bad. These active traders look for a broker that offers a reliable and inexpensive way to place orders. Once in place, they can follow the progress of the trade with regular quotes.

Swing traders will want access to live quotes (not the delayed quotes you see on many free news sites). Most brokerage accounts provide Level I Nasdaq quotes as part of their service. If not, you can find these quotes in a variety of places, most free. This is not a universal standard. There are some swing traders who are very aggressive and want intraday prices, in which case they will need a broker that can provide that level of service. A retail broker may not be adequate for these traders, in which case a trading platform with a direct access broker (see Chapter 12) is in order.

Basic brokerage firms offer deep discounts on commissions and can serve active traders' needs by keeping their trading costs low. If what you need is a firm that will provide you the means to place your stock orders and not screw them up, the basic brokerage firm/account may be for you.

Trading Tip

Many of the deep discount brokers offer even better deals for active traders who trade a lot and don't need customer service or investment advice.

Tiered-Commission Brokerages

Many brokerage firms have staked out a middle ground between the deep discounters and the modified full service brokers. These firms may offer some form of investment advice, but usually not an individual dedicated to your account. They have comprehensive research offerings or pair with an outside service to provide clients with research and analysis.

These firms may offer very low commissions, usually a tiered commission structure that is keyed to the number of trades you make. An active trader who wants access to research and someone to bounce ideas off of every once in awhile may find these firms' offerings are a good fit.

Full-Service Brokerages

While full-service brokerage firms as they existed in pre-1975 days are gone, you can still find many firms that are eager to work with you and your assets. Some traders may value the access to an investment professional for assistance or want to tap proprietary research that is available to clients with these accounts. What the firms are hoping you will do is put all your investment assets under their management (discretionary or not). For an annual percentage fee (usually paid quarterly), they will give you unlimited trades, access to a professional investment adviser, and other value-added services. The annual fee is determined by how much you place in assets under their management. One to two percent of assets under management per year is common.

> **Margin Call**
>
> What happens if your assets under management drop below the brokerage's minimum threshold? Before you sign on with an asset manager, make sure you won't be hit with retroactive fees and so on.

Traders may find this arrangement more beneficial and economical, but watch for extra fees and limits on trades of access to investment professionals. These can change the benefits of this type of account.

Your Choice

Many of the leading retail stockbrokerage firms offer accounts that range from deep discount to investment management. Your choice of a stockbroker should include the services offered as they fit your particular trading needs and as the firm qualifies in the other areas listed below.

Evaluating a Broker

Traders look for certain qualities in a brokerage firm. Not all traders rank qualities the same, but most would agree on some basics. The major stockbrokers offer a wide variety of services and are usually competitive in pricing for comparable services.

However, it is worth your time to shop. Most will let you try their website's interface through a demo account and many will let you paper trade to get a feel for their system and online trading. If this service is offered, take some time to try out the site. In many cases, you'll quickly get a sense of how well you can work with it—or not.

Working Online

Since most, if not all, of the interaction occurs through the company's website, it is important for the trader to find it comfortable and easy to navigate. The response time should be acceptable even during heavy trading. Given the popularity of BlackBerry mobile devices and other smart phones, the company should offer a robust mobile service. The trader should have a phone number that she can call to place trade if away from her computer or if there is a problem connecting with the website.

One of the harshest criticisms of online brokers is their vulnerability to an Internet disconnection or service disruption. Active traders who specialize in short-term trading often have a redundant connection as a backup. That may be overkill for swing and position traders, especially if they always use protective stock orders. However, in stressful market events of the past, online brokers have been swamped and unable to keep up with orders coming in via the Internet. Orders were running hours behind and in severe cases computer servers crashed, rendering the website inaccessible.

Market Place
In extreme market conditions, no broker may be able to keep up with orders. However, a very active day is not an extreme market condition. Consider it an extreme market condition if the exchanges drop five percent.

It is important to have a phone number, preferably one that is only available to customers, so you can call in orders if the Internet connection is lost or the computer system crashes. A phone line is not a good solution if there is no one on the other end to answer it. These are important questions to ask potential stockbrokers.

Ease of Use

It is remarkable that in this day and age, websites that are supposed to be "self-service" are designed so poorly that traders have a difficult time figuring out what they are supposed to do. There is nothing more frustrating than filling out a screen of information and clicking on "submit" only to get an error message because you put the date in the wrong format or some other silly mistake. Websites that don't tell you exactly what to do and in what format waste your time and could cost you money as you struggle to get a trade entered.

Navigation through forms should be intuitive, but with directions. Navigation from page to page and section to section should also flow logically and you should always be able to get back to the home page with one click from any other page. Accomplishing any task from making a trade to changing contact information should not take more than a few clicks to get to the correct screen.

Reliability

A critical factor in picking a stockbroker is how reliable is access to your account. If a storm knocks out the company's electricity, do they have a backup generator? What are the contingency plans if there is a natural disaster or other problem that affects only this firm?

Reliability goes beyond physical integrity—it includes fiscal integrity. Stockbrokers are highly regulated but you don't want to deal with a company that has a lengthy history of complaints from consumers and trouble with regulatory agencies. In the section below, you will learn which agencies regulate the securities industry and how you can check on a firm's background.

Advice and Management

If you are looking for advice and management skills from the stockbroker, how comfortable are you with what they offer? In some cases, this may be hard to determine in advance. However, firms with a history of giving inappropriate advice or mismanaging clients' funds will have a history with regulatory agencies. Stockbrokers are required to suggest investments that are appropriate to their client. The "prudent man" test is a generic appropriateness qualifier for investments. Stockbrokers are supposed to ask themselves if a prudent man would recommend this investment to a particular client.

> **Trading Tip**
>
> Before you sign on with an investment adviser, ask about their approach to investing. If all you get are a bunch of clichés, you'll probably want to interview someone else.

For example, it would be inappropriate to suggest to an elderly widow that she invest significant assets in a speculative high-technology stock. That same investment might be fine for a 30 something, however.

Another concern is stockbrokers recommending securities of companies they represent in other capacities. Often, large brokerage firms also help raise money for companies through secondary stock offerings and other means. When stockbrokers push these products, there is a conflict of interest—the stockbroker does not have the best interest of the retail customer first. There were several scandals on Wall Street where analysts for major brokerages were recommending the stock of clients.

If you are working with a stockbroker who is offering advice or investment suggestions, you should always be asking yourself who benefits from this investment more—the stockbroker or me?

Keep an Eye on Costs

When shopping for an online broker, active traders should be aware that advertised prices per trade might not be the whole story. Read all material carefully to determine what other fees or charges may apply. For example, you may see a very low per trade cost, but on further examination discover that you have to make a minimum number of trades to receive this rate. For an active trader, meeting this minimum may not be a problem. However, you shouldn't be locked into one rate that is dependent on making more trades than you planned to make.

Another popular marketing tool is free trades up front. The firm will give new customers 50 or more free trades to get them started in the account. However, these free offers often have a time limit for making the trades, which may not meet your calendar of events.

If the stockbroker provides certain quotes from the exchanges, you may be responsible for paying exchange fees. Exchange fees can run from a little over a dollar to more than $20 per month depending on the exchange and the depth of prices you want to receive. Some brokerages will waive the fees for large accounts.

Another common fee is an account maintenance fee, which may be charged on a quarterly basis, depending on your level of activity. This fee is supposed to cover preparing statements, mailings, and so on. If your account is dormant for a prescribed period, you may have to pay an inactive account fee.

Trading Tip _____

Active traders are effectively operating a business. As such, they must watch expenses. What may seem like just a few dollars in fees now will over time eat away at your return since they reduce your profitability.

Regulatory Agencies

The securities industry is highly regulated, yet with all the scandals that seem to fill the headlines, you may wonder if that is so. Unfortunately, people bent on cutting corners will usually find a way. The good news is most of them eventually are caught. It is the practitioners who dwell in that area between legal and illegal that cause the industry so much pain. These are the stockbrokers who put people in inappropriate products, who trade too often in discretionary accounts, who push company products over the customers' best interest, and so on.

The regulatory structure begins with the United States Congress. It created most of the structure and it passes major laws that affect how the industry operates. It also authorizes budgets for the Securities and Exchange Commission and other agencies involved in regulatory duties. The SEC is the top regulatory agency responsible for overseeing the securities industry. It registers new securities and handles all the filings that public companies must make, such as annual and quarterly reports.

Margin Call

The SEC aggressively prosecutes securities professionals who take advantage of the investing public. They also will prosecute individuals who attempt to trade on inside information or commit some other type of security fraud.

The SEC also oversees all of the stock exchanges and any organization connected with the selling of securities. It also has a strong anti-fraud unit that monitors advertising and marketing to make sure companies comply with strict rules concerning the sale of securities.

At the next level is the Financial Industry Regulatory Authority (FINRA). It was created in 2007 when the National Association of Securities Dealers merged with the regulatory functions of the New York Stock Exchange. This is an industry self-regulatory body that is responsible for policing the securities industry.

FINRA set standards for stockbrokers and other industry professionals and licenses them after comprehensive examinations. It has the ability to fine individuals and organizations for unethical behavior and can revoke licenses.

The organization is usually the place customers can take complaints of behavior they feel is unethical or illegal. FINRA also monitors trading activities of member firms to detect illegal trading patterns and other illegal activity.

The individual exchanges also have sophisticated regulatory oversight functions within their own operations. These include monitoring trades and other steps to see that customers get a fair deal.

Individual states also have securities divisions, although they are usually not as sophisticated as the FINRA. Often they handle complaints and register securities that will be sold within the boundaries of the state, although this will vary from state to state.

The final step of protection is at the brokerage level. Each firm is required to keep certain records and perform certain checks and audits of the operation to make sure their brokers are operating within acceptable legal and ethical guidelines.

Do You Need a Financial Adviser?

Some traders find that they don't have the time, energy, or talent to research and identify stocks for their portfolio, much less manage their money effectively. Their needs go beyond the scope of a stockbroker—they may need the services of a qualified financial adviser.

Most financial advisers want to look at your whole financial picture—all your income and liabilities. They want a complete picture of where you are financially so they can draw a map from where you are to where you want to go. Here are some of the benefits of using a financial adviser:

- **The big picture.** A financial adviser will develop a comprehensive profile of your financial status. This profile will identify areas of strengths and weakness.

- **An unemotional assessment.** The financial adviser will give you an unemotional assessment of what needs to be done. Money is an emotional topic for many people, which often leads to bad decisions.

> **Market Place**
>
> Active traders can lose sight of their overall financial picture if they are not careful. Retirement and estate planning are important exercises that can't be put off.

- **Allocate resources.** It is likely you have competing priorities, such as sending the kids to college while building a retirement fund. A financial adviser can help you allocate resources so both goals receive the appropriate share of dollars.

- **Minimize taxes.** Most investment decisions carry some type of short- or long-term tax implication. Your adviser can help you shape your investments in a manner that keeps taxes to a minimum and more of your dollars invested.

- **Estate Planning.** Careful planning will help ensure that your estate passes to loved ones in a manner that protects as much of its value as possible.

The plan may include options to reach your goals that involve different levels of commitment on your part (read that dollars). Generally, you can classify financial advisers two ways: by their method of compensation and by professional designations.

Method of Compensation

There are three basic ways you compensate financial advisers for their work: fee only, fee and commission or percentage of assets, and commission only. Each of the three methods has some good points and some weaknesses. In the end, you should choose the adviser you feel would do the best job for you and worry less about the method of compensation.

Fee Only

The fee-only adviser develops a comprehensive plan that lays out how you can reach your financial goals. However, it leaves the actual execution of the plan to you. The adviser doesn't sell any products or services other than the plan itself. Fee-only advisers usually produce the most comprehensive plan since this is their sole product. Fee-only advisers charge more than other types of advisers since they do not take any other form of compensation.

Fee and Commission or Percentage of Assets

The second method of compensation of financial advisers includes a fee and commissions. The fee, which is usually substantially less than what a fee-only adviser would charge, covers the cost of building the plan and commissions cover the cost of execution.

A variation on this compensation plan involves an annual fee based on a percentage of assets in your accounts. The fee compensates the adviser for monitoring your investments and making recommendations. The fee-plus adviser develops a plan for the customer that lays out suggested strategies for reaching the customer's goals. Because the fee-plus adviser receives compensation from executing the plan, the adviser is there to execute the plan. Fee-plus advisers may push certain mutual funds or life insurance products, for example, which may not be the best choice for your particular situation.

Commission Only

The third method of compensation is commission only. Financial advisers receive their only compensation from products they sell to you. I think you can see the inherent problem with this arrangement—it is in advisers' best interests to sell you something. A person who works on a commission-only basis is a salesperson. However, this is not to say that you can't work with someone on this basis. It will depend on the individual and your relationship.

Professional Designations

In many states there are no strict regulations regarding the terms "financial adviser" or "financial planner," meaning anyone can print up business cards using those terms. However, several professional designations are protected.

The top designations you should look for are:

- ◆ **Certified Financial Planner (CFP).** This is the top of the line in terms of professional designations. Before an adviser can carry this designation, they must complete three years of work in financial planning, take a course of study, and pass a comprehensive set of examinations. They must also meet certain ethical and educational standards.

Trading Tip

Active traders are less likely to need financial/investment advisers than the general public, but it may make good sense to employ an objective set of eyes to look at your total financial plan.

- ◆ **Chartered Financial Consultants (ChFC).** ChFCs must take courses of study on personal finance and pass exams.

- ◆ **Certified Public Accountant (CPA).** CPAs must pass exams on accounting and tax preparation to win the designation. However, you want a CPA who has also been awarded the designation Personal Finance Specialist.

If you decide to use a professional financial adviser, the most important considerations are the person's integrity and your relationship. Method of compensation and other factors are secondary to establishing a level of trust that will allow you to work with the adviser in confidence.

The Least You Need to Know

- ◆ Retail stockbrokers work fine for many swing and position traders. These stockbrokers should meet minimum expectations of usability and reliability.

- ◆ Basic brokerages provide discounted commissions, while tiered commission brokerages offer more services but with fees tied to the volume of trades you execute.

- ◆ Full service brokerages charge much higher fees, but provide comprehensive investment services, including advice.

- ◆ The SEC and FINRA are the primary regulatory agencies that cover the financial markets, setting rules for financial disclosure and broker conduct.

- ◆ Be cautious of unadvertised costs that can increase your trading expense with retail stockbrokers.

- ◆ Some traders find working with a financial planner helpful.

Chapter 12

Direct Access Trading

In This Chapter

- ◆ Direct access brokers
- ◆ What an advanced trading platform does
- ◆ Information features of an advanced trading platform
- ◆ Trading features of an advanced trading platform
- ◆ Choosing an advanced trading platform

A minivan and a sports car will both get you to the grocery store. However, if you want to enter a race, the sports car is clearly the better choice. A discount broker can take your order and execute it, but if you want to succeed in short-term trading, you will need something with more horsepower.

Advanced trading platforms offered by direct access brokers are sophisticated, high-performance portals to the market. Thanks to high-speed Internet connections, when you place an order through an advanced trading platform it goes directly to the market. Advanced trading platforms are wonders of information technology and give active traders equal footing with many investment professionals in terms of order execution and access to market news and data. If you are serious about a career as an active trader, especially focusing on short-term trading, you must be plugged into one of the advanced trading platforms. Without the advantages of direct access trading, you have no chance of surviving as an active, short-term trader for very long.

Platforms for Pros

The online brokers described in Chapter 11 will work fine for active traders who focus on swing and position trading, although some swing traders may want extra features, as we'll see in Chapter 19. Day and momentum traders require a much higher degree of sophistication. Their needs require multiple news inputs, along with pricing and volume information that is inside and away from the market. They require an order-entry system that is simple to use, but allows traders to specify exactly what they want to do and split-second order execution.

Trading Tip

If your goal is active trading as a full-time business, don't cut corners on the most important tools—your trading account.

Most important, advanced platforms are offered by direct access brokers. This means your order goes directly to the market and is not routed through a broker's system before eventually being placed into the market. The difference in timing is measured in seconds and may seem miniscule, but to the short-term trader it is an eternity.

Software and Hardware

Most advanced platforms download a significant amount of software on to your computer so it will run faster—the alternative is a Web-based platform, which is discussed below. With the software residing on your computer, you get the benefit of superior performance without many of the dangers and limitations of Web-based programs. A robust computer and display is recommended to take full advantage of the capabilities advanced trading platforms offer. Large flat-panel monitors are easier on the eyes and many traders use more than one. Hardware is covered in more detail in Chapter 22.

Advanced Platform Providers

The market for advanced trading platforms is competitive. A number of good companies provide direct access to the markets. I've listed some of the better known providers in Appendix A. Almost all of the direct access providers offer some type of demo account that will let you try out their software. Take advantage of these offers to see which platforms work the best for you. If you live in or near a major metropolitan area, there's a good chance you can find a trade show for investors. Many of the providers will attend and offer demonstrations of their software.

Major Components

Advanced platform providers differ in screen layouts and other details, but most will offer the following basic services in some form:

♦ Order execution

♦ Nasdaq Level II prices

♦ Time and sales prints

♦ News feeds

♦ Charting

♦ Account management

♦ Screening

♦ Markets

♦ Alerts

> **Market Place**
>
> Advanced trading platforms let you add on components that you need. Many of the services they offer can be bought individually, so if you don't need them, you aren't charged for them.

These are the main features advanced platforms should offer, although not all will be configured in the way described. Some platforms may have additional features.

Order Execution

Everything else an advanced trading platform does is really secondary to order execution. This function is what enables active traders to compete with investment professionals and survive. For short-term traders, hitting a single key to initiate a buy or sell order is what makes it possible to grab small profits dozens of times each trading day. Unlike regular online brokers, the order sent through an advanced trading platform goes directly to the market via Electronic Communication Networks (ECNs) or to market markers or specialists. The difference can be measured in seconds, which in the business of short-term trading is forever.

This shows the order-entry screen for equities from the Interactive Brokers' Trader Workstation. Many of the fields can be pre-assigned to the trader's default values.

(Photo courtesy of Interactive Brokers.)

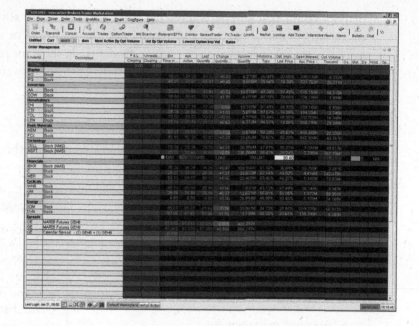

Many of the advanced trading platforms offer single-key order entry with a default number of shares (if you're trading equities) assumed. You can configure the system to automatically generate a limit order when you click on an ask price (more about limit orders in Chapter 13). You can then click on a bid price to generate a limit sell order. If you have correctly bracketed the price, no matter which way it moves, one of your orders will be filled. When the order is filled, you place a stop limit order on it to protect against a loss and a closing order to make your profit goal. All of these orders can be entered and executed with a few clicks because of the way you have configured the system.

> **Margin Call**
>
> Short-term traders learn quickly that if they are not careful in entering orders, market makers will take advantage of them and their order will not be filled at the price they expected. Always use limit orders, which specify an exact price for your order.

With some experience, you'll learn the best way to route your order, whether it is through an ECN, market maker, and so on. This is a level of control that can mean better execution of your order and more profit for you. You stay in greater control of your business and keep more of your money.

When we look at short-term trading in more detail in Chapters 17 and 18, you'll see how the power of order execution through advanced trading platforms makes this form of active trading possible and profitable.

Level II Prices

Level II prices give you insight into trading activity on all Nasdaq stocks. You get more that just the latest quotes—you see all the orders that are away from the market on the bid and ask side. Level II quotes tell you who is entering the quote and for how many shares. Among other things, this information lets you watch the ratio of buyers and sellers by the number and size of order. Along with other information, this gives you a clue about the direction the stock's price may be headed.

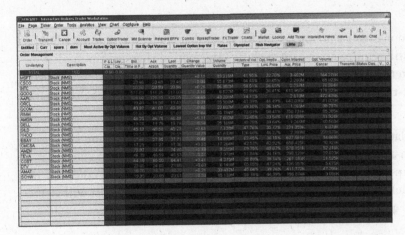

This shows Nasdaq Level II stock quotes from Interactive Brokers' Trader Workstation. Level II quotes show prices inside and away from the market.

(Photo courtesy of Interactive Brokers.)

Each Nasdaq stock has a market maker that is responsible for providing liquidity and maintaining a market for the stock (some stocks will have more than one). With some studying, you will be able to identify this market maker, known as the *ax* in trading jargon. Smart traders will usually want to place their order through the ax because that's where the best prices are found.

Without Level II prices, you would not know where your best price was.

While Level II is an important source of information, it can also be used for tricks. Large orders can be broken up to hide a big buy or sale. Professional traders may enter large orders to trick inexperienced traders into certain positions. We'll explore this further in Chapters 14 and 17.

def•i•ni•tion

The **ax** is a market term for the main market maker for a Nasdaq stock. The market maker is responsible for creating an orderly market for a stock and must be willing to either buy or sell the stock if needed. You usually get the best prices from the ax.

Time and Sales Prints

Before computers, trades were printed out on ticker tapes. The term prints has hung on and that information is still very important to active traders. It is formally called the Time and Sales display and it records the price and time of trades. The display records transactions by the minute so you can see if there is a change in sentiment about a stock. A falling price indicates fewer buyers are in the market, for example.

News Feeds

Short-term traders don't have the huge need for news that traders with longer hold times do, but they still require an eye on specific information that can tip market prices. If the short-term trader is trading securities related to market indexes (E-Mini futures or exchange-traded funds, for example), any news that might shake the market is important.

Advanced trading platforms let users configure news feeds to their trading strategies. If you are trading in a certain stock sector, you can set the news feeds to check for important changes in that area or to pick up specific keyword articles (a company or industry, for example). You can keep a window open on your desktop that will alert you if your keyword appears in a news story.

This shows how you can park a window to monitor news feeds on your desktop from Interactive Brokers' Trader Workstation. You can select news feeds to cover the securities you are trading.

(Photo courtesy of Interactive Brokers.)

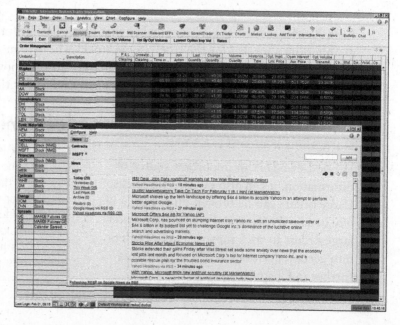

You won't grab the news before everyone else if you have your news feeds functioning, but you may catch something a few seconds before everyone in the market realizes what is going on and profit from it. Even if you aren't the first to know, you don't want to be the last to find out about a major piece of market-moving information.

Trading Tip _____

You will want to monitor news feeds related to securities you are trading. For example, if you are trading in the technology sector, keep an eye on important technology indexes and sector news channels.

Charting

Charting is the visual tool most often used by short-term traders to determine buy and sell signals. Most advanced trading platforms offer some form of charting software, but you will have to determine if it is adequate for your needs. Some traders prefer to use an information platform (see Chapter 10) that will be more robust in many cases. Many traders have this system running on a different monitor.

If you use the charting offered through the advanced trading platform, be sure it is using live prices and it is dynamically updated. You will develop charts that work the best for your trading needs and the platform should remember these configurations so you're not re-creating them each time you need one. Charts are covered in more detail in Chapter 15.

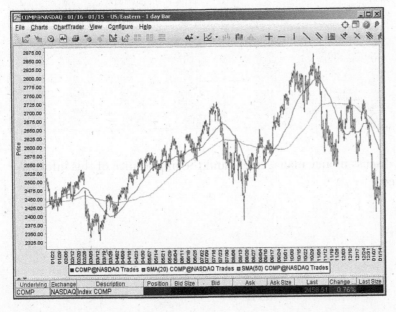

This shows a daily chart with 20- and 50-day moving averages from Interactive Brokers' Trader Workstation. Charts are the visual tool that short-term traders use to catch buy and sell signals.

(Photo courtesy of Interactive Brokers.)

Account Management

Account management is more important than many beginning traders realize. This function on an advanced trading platform keeps you informed on where you are financially and what your current margin position is. This is extremely important if you are doing short-term trading at the clip of 50 or more trades per day. You won't be able to keep the information in your head, and if you don't follow your progress, you can get in trouble quickly.

Most traders set a daily limit on losses—if they lose a certain percentage of their trading capital during one trading session they stop for the day. There is a danger that when you are down, you try harder to catch up, which usually leads to bad trades. The account management function, which can stay open on your desktop, keeps you up-to-date on your progress.

This shows an account management window from Interactive Brokers' Trader Workstation. It is important for traders to keep track of their position, margin, and cash balances.

(Photo courtesy of Interactive Brokers.)

In Chapter 23, we'll discuss money management and the importance of this information will be reinforced.

Screening

Stock screening is a way of sorting through the market and selecting a group of stocks based on a set of criteria. Traders use screening to identify potential trading opportunities. Many start the day off (or end the day) with a screen looking for stocks that behaved in a certain way during the previous trading day.

For example, a screen might look for stocks that opened with a large gap that was higher than the previous day's close. Another possibility is stocks that closed at new 52-week highs.

The screening tool will usually return in current price information plus news links, which could explain some price changes.

> **Trading Tip**
>
> Stock screens are available free at a number of websites. However, most advanced trading platforms have a more robust screen capability. Some offer predefined screens that active traders may find useful.

Markets

When considering a direct access provider, think carefully about your current and future trading plans. Most direct access providers let you trade a wide variety of securities through their advanced trading platforms. However, be sure the provider you choose has access to all the markets you want to trade.

Not every provider is licensed to trade futures, for example. Trading futures and options is a specialized service that requires a different type of quote and order entry. Do you want to trade on the forex? What about trading on foreign exchanges? Before you sign on with a direct access provider, make sure all the markets you want to trade in are covered.

Alerts

Alerts are an extra pair of eyes that help traders keep watch on action over multiple securities. Alerts on an advanced trading platform are more than alarm bells; they can be set to initiate action—if you wish. Many short-term traders track multiple securities at once and will trade only those that hit certain marks. Alerts can help traders know when the time is right for action.

Traders can monitor certain stocks and set alerts to trip when the price hits a specific mark. For example, you could set an alert that when the price of XYZ drops by $4 per share, the alert will notify you. You could also set the alert to enter a limit buy order when that same event occurred. The condition could also be a percentage change as opposed to a dollar amount.

Alerts can also monitor volume on a list of stocks alerting you to rising or falling volume. Changes in volume can indicate a switch in price direction or momentum. Other alerts include widening or narrowing of the bid-ask spread on selected stock; profit or loss alerts tell you when a trade has hit a specified gain or loss; and combinations of alerts. Combination alerts could include a change in price accompanied by a specified change in volume.

> **Margin Call**
>
> Alerts can be extremely helpful, but don't rely on them for everything. You may believe you have set the conditions correctly, but a small mistake can prove costly. Test alerts that trigger buy or sell orders.

Alerts can be moved from day to day and stored for reuse as needed. They should be easy to edit. However, if you use alerts with actions, be careful to review the conditions on a regular basis to make sure they still reflect your trading preferences.

Demos

Download demo programs and try them out to get a feel for how each advanced platform works. This will be the main tool of your active trading business and it should be comfortable to work with. However, don't expect to master these programs in an evening. They are sophisticated systems that can process tremendous amounts of data. You should see the logic of how it fits together quickly and the details will come with practice.

Practice is important because when the market is active, as it always is for the short-term trader, there is no time to consult help files to figure out basic instructions. Although it may be tempting to "go live" with an advanced trading platform after a few hours of navigating around the features, that would be a mistake. You may pay dearly if you are in a tight spot with the market going against you and no clue where to click next.

What It Costs

As you might imagine, advanced trading platforms and the services on a direct access provider aren't inexpensive. The costs vary from provider to provider and depend on how many optional services or features you add to basic packages and how much you trade. There are several approaches to charging for advanced trading platforms. Some vendors charge a fee for use of the software, while others do not. Feeds from Nasdaq Level II, various other exchanges, commodity exchanges, and so on can add up. In most cases, you only subscribe to the data you need. If you aren't planning to trade commodities, you aren't required to buy a data feed from the exchange.

Commissions are either a flat fee or are based on a per share price for equities on option contracts. Volume is the name of the game and the more volume you generate in trades, the lower your commissions will be. In some cases, direct access providers will lower or drop other fees for traders who are generating large commissions each month. It is smart to get a complete list of all fees charged by the direct access broker, including exchange fees passed through by the broker to you. Be certain you understand all the fees and when they apply. Trading over an advanced trading platform can be expensive for active traders.

> ### Market Place
>
> Because direct access providers structure their fees in different ways, it may be difficult to do an "apples to apples" comparison. If you are confused about fees, ask for clarification. If you have trouble getting questions answered, you may want to try another provider.

Start-Up Capital

Most direct access providers set minimum initial capital in the $3,000 to $5,000 range. However, remember the SEC will require you to deposit a minimum of $25,000 if you meet the qualifications of a day trader. Some direct access brokers could set that minimum higher.

Realistically, active trading for a living is like starting a business and you should plan to invest substantial capital into the venture. This capital should be money you can afford to lose without losing your home or robbing your child's college fund. A good starting place is a minimum of $25,000 of investment capital; more would be better.

Choosing an Advanced Trading System

There are a number of excellent advanced trading systems on the market. The best way to select one is to work through the demos and see which system seems most intuitive to you. A good recommendation from a respected trader is a good place to start, but just because a system works well for one trader doesn't mean it will work well for you. If you begin trading with one system and it's just not coming together, don't be shy about switching. A good trading system is your best tool to make a profit.

Web-based programs offer many of the same features as advanced trading platforms that download much of their software. Active traders who aren't doing short-term trading may want to consider a Web-based system. This would include swing and position traders who may not need all the bells and whistles of the full-featured advanced trading platform. These systems are often referred to as hybrids since they cross between a regular online broker and advanced trading platforms.

Margin Call _____

Be wary of systems that promise advanced features at very low costs—it could be there are hidden fees or charges that you will discover once you sign up and begin trading.

Hybrid trading systems may offer some of the same features as advanced trading platforms, but not all. Short-term traders will probably not be satisfied with the depth of order execution and less robust features. Many of these systems can't trade derivatives or commodities.

In addition to the limited features compared to an advanced trading platform, Web-based applications are subject to irritating problems such as dropped connections, slowdowns, and other delays.

On the plus side, hybrid systems are much less expensive than advanced trading platforms and may make a good transition from online broker to advanced trading platform. Swing traders in particular may find the Level II quotes helpful, even though they may be able to get those quotes cheaper or free other places.

The Least You Need to Know

- Advanced trading platforms put precise information and trading power on your computer's desktop.

- Information organization and presentation is a strong point of advanced trading systems.

- Advanced trading systems let you issue trading orders with single clicks, saving time and making you money.

- Advanced trading platforms come in many configurations to meet the needs of a diverse group of traders.

13

Market Orders You Must Know

In This Chapter

- ◆ Active traders use special orders to buy and sell securities
- ◆ The importance of limit and stop limit orders
- ◆ Using buy and sell orders with margin
- ◆ Short selling is buying backwards

Market orders are the tools that active traders use to help secure a profit or protect against a large loss. If you don't know how to use these tools, you will have little chance of succeeding in active trading.

Buy and Sell Orders

The two basic orders are, of course, buy and sell, but don't think that's where it ends. In fact, if you are new to trading, this is the place where you will see profits diminish and losses increase. The system of orders has not changed much in many years. Traders use many of the same orders their fathers used and the system works well for those who know how to use it.

Knowledgeable traders need precise entry and exit points to ensure profits and cut losses. As noted in earlier chapters, short-term traders make a living hitting small profits multiple times each trading day. To be successful, short-term traders need the precision of special market orders to get them in and out of a position at the price that's right. Special trading orders aren't foolproof, as we'll see in a moment. Market conditions can conspire against a trader to make it difficult to enter or exit a trade at the precise moment and price she wants.

The Market Order

A market order to buy or sell goes to the top of all pending orders and is executed immediately, regardless of price. If you look a Nasdaq Level II pending orders for a stock during the trading day, you will see a number of orders to buy or sell arranged by price. The best ask price, which would be the highest price, is on the top of that column, while the lowest price, the bid price, is on top of that column. As orders come in, they are filled off these best prices. If an order with a better bid price comes in, it goes to the top of the list.

When a market order is received, it gets the highest or lowest price available. In other words, when you submit a market order to buy a stock, you pay the highest price on the market. If you submit a market sell order, you receive the lowest price on the market. Active traders love people, usually novices, or investors unconcerned about nickels and dimes of the price, who use market orders because they represent easy money.

def•i•ni•tion

Slippage is the difference in the bid-ask spread from the time a trader enters an order to the time it is filled. Another form of slippage involves the market maker upsetting the applecart with a change in price to take advantage of an upcoming market order.

In most cases, active traders avoid using market orders. Not only will you pay top dollar or get bottom price, but you will pay for a little mischief known as *slippage*. Slippage occurs when a market maker changes the spread to his advantage on market orders. This is a questionable practice, but beware that you may pay a small premium, which is the market maker's extra profit, if you use market orders to buy and sell securities.

When to Use Market Orders

Is there ever a time when a market buy or sell order is okay? Absolutely. If you are caught in a short position and the market is moving against you, it's time to bail out in a hurry and not worry about slippage. We'll discuss short selling in detail later and you'll see there are situations where escape from a position is more important than anything else.

There are other times when experienced active traders use market orders. Momentum traders may use market orders if they sense a fast-moving stock is taking off and they want to ensure a position. Using some of the limit orders discussed below may mean they would miss the move because the stock is climbing away from their price. When we look at momentum trading in Chapter 18, you'll see the risky and fast-moving trades these active investors make to catch a stock on the move.

For most active traders, the use of a market order is a judgment call. Is it more important to buy the stock (or sell it) or to get in (or out) at a specific price? In most cases, active traders are very concerned with controlling entry and exit prices; however, as noted above, there will be times when buying or selling the stock is more important than price. The danger for active traders is convincing themselves that they have to own a "hot" stock at any cost and using market orders to grab shares. This was a tremendous problem during the dot.com boom when amateur traders assumed the price was always going up so it didn't matter what they paid. The tech crash of 2000 was a rude awakening to many.

Margin Call

Thanks to electronic communication networks and other high-speed innovations, small market orders can zip into the market without much warning and be filled. Use caution, however, that frequent use of market orders doesn't alert other traders to your strategy. If your strategy is identified by other traders (using Level II screen information), they may attempt to trick you into a quick buy or sell with misleading orders.

Placing a Market Order

Placing a market order is saying you want to buy the stock regardless of price. If you were giving a verbal order to your stockbroker, it might go like this:

> Buy 200 shares of IBM at market.

Assuming you are using an online broker or an advanced trading platform, the order is entered on the order screen. Most active traders have default trade parameters set up so they can quickly execute their typical trades. If a market order is not a typical order, some adjustment is made.

If the stock is actively traded, a market order will be filled almost instantly unless there is an unusually high volume in this particular stock. However, in a fast-moving market even almost instantly isn't fast enough to ensure that the price you saw when you placed your order is the exact price you receive. If your trade isn't filled at the price you thought it would be, you are the victim of slippage.

Slippery Slippage

Slippage occurs when the price of an executed trade is different from the order you submitted. For example, you enter a market order to buy 100 shares of XYZ at $33.25 per share. When you get your confirmation of the trade, you notice you paid $33.30 per share. What happened? You are the victim of slippage.

Slippage comes in two forms. The naturally occurring slippage is when the stock is moving rapidly and even Level II quotes and order entry are not quite synched with executions. The ask price of the stock may have gone up, thanks to other orders arriving a fraction of a second before yours.

The other form of slippage is not so natural and happens when a market maker takes advantage of a market order in a slow-moving market and drops or raises his price to put a little extra commission in his pocket. (The difference between the bid and ask prices—the spread—is the market maker's commission.)

A few cents per share doesn't seem like a big deal, but if you are an active trader, especially a short-term trader, these few cents can add up to real money in a hurry. This is money out of your pocket. If you aren't careful how you use orders when buying and selling stocks, slippage will slowly put you out of business.

Slippage Protection

Active traders protect against slippage by specifying a price at which they will buy and sell. With these types of orders, it makes no difference whether the stock's price moves before the order hits the market. It also prevents market makers from taking advantage of market orders and inching the price up or down for a little extra profit at your expense.

Limit Orders

The limit order limits the price you are willing to pay or the price at which you are willing to sell. You are telling the market you will sell (or buy) at this price. Unlike the market order, the limit order may or may not go to the top of the list. If the price on your limit order is the best ask or bid price, it will go to the top and may be filled very quickly. If it is not, it will slot in among the other orders that are away from the market. As other orders are filled, your order may work its way to the top. On the other hand, better orders may come in and push your order down the list.

Trading Tip _____

Limit orders are a trader's best friend because they provide discipline to buying and selling and fix a price the trader can live with.

The important point for active traders is that your order will only be filled at your price or better. Active traders learn quickly that the potential for profits is greater at certain price points, but not less at others. If they can capture a security at the price they want, it is usually because the stock is moving in a direction that the trader believes offers a quick profit. Many active traders use limit orders or some variation (see below) almost exclusively.

Placing a Limit Order

A limit order, whether given to a stockbroker or entered into your advanced trading platform, has the same five components:

- ◆ Buy or sell
- ◆ Number of shares
- ◆ Security
- ◆ Order type
- ◆ Price

For example, if you wanted to buy 100 shares of XYZ using a limit order, here's how you would express it:

> Buy 100 shares XYZ limit 33.45

This order tells the market you will buy 100 shares of XYZ, but under no circumstances will you pay more than $33.45 per share.

Limit Orders Not Absolute

An important point to remember about limit orders is they are not absolute orders. Your limit order to buy XYZ at $33.45 per share can't be filled above that price, but it can be filled below that price. If the stock's price drops past your limit before it is filled you could pay less than $33.45 per share. It works the same way on the limit sell order. If you enter a limit sell order for $33.45, it can't be filled for less than that amount. However, if the stock rises above that price before your order is filled, you could receive more than your limit price.

The simple limit order could be a problem for traders or investors not paying attention to the market. For example, you enter a sell limit order on a stock that is a few dollars per share over the market price and a buy limit order a few dollars per share under the market. This way you will make a profit if the stock rises and add to your holdings if the stock dips. Not a particularly inspired trading strategy, but one that seems to have your bases covered. You take off for a long weekend and return on Monday to find your sell limit order has been filled. You are happy with your small profit until you notice that the company is a merger target and the stock has jumped $15 per share. Unfortunately, your limit sell order got you out of the stock with a $2 per share profit, leaving $13 per share on the table. You can imagine the reverse of this scenario if the stock dropped like a rock and your buy limit order filled as the stock was in a free fall.

The point is simple limit orders are excellent tools, but they are not foolproof. Active traders can use more sophisticated orders when the need arises.

> **Trading Tip**
>
> It will take some experience to know where to set limit orders.
> If you set limit buy orders too low they may never be filled, which does you no good. The same is true for limit sell orders. With some experience you'll find the spot that gets you a good price and your order filled.

The Cost of Limit Orders

Using limit orders has a price, at least with some brokers and direct access providers. In many cases, market orders carry a much lower commission than limit orders. Added commissions mean extra profits will be needed to cover that overhead. Now that stocks are traded in decimals, the bid-ask spread on actively traded stocks may be just a penny. For an actively traded stock, you may not see any slippage for a market order. Active traders may find that the lower commissions for market orders (compared to commissions charged for limit orders) make up for any penny slippage that may occur. Experience will teach you when a market order placed in a fast-moving market may make more sense than a higher cost limit order. Be sure you understand any extra charges for limit orders or the other orders, which follow to avoid nasty surprises on your account statement.

> **Margin Call**
>
> Commission and fee structures of brokers can be very complicated. Be certain you understand all the charges associated with the different types of orders. Remember to add these costs into your business expenses when calculating your profit.

Stop Orders

A hybrid order that many active traders use extensively is a stop order—also known as a stop loss order. The stop loss order combines attributes of market and limit orders. It can be used to sell or buy, but is most often used to sell (thus the stop loss name).

Limit orders are executed when the price is hit and market orders are executed as soon as they are entered into the market. The comparison is a limit order guarantees price, but not a fill and a market order guarantees a fill, but not a price. The stop loss order does nothing until the stock hits the stop loss price and then it becomes a market order and is filled at the best available price.

Active traders use stop loss orders to protect a position. Here's how they would enter a stop loss order:

> Sell 100 shares XYZ at 33.45 stop

This tells the market that when the price of XYZ drops to $33.45, this becomes a market order to sell 100 shares at the best available price. Unless the stock is in a free fall, the active trader should get close to $33.45 on the order fill. Frequently, traders will use this order to protect a profit in a stock. Rather than constantly watch the price, the trader can set a stop loss order and be confident she will get a good fill if the stock retreats to the point she designates.

Better than a simple stop loss order is the trailing stop. Swing and position traders can use trailing stops to protect profits of rising stocks without having to watch the securities on a daily basis. Most advanced trading platforms can set up trailing stop orders.

> **Trading Tip** _____
>
> Some traders use stop loss orders when they are going to be away from the market for several days and unable to check on prices. This order protects them from a disastrous loss when they aren't looking.

Trailing Stops

A trailing stop order is like a stop loss order except it moves with a stock that is increasing in price. The stop loss order follows the stock price up by a specified amount or percentage of the price. The idea is to let a rising stock keep going and accommodate typical fluctuations in price while protecting most of your profit.

For example, you could set a trailing stop order on a stock that would be triggered if the stock dipped by 10 percent. If you put such a trailing stop on XYZ and the price climbed to $40 per share, the stop loss order would not be triggered unless the price dropped to $36 per share ($40 × 10% = $4; $40–$4 = $36). If the stock rose to $42 per share, the stop loss would not be triggered until the stock price dropped to $37.80 (90% of $42). As long as the price does not back up 10 percent, nothing happens. If the price does back up to the trigger, the stop loss becomes a market order and is filled at the best available price.

Using Buy Stop Orders

Some traders use stop orders on the buy side. They may be interested in a stock, but only if it makes a move up. They may believe the stock is due for an upward swing, but rather than buy and hold for something that may happen in the future, they will enter a buy stop order.

Trading Tip

Trailing stops can be automated on most advanced trading platforms to follow a stock's price up. This order is one of the most helpful in protecting your profits in a rising stock.

Like the sell stop order, the buy stop order doesn't do anything until the trigger price is hit. For example, if a trader feels a stock will move upward she would enter a buy stop order above the current market price by some amount—usually not a lot, but enough to confirm an upward trend and not just a typical intra-day price fluctuation. If the stock hits the trigger price, the stop buy order becomes a market order and is filled at the best available price.

Traders use buy stop orders to protect themselves against a short position gone bad. Selling short can leave a trader in a dangerous position if the stock begins rising sharply. A buy stop order will close the trader's short position out on a rising stock. More about short selling below.

Stop Limit Orders

Stop orders convert to market orders when the trigger price is hit. A variation of stop orders converts to a limit order when the trigger price is hit. This order gives the trader more price control than a market order, but risks not being filled because of the limit price. Here's how a stop limit order might be entered:

Buy 100 XYZ stop 33.45, limit 33.39

This order becomes active when the price of XYZ hits $33.45, but says the trader will buy 100 shares at $33.39. The trader is hoping XYZ is on the way to a big move and is counting on grabbing shares when the stock dips slightly. There is a risk the stock will keep going up and your order won't be filled. Active traders who watch the market closely probably won't find much benefit in these orders.

Margin Call

Be careful of too exotic market orders that may become confusing in their execution, especially if they are designed to be triggered by an outside event—a stock's price, for example.

Trading Tip

Many advanced platforms and brokers that handle short-term trading consider most trades good for the day and if the trade hasn't filled by the end of trading, it's canceled. You can enter a good till canceled order, which will usually stay open for 90 days.

Margin Orders

Most advanced platforms allow you to set up a default margin trade. You can choose or change the percent (up to 50 percent) of the amount you want to borrow. Margin trades are instantly checked against your equity to confirm you have enough for the trade. Active traders who make multiple trades during a day will keep their account management window open on the desktop of their computer. Real time updates show traders exactly where they are with their margin and cash positions. They can also see what margin is available to them. If an attractive opportunity presents itself, but equity is low, the trader may choose to liquidate a position that has less appeal to increase equity in the account.

Market Place

Regulations concerning margin and margin requirements change frequently. Double check with your broker concerning the most recent laws in place on short-term, momentum, swing, and position trading. Ask specifically about margin and the requirements for a margin account.

Active traders want to keep an eye on the minimum maintenance requirement to avoid a margin call, but also to avoid having the broker freeze the account to any further margin trading. Fortunately, advanced trading platforms will keep track of this requirement based on the broker's requirements and regulations. This is helpful to traders in a fast-moving market who don't have to do the calculations manually.

The Minimum Maintenance Requirement

Even though most active traders will use systems that calculate the minimum maintenance requirement for them, it is helpful to know how the calculation works. If you want to buy 100 shares at $50 per share and use 50 percent margin, you will put in $2,500 cash and borrow $2,500 from your broker, which requires a 35 percent minimum maintenance margin. Of the $5,000 account value, $2,500 is equity. If the stock drops to $40 per share, the account is now worth $4,000. However, you still owe your broker $2,500, so the equity is only $1,500. That leaves your equity at 37.5 percent ($1,500 ÷ $2,500 = 0.375). You are still within the minimum maintenance requirement, but just barely.

If the stock's price drops to $36 per share, the account is now worth $3,600. When you deduct the debt to your broker of $2,500, you are left with $1,100 in equity or 30.5 percent, which is below the minimum maintenance requirement. You will get a margin call to bring up the equity in your account to the minimum maintenance amount. Some brokers may not give you the courtesy of a call, but will liquidate all or part of your holdings to pay themselves back.

If your brokerage system does not automatically calculate and update minimum maintenance margin for you, be very careful how you use margin. Unlike a cash investment in securities, it is possible to lose more than you have invested with a margin account. This is an important point and should be carefully considered before you jump into heavy reliance on margin to support your trading needs.

Margin Trading Reminders

Using margin in your trading is a way to extend your purchasing power. When trading tiny profits, as short-term traders do, you'll need to trade big lots to earn enough on each trade to make it profitable (after commissions). Margin makes it possible to do this, but it can also amplify your losses if the trade goes bad.

Not all stocks are marginable. Your broker maintains a list of stocks that can't be bought on margin. Regulations prevent you from buying new issues, penny stocks, and others on margin. Check with your broker for these rules.

It is also important to remember that margin isn't free. If you hold a margin trade overnight, your broker will charge you interest on the amount you borrowed. That interest is another expense that will eat into your profits. Unless a stock is on a steady climb, interest charges on a margin loan along with commissions will consume any profits.

Trading Tip _____

Margin trading is a useful tool, but you must practice careful money management or, like a credit card, you can over use it.

Selling Short

Selling short, another margin transaction, is an order that puts you in position to profit when a stock falls in price.

Short selling is a popular tool for active traders because it gives them the opportunity to profit on both sides of a stock's price cycle. Traders can grab profits as the price goes up and then reverse their strategy and take profits as it reverses. Of course, it sounds easy reading about it in a book, but the reality of making it happen is possible, although profits are not a given and traders lose money attempting this strategy.

Because short-selling is a margin transaction, the broker will charge interest on the value of the borrowed shares. If the price of the stock rises instead of falls, traders are faced with buying higher priced shares to replace the lower priced shares they borrowed and will suffer a loss. If the difference between the price of the borrowed shares and the market price is great enough, traders may experience a margin call.

Traders exit a short sale position by buying an equal number of shares to replace the borrowed shares. On many trading platforms, you may find a *buy to cover* option. This lets the system know you are covering a short sale with this order.

def·i·ni·tion _____

Buy to cover is an order you can execute that will buy an equal number of shares of the stock you shorted. Buy to cover is often a simple click of the mouse on advanced trading systems.

For traders who hold positions more than one day, there are some risks in selling short. Of course, the price of the stock could rise, forcing you to buy back shares at a higher price and creating a losing trade. This can get out of hand when a company that has been the target of short sellers turns in some good news and the stock blips upward. The short sellers begin covering their positions by buying shares. The more short sellers that cover, the higher it drives the price. The higher the price, the more short sellers are driven to cover. The feeding frenzy pushes the stock's price up in a hurry. This is known as a short squeeze and the folks on Wall Street who don't like short sellers enjoy seeing them squirm.

The stock market is geared to growth and profits. The focus is on the positive and, in general, the market favors growth over time. So short-selling is against the general market trend. As such, it is probably a difficult standalone strategy, however most active traders take advantage of it during their trading.

The Least You Need to Know

◆ Market orders guarantee a fill, but not a price.

◆ Limit orders guarantee a price, but not a fill.

◆ If you want to protect profits or prevent a loss, use limit orders of some type.

◆ Margin trading and short selling are risky, but legitimate tools of active traders.

14

Using Level II Screens

In This Chapter

◆ Nasdaq Level II screens provide detailed pricing

◆ Level II screens let short-term traders see market

◆ Charts translate data into information

◆ Expense is not prohibitive and information is necessary

Information is the active trader's best tool. If you're going to compete in the intraday trading frenzy, you must have access to the same information as your competitors. That means detailed order and price information on securities you want to trade.

Throughout this book, you have heard Nasdaq Level II price screens referenced for short-term traders. In this chapter, we'll look into the system and discuss its place in your active trading system. Charts that use detailed quotes (both intraday and moving averages) provide short-term traders visual representations of massive amounts of information that is easy to digest and act on. Having a large amount of information in front of you is only beneficial if you can quickly organize it on your computer's desktop for easy retrieval and comprehension.

Level II Screens for Short-Term Traders

Nasdaq Level II screens give active traders a live view of market activity in a stock. You see the orders, not just the bid and ask prices (which is all the information provided by Level I quotes).

Even though the quotes are called Nasdaq quotes, all traded securities on all exchanges are reported through this system. The transparency of pricing and orders is not complete, but Level II screens do give everyone connected the same view of the market during intraday trading. By transparency, I mean all participants in trading see the same information with the exception of market makers and market specialists. These professionals have access to Level III screens, which display order flow and other information relevant to maintaining a stable market in the security. The playing field will never be completely level because professionals such as market makers and specialists, large institutional traders, pension funds, mutual funds, and so on can still move the market. (More about how they do this in subsequent chapters. In Chapter 17, we'll look at how some professional traders and others can use tricks to fool you and novices into bad trades using Level II screen information.)

> **Trading Tip**
>
> When you see stock quotes, you can identify issues traded on the New York Stock Exchange by their three-letter ticker symbol (IBM). Stocks traded on Nasdaq have four-letter ticker symbols (MSFT).

Not all active traders need the power (and expense) of Level II screens. If you plan to stick with swing and position trading, you probably don't need the detail of Level II screens. As we'll see when we look at those strategies, trading at that pace is much more focused on price moves over longer holding periods—days, weeks, or months. There is little need for intraday prices.

However, many active traders will find themselves looking at short-term opportunities as well as the longer perspectives of swing and position trading. If you do enough short-term trading to justify the use of a direct access broker, which will give you Level II quotes, the research and charting power will help you with swing and position trading, also.

For active traders who trade short term, Level II screens are your most important source of information, although many traders look to charts generated by intraday pricing and volume for trade signals. In a fast-moving market, the numbers on Level II screens will be changing very fast. Charts often make it easier to see what is happening and so you can plot your next move.

Short-term traders must have Level II screens—there is no substitute. There is almost no chance of success for people who attempt short-term trading with a regular discount brokerage account. You will always pay more than necessary for your buys and receive less than the best possible price when you sell. That doesn't make for a winning strategy.

Margin Call

A strategy of earning your way into a short-term trading career has little chance for success. It is no different than starting a business with no capital. Neither indicates a real commitment to succeed.

What You See Onscreen

It is important to note that direct access providers and services that sell Level II services may format their displays slightly different from what is described here. Some providers include graphic displays, while others may not include some of the information I describe.

Most direct access providers show you two columns of prices—the bid and ask. At the top of the columns are the best current prices. These are the "at market" prices. If you bought or sold at this very instant, these are the prices you would likely receive. You can't say for sure you would receive those prices because another factor besides price is supply. In other words, how many shares are available at that price? If your market order is only one of many, it may not be filled before the supply at that price runs out and/or the price changes. Market orders are processed in the order they are received.

Market Place

Short-term trading is different from investing. You are trading against others who also want the best price for the same stock. Arm yourself with the same or better weapons and you have a chance at success.

The prices under the best bid and best ask price are listed in order of how close they are to the best price. For example, if the best ask price is $25.35 per share, the next one might be $25.33 per share. When the supply of shares at $25.35 is gone, then $25.33 becomes the market price. If new orders come in above $25.33, they will become the new market price.

Digging Deeper

You'll notice that there is much more information than just prices, and every bit of it can be helpful to short-term traders who know how to read it. Short-term trading is a battle of wits and nerve. Successful traders arm themselves with every weapon they can. As you study Level II screens, you'll learn which areas are important and how to find the information you need quickly. This is one of the most, if not *the* most, important skills to learn first, before you attempt short-term trading.

What does the Level II screen tell you? Across the top, you'll find Level I price quotes, which you remember is the most recently traded price for the stock. You'll also find the previous closing price, the high and low for the day, the volume, and the size of the last trade.

This shows a Level II screen for Apple (AAPL—Nasdaq) from Interactive Brokers's Trader Workstation. As you can see, the orders are building on the ask side of the screen, indicating that more sellers are in the market at this particular moment. This may indicate that the price is headed down.

(Photo courtesy of Interactive Brokers.)

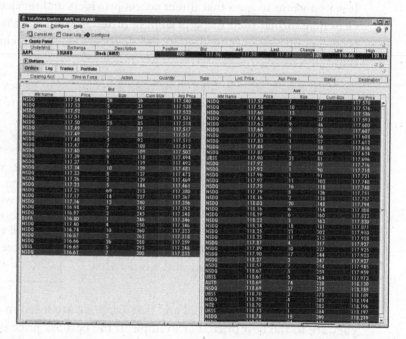

Under both the bid and ask columns you will find three columns of information:

- ◆ **Order.** The first column shows you which market maker, specialist, or Electronic Communications Network (ECN) has placed the order. This is useful information, which we'll spend more time on in Chapter 17. ECNs are anonymous ways for institutional investors to hide their actions, and by breaking a large order up into several smaller orders, they try to hide potentially price-changing actions.

◆ **Price.** The bid or ask price is listed in the middle column. Notice how the spread between the bid and ask price changes as the prices move away from the inside price. The prices at the top of the bid and ask columns are the best available at that moment. If you submitted a market buy or sell order at that exact moment, you would get these prices. Notice how many other orders are lined up under the best bid and ask at the same prices. These would be filled in order. Right below those best prices is another level of prices, below that another level, and so on.

◆ **Size.** The size of each order is listed in the third column. The orders are listed in hundreds, which is called a round lot. So an order with a 5 is for 500 shares. There are some special designations for larger orders, which we'll cover in Chapter 17.

The final item is the Time and Sales screen, which may be a separate screen or part of the Level II screen. This report, which is continually updated, shows actual transactions as opposed to orders so you can follow completed trades. The actual trades reported on the Time and Sales screen will tell you if the stock traded up or down from the previous trade (by its color) and the price.

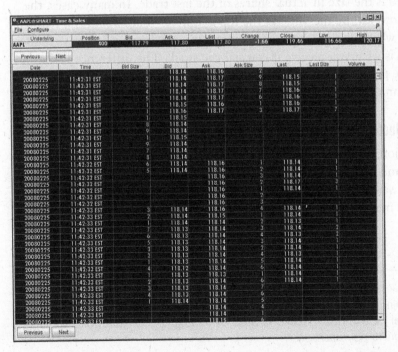

This shows a Level II screen recording Time and Sales for Apple (AAPL—Nasdaq) from Interactive Brokers's Trader Workstation. This screen tracks actual sales by the minute and is one the short-term active trader refers to constantly during the trading day. Different colors mark whether the trades were inside the ask or bid or outside.

(Photo courtesy of Interactive Brokers.)

Trading Tip _____

As you master elements of the advanced platform you choose, you will find the desktop of your computer crowded with open windows. It is important that you limit open windows to those screens you need to look at every minute and minimize the rest.

Let's look at all of these areas in more detail to discover what they tell the short-term trader.

Level I Quotes

The Level I quotes across the top of the Level II screen contain more information than the trading novice might think. The information is packed into a relatively small area, so it is important that you become familiar with where the data items are located.

At the top, you will see the "Last" quote, which is the last trade for this stock. This represents an actual sale; the number indicating how much the price changed is listed under "Chg." Next to it tells you how much the trade was up or down from the previous trade. Also listed is the size in actual shares of the last trade. In many cases, the price for the last quote will be the same as the top ask price—but not always. Remember, the ask price is what you pay for the stock if you want to buy—it is always higher than the bid, which is what you receive if you sell the stock. The difference is the spread. At the inside price, the bid-ask spread shouldn't be too far apart—no more than a couple of pennies. We'll see why that's important in Chapter 17.

Opening and Closing Quotes

Also in the top section, usually in the Level I price information, is the opening price for today's trading and the closing price for yesterday's trading. When there is a difference, the stock is said to _gap_ at open. If the gap is modest, it probably doesn't mean anything except the market specialist is adjusting for volume or some other technical correction.

def•i•ni•tion _____

Gap is a term used to describe a jump (up or down) in price from the closing price to the next day's opening price. Gaps also occur during intraday trading when prices skip up or down. Several factors, both good and bad, can cause a gap. Gaps are warning signs to active traders to pay attention.

However, if the gap is large, it may be due to news about the company, economy, or industry that was released after the market closed the previous day. Traders are reacting to the news by lowering or raising expectations when the market opens the next day. We'll see in Chapter 17 that gaps can play an important role in short-term trading.

Prices and Volume

The Level I area also contains the current best bid and ask price along with a ratio of orders on both sides. This is important information, because it can tell you at a glance if orders are building on one side or the other. For example, if the screen reported a ratio of 350 × 1,200, that means there are 35,000 shares at bid prices and 120,000 shares at ask prices. This tells you that more traders are looking to sell than to buy, which could mean prices will move lower because of the imbalance in order size—lower supply of buyers (35,000 shares) and higher supply of sellers (120,000 shares). By watching this section, you will be able to keep up with the flow of orders from buy to sell or sell to buy. This information will help you determine which direction the stock's price is headed.

Another set of price numbers is the current day's high and low. These numbers give you a frame of reference concerning the price range where the stock is trading. Momentum traders will find this information helpful. You will also get a volume number for the day that is constantly updated. If you follow the same stock with any frequency, you know when it breaks out of its normal range patterns.

Bid and Ask Columns

The bid and ask columns are identical in format. The first column is the code for the entity placing the order. Some orders will come from market makers or specialists depending on the exchange, while others are placed by ECNs. With some experience, you will quickly recognize which entity is placing the order. This can be important because some big players may try to hide their moves by going through an ECN. (You can place your order through an ECN too, if you wish.) Most advanced platforms will let you specify how to route your order. This can be important when dealing with a market maker who controls a particular stock, as we'll discover in Chapter 17. There is a list of major players in Appendix A.

Trading Tip

The market maker responsible for a particular stock is called the ax. You will often get a quicker fill by placing your order through the ax than other routes.

Like prices are grouped together in the order in which they are placed. The closer the price is to inside the market, the closer it will appear to the top of the list. Different shading shows you where there are levels or tiers of orders at the same price. This gives you an idea about supply and whether your limit order has a chance to be filled.

The size column tells you how big the order is in round lots of 100 shares. Some systems will display the size by the actual number of shares—5,000, for example.

Time and Sales Screen

The Time and Sales Screen is usually positioned to the right of the Level II quotes. This screen records the price and size of each sale. The screen is divided into minutes. Other providers list the price with the actual time and the size.

When the price ticks up it appears in green, and when it ticks down it appears in red, following traditional market-reporting colors.

TotalView for Even More Information

Nasdaq offers an additional service to augment Level II quotes called SuperMontage TotalView. SuperMontage is the electronic order execution system Nasdaq uses. The exchange was created as an electronic market, and this is the latest version of its processing system.

Its TotalView product looks deeper into the orders than Level II does, approaching the detail previously available only to market makers and other exchange professionals. For short-term traders who are deeply into the fine art of trading against major market players, this is a must-have piece of information.

Margin Call

Be careful of "analysis paralysis," which happens when you load up with information and spend more time studying than trading. Short-term trading is about taking the best information you have on intraday pricing and making a decision. It's not guessing, but it's not an extended study either.

Most beginning active traders should focus on mastering Level II screens first and become comfortable with reading and understanding how they work before attempting TotalView. Once you are up to speed on Level II, you can try TotalView and see if the additional information is worth the extra cost. Several providers will give you a free trial. Check with your direct access provider about its policy.

What You See Can Be Confusing

Level II screens can appear to be a blur of numbers for an actively traded stock. Prices change and orders are filled several times a second. As we discuss in Chapter 17, you must have a plan before the market opens or you will make bad decisions in the heat of the moment. Things do happen that call for a change of plans or a reversal of plans, but you will not last long as an active short-term trader if you simply react to the market every day.

Level II quotes can tell you if the market is building depth on the buy or sell side, and that information is important in your trading decisions. You can watch the flow of orders go from one side to the other as the buyers or sellers take hold. Combine this with a screen that shows the short interest (how many traders are betting the stock will go down) and you have some useful information about where prices are headed.

However, you probably won't see much of this the first time you look at Level II quotes of an actively traded stock. It will take some time and practice to develop an understanding of what the numbers represent and who the players are. This is why it is so important to paper trade until you develop that understanding—if not, it will be an expensive lesson.

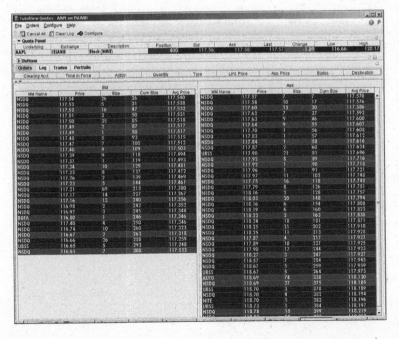

This shows a Level II TotalView screen for Apple (AAPL—Nasdaq) from Interactive Brokers's Trader Workstation. This is the first of three screens to show how quickly the order balance can change. The three screens were taken in sequence over a period of just a few minutes. In this first screen, we see the orders are heavier on the ask side of the screen (the bottom is cut off from view).

(Photo courtesy of Interactive Brokers.)

In this second screen, we see that the orders now appear roughly balanced between bid and ask; however, if you can read the cumulative size of orders, the ask still outweighs the bid side significantly.

(Photo courtesy of Interactive Brokers.)

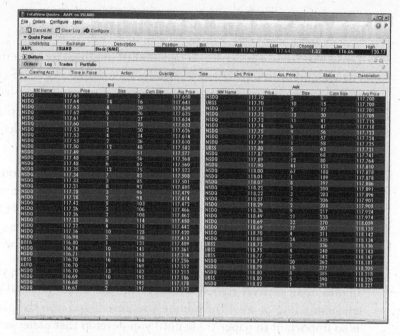

In this last screen, we see that the orders have swung from heavily weighed on the ask side of the screen to about even with the cumulative bid size. All of this changed in a matter of minutes.

(Photo courtesy of Interactive Brokers.)

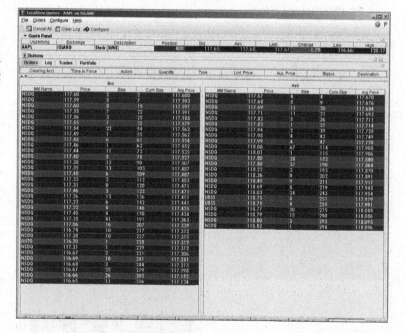

Using Level II Information

Do short-term traders trade off Level II information alone? Some undoubtedly do; however, many use charts that combine intraday prices and other indicators to observe buy and sell points. Most direct access systems let you enter your trades directly from the Level II screens. This gives you pinpoint accuracy in your price and the best chance for order fill. (We'll discuss more about buy and sell signals and order entry in Chapter 17.)

Level II services are available from all direct access providers, either as part of their standard packages or as an add-on feature. You can also subscribe to Level II information independently through a number of providers. Be cautious when looking for an independent source of Level II quotes so that you don't get "Level II–*like*" quotes.

 Trading Tip _____

Level II quotes move as fast as the stock trades. Practice on a stock that is not highly traded to get a feel for the screen and then move to more actively traded issues.

Prices for Level II services are all over the place. Many brokerages price them from $15 to $50 per month and then waive the fee if you execute a minimum number of trades per month. Independent vendors may charge $15 per month and up. Vendors also pass on an exchange fee of approximately $9 per month. The Nasdaq TotalView is often offered at about the same price. However, this is a very competitive market, so it pays to shop.

For most active investors, you will get the service through your direct access provider because you'll want it integrated into the order-entry system. Be certain you understand the pricing for the quotes and any additional fees (such as exchange fees) that may be involved. The money you spend on Level II screens is a necessity if you want a chance to succeed as a short-term active trader.

The Least You Need to Know

- ◆ Short-term active traders must know Level II screens.
- ◆ Level II screens give traders a view of the whole market.
- ◆ Traders can see depth building on the buy or sell side.
- ◆ It takes practice to read and understand Level II screens.

Chapter 15

Using Technical Analysis

In This Chapter

- ◆ Technical analysis and trends
- ◆ Counting on price trends
- ◆ Support and resistance
- ◆ Using moving averages

What will be the share price of IBM stock on the first trading day in July two years from the day you read this? The answer is: No one has a clue. However, if you ask a short-term active trader at 10 A.M. on any trading day what IBM's stock is going to do in the next 30 minutes, the trader would have a good shot at the correct answer. Lucky guess? No, the trader would have been looking at his charts and plotting IBM since trading opened. He would know whether the stock was trading in a narrow range or trending up or down. If the stock followed its trend, the trader would have a good idea where it would be and figure out a trading set-up to profit from it.

Many short-term traders use technical analysis to identify trading opportunities—when to buy and when to sell. Intraday prices from Level II quotes and historical prices are used to construct charts, which illustrate what prices are doing at that moment. Short-term traders learn to construct charts to provide immediate information on changes in price trends.

The Trend Is Your Friend

There is an old market cliché that the trend is your friend. For investors and traders with longer holding periods than one day, that may not always be true. However, for short-term traders, correctly identified trends are where you make money.

Technical analysis is about trends or cycles in stock prices. The premise of technical analysis is that by studying the supply and demand forces at work on a stock (or other type of security) you can see suggestions of future price direction. The supply-and-demand forces at work in the market are the emotions that drive expectations of future profits or losses. If some investors and/or traders expect a stock to be worth more in the future, they will buy now and that pressure will possibly increase the price. However, if more investors disagree with that rosy picture and predict losses in the future, they will sell and put downward pressure on the stock's price. If there is more supply than demand, the price will keep falling until it reaches a low enough point to encourage a trader or investor to buy.

> **Market Place**
>
> Market pundits are like the weather forecasters—they are much more accurate in the very short term, but not so much as time stretches out. Technical analysis can help predict short-term price changes, but is not much use for long-term forecasting.

Technical analysis differs from fundamental analysis in that it does not attempt to measure a company's value. Fundamental analysis is more appropriate for investors or traders with longer holding periods—more than six months, for example. Fundamental analysis can identify under- or overvalued stocks and suggest an appropriate price based on its intrinsic value. Buy-and-hold investors use fundamental analysis almost exclusively.

> **Margin Call**
>
> Buy-and-hold investors make up the majority of people who invest in the stock market. As a long-term strategy, it has worked well for those who have followed the rules of diversification and asset allocation. It is important to know the difference between trading and investing. Don't trade with your retirement fund or child's college fund.

Technical analysis employs a number of tools to identify trends, cycles, or patterns in a stock's price. The premise is that these will repeat themselves barring the intervention of an unforeseen consequence (a merger or hostile takeover, for example). By plotting historical price and volume data, a trader can spot trends as they develop and capture profits by entering the position at the earliest possible moment. Short-term traders use one-minute charts, among others, to watch a stock's movement and to identify when it is beginning or ending a cycle or trend.

The Price Tells All

Technical analysis works, its proponents say, because the market prices all fundamental and economic factors into the price of the stock. This means the stock's price is the best gauge of a company's value at that particular point in time. Market pros like to talk about the market "discounting" certain factors. What they mean is those factors are already reflected in the price of the stock. If the technical analysis proponents are correct, a stock's price is all the current information you need. Any change in a stock's price, barring some change in circumstances, reflects the adjustment to new market conditions, specifically supply and demand.

If demand is high for the stock, the price will rise. Sellers realize that selling a sought-after commodity of limited supply will allow them to raise prices. The psychological and emotional aspects of buying and selling stocks are very much a part of technical analysis.

However, not everyone is convinced that the premise of limited supply and known price is correct. Value investors who look for stocks that are languishing, but have no serious fundamental flaws, do not hold the idea that all stocks are correctly priced by the market. Their strategy is to buy the underpriced shares and hold them until the market gets around to correcting the price upward. This process could take a long time, however.

> **Margin Call**
>
> For investors, it sometimes makes sense to buy when others are selling and sell when others are buying. However, for the short-term trader, going against the trend is usually a bad idea. Investors can be contrarian because they have time on their side. Traders must take profits quickly.

Technical analysts believe everything has already been factored into the price and all that is left to do is to discover the trend. Price trends will repeat themselves and technical analysis can identify them. By analyzing price trends, traders can profit by buying or selling with the trend.

Must You Use Technical Analysis?

Can you be a successful active trader without using technical analysis? Yes, you can, and a number of traders use other tools or don't rely on technical analysis exclusively. It is possible to be a scalper—a very short-term trader—without using technical analysis. You can also be successful as a momentum trader without technical analysis. Swing and position traders most definitely can do well without technical analysis.

However, many active traders find technical analysis an extremely helpful tool that provides an objective way to determine entry and exit points. You can succeed by trading on Level II quotes alone, although for very active stocks, this can be challenging. Scalping and momentum trading are all done in a single trading day. The market and market information moves quite rapidly.

Using technical analysis to help you decide where to get into and out of a position is important to many active traders.

Charts and Patterns

Some traders use charts exclusively for their short-term trading decisions. They follow a stock through charts, which they set up in advance to have the right parameters. Some of these traders use nothing but their charts for trading guidance and don't want or need any fundamental analysis.

Trading Tip

Some advanced trading platforms will let you enter trades directly from charts.

For these traders, charts are everything. They have their favorite types and look for certain setups or patterns in a stock's price trends to direct their trading activity. There is no doubt that following charts can prove valuable to traders, if the charts are set up correctly and the trader understands what they mean. However, charts aren't perfect. Despite the notion that the price reflects everything known about a stock, charts can't anticipate a major economic loss, a union strike, an unfortunate court ruling, or one of a hundred other events that can push a stock's price up or down. We'll take a more detailed look at charts in Chapter 16.

Repeating Patterns

Proponents of technical analysis believe that price movements tend to repeat themselves barring the introduction of an unexpected influence. It is this tendency toward repetition of pricing patterns that technical analysis relies on to predict future price movement.

The most basic pattern of a stock's price is the peak and valley. In simple terms, a stock creates a peak and valley pattern each day it is traded. It has a high and low for the day. It may close at the high, low, or somewhere in between. If the stock is very actively traded, there may be several points' difference between the daily high and low. A stock that is thinly traded may have only a slight or no change in price during the day.

This same pattern can be tracked over days, weeks, months, or years. Obviously, the more periods you track, the more peaks and valleys you will observe. If, over time, the highs are higher and the lows are higher than previous lows, your chart will show an upward inclination. If you plotted a line on your chart using lows, you would see that the stock is rising in price. This would be obvious without the line, but adding the line gives you a better graphic idea of the angle of ascent. The line represents support for the uptrend or a floor.

The Uptrend

Stocks following this pattern are in an uptrend—they are not bumping against any ceiling in their price that will hold them back. Over a long period (months), you will often see the stock rise, and then back off slightly, only to rise even higher. This three-steps-up-and-one-step-back pattern is typical of a stock on an uptrend. The periodic retreat is often caused by profit-taking, which will cause prices to drop momentarily.

> **Market Place**
>
> It is easy to remember what support and resistance are to stock prices if you think of support as being under the price and holding it up. Resistance is the roof that resists the price climbing any higher.

Active traders want to spot uptrends early and ride them as long as possible. Some uptrends may last a very short time; if you're trading intraday, you will want to get in and out in a hurry. These short-term traders are grabbing profits in the daily cycle of highs and lows. While it sounds simple to buy the low and sell the high, it is much more complicated than that. We'll look at trading strategies in Chapter 17.

The Downtrend

Trends can be down as well as up. The downtrend is defined by lower lows and lower highs. When you look at a stock over a longer period, you will often see both trends on the same chart. This trend up, then trend down, is also a pattern. It is a particularly important one for traders to understand because, with some exceptions, most stocks don't continue up or down forever. Some companies will go bankrupt and their stock will be worthless, so it is possible to go to zero. It is rarer that a stock will continue to climb forever. However, a number of companies have uptrends that run for years.

Traders are often more comfortable with uptrends, but there is money to be made with downtrends as well and they shouldn't be ignored. Shorting, which we discussed in Chapter 9, is a way to make money when a stock's price is trending down.

Sideways

The other trend possibility is that the stock will neither go up or down, but trade in a narrow range for a period. The sideways trend is a place where a form of swing trading can be employed under the right circumstances. If the stock is reasonably consistent in staying in the channel, the swing trader can play the stock going up and coming down.

Sideways may not be a bona fide trend, but the absence of one. When investors and traders are undecided about a stock, the stock may sit in a price range for some time until the buyers or sellers have a reason to act. This is also known as *consolidation* and when a stock breaks out of consolidation, traders have an opportunity to profit.

Consolidation doesn't mean for sure that a trend is about to reverse itself, but traders should be looking for other indicators. Although some of its adherents treat it as such, technical analysis is not a precise science—there are too many influences that can change the course of a stock's price movement.

def•i•ni•tion

Consolidation is when a stock trades in a narrow price range without any clear direction from buyers or sellers. The active trader has profit opportunities when the stock breaks resistance or support as the volatility usually increases markedly.

Another Sideways Pattern

Of course, stock prices don't always form neat patterns on charts for us to quickly analyze. At times, prices jump up and down without seeming to establish a direction either way. This is another form of moving sideways and is usually a nasty place for traders. Such a pattern suggests a lot of indecision in the market, and that is dangerous for traders. When investors and traders are acting erratically toward a stock, it's a good time to sit on the sidelines and wait until the stock breaks toward the buyers or sellers.

Support and Resistance

We have talked about support and resistance on several occasions, but its importance in technical analysis cannot be overstated. Identifying and understanding these two concepts is key to making profitable trades. The idea of support and resistance is there are certain price points that a stock will not easily fall through or push above.

When a stock's price does break through either support or resistance, it signals the beginning of a trend in that direction. This involves investors' psychology more than any fundamental or factual reason.

As a practical matter, support and resistance are often not single numbers but zones that function as roofs and floors. It is important for short-term active traders to identify support and resistance of the stock they are trading and watch for significant changes.

For example, investors seem reluctant to broach round numbers. As the price approaches a round number, investors tend to sell shares, causing the price to fall back—making the round number a difficult resistance level to crack. Likewise, when the share price falls close to a round number, buyers will step in and purchase large amounts of stock, raising the price. This keeps the round number at the support level. Active traders use support and resistance knowledge to enter trades. We'll discuss this strategy in Chapter 17.

> **Market Place**
>
> Support and resistance are important concepts for traders, but they can help investors, also. If investors are is preparing to sell a holding, they should study where the stock is trading to see if it is showing signs of breaking support or resistance. Their conclusions may affect the timing of their sale.

Round numbers aren't made of iron and are breached when buyers or sellers see a compelling reason to move. When this happens, and support or resistance is broken, the volatility of a stock can increase and traders may find interesting profit opportunities.

Frequently, when support or resistance barriers are breached, they take on the opposite role. For example, if a stock bursts through resistance, the old resistance level may become the new support level.

Speaking Volumes

Breaking the support or resistance barrier by itself is not enough to confirm a breakout or reversal. The breakthrough must be on strong volume, meaning a significant number of shares traded. If the price pokes through resistance, but volume is below the stock's normal daily volume, assume that it is a fluke and wait for more confirmation.

> **Margin Call**
>
> Volume is, unfortunately, often overlooked in the decision-making equation. Volume is the verifying data that a move through support or resistance is for real or not.

The importance of strong volume is obvious—buyers or sellers are making a move and traders should always pay attention when that happens.

It is easy to track volume, so there is no excuse for being fooled by a price change that breaches either support or resistance on weak volume. Many charts feature a volume bar across the bottom, which will show you whether this is a legitimate breakthrough or an aberration that won't hold.

Moving Averages

We discussed moving averages in Chapter 4, but need to expand on them in this chapter because they are an important part of technical analysis.

Long- and Short-Term Moving Averages

Moving averages are a way of looking at prices over a period and smoothing out the peaks and valleys. A moving average takes the closing stock prices for the stated period and averages them (simple moving average). As a new period is added, the oldest period is dropped and the average is recalculated. Thus a 20-day moving average would take 20 days of closing prices and average them. The next trading day, the oldest price is dropped, the newest closing price is added, and the average recalculated. These data points are plotted on charts to help traders see price trends over time more clearly.

The longer period you use, the flatter the line becomes since more numbers are used in calculating the average. A 50-day moving average would look flatter than a 10-day moving average, for example. Sharp price changes can skew a short moving average to be misleading. Longer-term moving averages help traders verify the strength of a trend and its direction.

Trading Tip

Charting software makes it easy to look at many different varieties of charts, including different data sets. Find the right combination for you and save those settings in your software so you can easily retrieve the chart when you need it.

There is value to giving more weight to recent data than older data, especially in longer moving averages. Exponential moving averages use a weighed calculation to give more importance to recent prices.

All major charting software will place these averages on charts for you so you don't have to learn the math or dig up historical price quotes.

How to Use Moving Averages

Moving averages are more than decoration for your charts. They represent key information that can tip you to important trading opportunities. How moving averages display with current prices and how they display with other moving averages of different time periods tell you much about price movement.

You should expect shorter term moving averages to more closely reflect current prices. This just makes mathematical sense. As noted above, the longer the term, the flatter or less reflective of current prices the moving average will be. When current prices are above the long-term moving average (50 days or more), you have a confirmed uptrend. When prices are below the long-term moving average, it's a downtrend.

It gets more interesting when you add a short-term moving average to a chart with a long-term moving average. For example, if you have a 15-day and a 50-day moving average plotted on your chart and the 15-day average is above the 50-day average, which signals an uptrend. If the longer average is above the shorter average, that signals a downtrend.

When prices cut through an important average, such as the 50-day average, traders should take that as a signal that a trend is reversing. For example, a stock on the uptrend suddenly drops through the 50-day moving average—this is a reversal of the uptrend and traders should look for the price to fall farther.

Crossovers are when moving averages intersect and change places—the one below becomes the one on top. For example, if you see the 10-day average crossover from under the 50-day average to above, that is a strong signal of an upturn. The longer the averages, the longer the trend is likely to last.

> **Market Place**
>
> Moving averages not only help you see trends, but help you see trading opportunities or traps. Watch out when short-term averages fall below long-term averages, for example—that signals a downturn.

Moving averages can also be strong support or resistance areas, especially the longer-term averages. The 200-day, which is considered a trading year, is the strongest moving average. A stock that falls through that support may be on its way to a serious downward trend. Likewise, popping through a 200-day average on strong volume is a definite statement toward an uptrend.

Using Technical Analysis in the Real World

Technical analysis is a powerful tool, especially for the short-term trader, as we'll see in Chapter 17. Those who practice technical analysis can't imagine trading without their charts. Some skeptics are not sure technical analysis is any more effective than reading tea leaves. The truth is probably somewhere in between.

While technical analysis does offer some insight into short-term price movements, it is not particularly suited for picking long-term investments. Buy-and-hold investors are probably better off sticking with fundamental analysis, which does offer some hope of playing out over a longer period. On the other hand, technical analysis has been around for a long time and is used by the most respected brokerage houses.

Short-term active traders would do themselves a favor to learn more about technical analysis than room permits in this book. Only you can ultimately decide if it is a tool you can use effectively in trading.

The Least You Need to Know

- ◆ Technical analysis is about profiting from trends.

- ◆ Support and resistance are important concepts in using technical analysis.

- ◆ Breakthroughs must be supported by substantial volume.

- ◆ Moving averages help traders spot changing trends.

Chapter 16

Charts and Indicators

In This Chapter

◆ Short-term traders often favor a particular type of chart

◆ Some charts are easier to read than others, but carry more information

◆ Technical indicators inform traders of major changes in price or direction

◆ Charts and indicators both need interpretation

Technical analysis as expressed in charts and certain indicators is one of the most common tools used by short-term traders. Charts provide a quick, graphic representation of what is happening with a stock and suggest a course of action (buy or sell). Indicators, which may show up on charts, provide the same type of information for quick decisions. Short-term traders who use technical analysis swear by it, while some buy-and-hold investors who use only fundamental analysis would put the same faith in astrology. Charts and indicators are subject to some interpretation and may not be read the same way by two different traders.

Worth a Thousand Words

Charts, which are used in many applications other than investing, can deliver a lot of information quickly and in a format that is easy to comprehend. Science, politics, business, or other areas have found that charts convey complicated and detailed information in a manner that is much easier to understand than the raw data. There is a place for analyzing the raw data, but if your point is to show sales growth over the past 12 months, a well-done chart will accomplish that quickly and in a manner that everyone can comprehend.

Trading Tip

Technical analysis is a skill traders must practice to improve. Since there is a certain amount of interpretation, practicing with paper trades makes good sense.

The same concept applies to technical analysis of stocks. Short-term traders need to grasp large blocks of data in a way that shows a comparison to other blocks of data. Long columns of numbers aren't the answer, but a chart can tell traders exactly what they need to know in a matter of seconds.

It is important to understand that technical analysis and the charts it generates is not an exact science. Charts do not predict with scientific accuracy what a stock's price will do next. The information represented on the chart is historically correct, but interpreting the patterns to form a trading strategy is a very subjective exercise. Technical analysis is predicated on prices moving in trends and these trends repeating themselves. If these conditions are correct, chart patterns may (or may not) predict which way a stock's price will move next.

Margin Call

If you want to make money as a short-term trader, you must train yourself to focus on the information that is relevant to the stock's price right now, not at some point in the future. Any other information or analysis will cost you money.

Investors who come from a fundamental analysis background may have trouble adjusting to the different information needs of the short-term trader. Analyzing financial statements is irrelevant to short-term trading. It will hurt the trader because it slows down the process and introduces information that has nothing to do with the price of the stock in the next five minutes.

Charts Explained

Most charts used in technical analysis have the same basic format. The bottom axis is the timeline, which can be months, weeks, days, or minutes. The axis on the right is usually the dollar value of the security. Price points are plotted along the chart and often connected in some manner, such as by a line. The result is a chart that follows the price of the stock over a set period. In most cases, a simple chart will plot the closing prices of a stock. We'll explore the more complicated (and useful) following charts.

One math consideration when viewing charts is whether you are looking at a simple mathematical chart or one that is *logarithmic*. You should be aware of the difference. Most charts plot the price on the right axis in equal units (for example, $5, $10, $15, $20, and so on). This means that as you plot the graph, it shows no difference between a stock that moves from $5 per share to $10 per share and a stock that moves from $20 per share to $25 per share. Mathematically, they are the same; both moved up $5 per share. However, when the stock went

> **Market Place**
>
> Math can be tricky, but it is worth it to slow down and pay attention to how numbers are used or represented. For example, the Dow is roughly 10 times larger than the S&P 500 index, so comparing point changes in the indexes doesn't make sense. However, looking at the percent change is a valid comparison.

from $5 per share to $10 per share that represented a 100 percent increase. When the stock went from $20 per share to $25 per share that only represented a 25 percent increase. The logarithmic chart reflects percent changes and would show a larger space between $5 and $10 than it would between $20 and $25. Percentage change is more meaningful since it represents the magnitude of the increase or decrease.

def•i•ni•tion

Logarithmic charts, or price scales as they are also known, reflect the percentage change in prices rather than the actual dollar amount of change. A stock price that moves from $15 to $30 per share would be represented by the same amount of space on the chart as a move from $3 to $6 per share. Both represent an increase of 100 percent. This is the preferred measurement by most traders because actual dollar changes do not show the magnitude of change.

The Importance of Volume

Most charts also include a section across the bottom that details trading volume for the period represented on the chart. This chart within a chart has its own scale of size. It helps traders see the strength or weakness of price movement based on trading volume. Strong volume confirms trends, while weak volume may indicate a false start or the end of a trend.

It is not uncommon to hear that everything is in the price, but without sustaining volume, prices changes can be false signals. Don't ignore volume and the volume indicators we'll discuss later.

What Charts Tell Traders

Charts signal two conditions for stock prices: the continuation of a trend or the reversal of a trend. If you think about it, those are the only two things that can happen to a stock's price—it will either continue in the same direction (up, down, or flat) or it will reverse direction. For short-term traders and some swing traders, this is all the information they need to trade. A continuation signal may mean buy or sell more shares (depending on the direction), while a reversal signal tells traders to buy or sell depending on their position.

The Three Basic Types of Charts

Which are the best charts to use? That's a matter of personal preference, but beginners should get to know the three basic types of charts and decide for themselves. The charts differ in the amount of information they deliver. Some traders want to strip information down to the essentials, while others believe that a little more detail means the difference between good trades and guesses.

Trading Tip _____

Don't make your mind up on any type of chart until you have worked with it using live data or in a simulation of live data. Paper trading with a chart until you see its potential is the best way to discover those tools that work for you.

The Line Chart

The most basic type of chart is the line chart. This chart takes a period and plots the closing price of the security on the chart. The points are connected by a line so you can instantly see where the stock has been and whether its most recent activity has been up, down, or flat.

The line chart's advantage is its simplicity. There is little to interpret, and you get a quick picture of the stock's history over the period covered. When you combine other indicators, such as moving averages, the chart becomes more valuable and provides buy or sell indicators.

In this example, a line chart is combined with an accumulation/distribution line. We'll discuss this indicator more later in the chapter, but be aware that it measures buying and selling pressure on the stock.

This is a one-year line chart for Yahoo! from Interactive Brokers's Trader Workstation. The line chart is the simplest chart to use and provides the least amount of information. The accumulation and distribution chart across the bottom tracks selling pressure on the stock. On this chart, the trend roughly follows the price. If the A/D line were to turn another direction from the price line, it would signal a change in the trend.

(Photo courtesy of Interactive Brokers.)

The Bar Chart

The bar chart expands the amount of information included, but sacrifices some of the readability of the line chart as it does. The bars in this case are vertical lines that represent the stock's high and low for the trading period. A horizontal line to the left indicates the opening price and a horizontal line to the right is the closing price. If the stock closed up for the trading period, the bar is shaded black or blue. A losing day will shade the bar red.

On up days the line to the left should be lower than the line to the right. If the opening price is also the low price, you may not see a left horizontal bar.

If the chart covers a number of periods, you can spot trends, but the vertical bars may make it harder to see what is happening. Some charting software will draw lines on bar charts connecting the price points you request (closing numbers, for example).

This is a three-month bar chart for Google from Inter- active Brokers's Trader Workstation. The bar chart adds a significant amount of information; however, some find it difficult to read if there are many bars. The vertical bar marks the high and low price for the day. The left horizontal mark is the opening price and the right horizontal mark is the closing price.

(Photo courtesy of Interactive Brokers.)

Candlestick Charts

Candlestick charts deliver the most information and may be the easiest to read. Candle- stick charts have been in use by various traders since their perfection by a Japanese rice broker in the seventeenth century. The name comes from the obvious shape of the markers on the charts, which resemble a candle with the wick exposed at both ends. Each part of the marker delivers information about the stock's price in the period cov- ered by the chart.

It takes some practice, but reading candlestick charts is much easier than bar charts with their tiny horizontal lines. The upper and lower wicks are called shadows and mark the stock's high and low. The shadow's length is determined by the relative dif- ference between the stock's high and low and the stock's open price. For example, if a stock opens at 30 and the high for the period is 35 and the low is 28, the upper shadow will be proportionately longer than the lower shadow.

Another key piece of information relates to the body of the candle itself. If the body is white or clear, it means the stock closed above its opening price. If the body is black, it means the closing price was lower than the opening price. A note of caution: not all chart providers use these coloring conventions, so check with the vendor regarding its color designations.

These are the absolute basics of candlestick charts. Interpreting patterns on the charts is where the real power for traders lies according to charting proponents. The candlestick forms may change as different price conditions emerge. For example, if a stock opens at its low for the trading period and never drops below that point before close, the candlestick will not

> **Market Place**
>
> Good charting software, whether through your direct access provider or a stand-alone application, will make understanding and using charts easier and quicker.

have a lower shadow. That form is called a shaved bottom. If the reverse is true (stock opens at high and never moves above that mark), the form will have no upper shadow and is known as a shaved head. If a stock's opening and closing price are the same, the pattern is known as a doji.

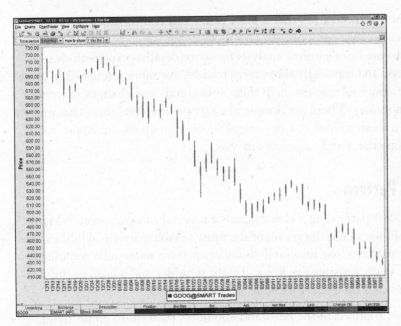

This is a three-month candlestick chart for Google from Interactive Brokers's Trader Workstation. The candlestick chart is one of the oldest forms of communicating market prices. It takes some practice to become comfortable reading, but the candlestick is very popular with technical traders. Vendors use different colors to indicate up closes from previous days and other important information.

(Photo courtesy of Interactive Brokers.)

Trend Lines

In Chapter 15, we talked about support and resistance. Support is the lower price that acts as a floor holding up the stock, while resistance is the upper price that is difficult for a stock to push through. When a stock trades between these two values, you can see the range defined by the support and resistance trend lines. Most charting software will draw lines connecting all the low prices and all the high prices. This gives you a visual trading range where the stock trades until it pushes through either support or resistance. Trading in this range can be profitable for short-term traders who buy at support and sell at resistance.

If a stock is trending up, your chart with lines connecting support values and another line connecting resistance values will angle up from left to right. This chart will reflect the upward movement of support and resistance values. If the stock is trending down, the parallel lines will slope down left to right.

Chart Patterns

Chart patterns tell active traders whether a price trend will continue or reverse, according to technical analysis proponents. (It's more complicated than that, but you'll need a book devoted to technical analysis for more detailed explanations.) Because active traders, and especially short-term traders, are more interested in price direction than value, any tool that can help them spot trends and changes in trends will help make them money. There are dozens of chart patterns and signs that purists follow. We only have room to look at a few samples here, but check out Appendix A for more resources on charts and technical analysis.

Head-and-Shoulders Pattern

The head-and-shoulders pattern on a chart signals a reversal in a price trend. Many technical analysis followers consider it one of the most reliable patterns. Unlike some of the more esoteric patterns, the head-and-shoulders pattern name tells you exactly how to recognize it. With a distinctive left and right shoulder and a head in the middle, the pattern stands out on a chart without too much nuance.

There are two major variations of the head-and-shoulders pattern. In an up trend, the head and shoulders are in an upright position on the chart. While in a downtrend, the pattern is inverted. Again, not much is left to the imagination for the basic patterns.

The basic head-and-shoulders pattern actually has four parts—the three mentioned above (left and right shoulders, plus the head) and a fourth component known as the neckline. The neckline is important because it is prices breaking through this level that signal completion of the pattern.

Head-and-shoulders patterns are considered trend reversal signals as stated above and tend to appear at the top of an uptrend in prices or at the bottom of a downtrend. Technical analysis proponents believe the reversal will commence when the head and shoulders pattern is completed.

That completion is the fourth step in the process that creates the pattern, which

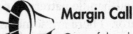
Margin Call

One of the dangers of charts is that not all patterns take shape in the classic manner that makes them easy to identify. What may look like a certain pattern may just be close to the shape, but sending you the wrong signal.

begins with the left shoulder as it hits a new high, then backs off to a new low. This forms the left shoulder. The price then hits a higher high, which is the head, before falling back to another new low. The third step is another high, but not as high as the head, which creates the right shoulder. The fourth and final step completes the pattern and begins the trend reversal. This is when prices fall off the high that created the right shoulder and keep falling through the neckline. Technical analysts believe this signals the completion of the trend reversal.

For stocks that have been in a downward trend the head-and-shoulders pattern is inverted, but the same process occurs to complete the reversal of the trend. When this happens, technical analysts believe the stock is headed up.

Cup-and-Handle Pattern

The cup-and-handle pattern signals the continuation of an upward trend. Active traders can profit from this pattern, which is characterized by a pause and dip in price before a resumption of the upward trend. The cup-and-handle pattern may be more appropriate for swing and position traders as it can signal a longer term price pattern.

As you might guess, the cup-and-handle pattern looks like a cup and handle with a rounded cup and a moderate downward move marking the handle. The cup is made by prices falling off a high and gently sliding down into the bottom of the cup before rising to form the right side of the cup.

The handle is formed by prices retreating from the high of the right peak forming the cup. Usually chart watchers expect no more than one-third retrace from the right-peak high. This brief dip gives form to the handle and sets up completion of the pattern. When the pattern is complete, prices will continue their upward trend.

The cup-and-handle pattern is on par with the head-and-shoulders pattern as a reliable indicator. There are some indicators about the cup-and-handle pattern to watch. If prices have had a large run-up before the pattern, there may not be a large surge following completion of the cup and handle. The pattern may signal some remaining enthusiasm by buyers, but with limits.

Other Signals

We have barely scratched the surface of charts and technical analysis. Active traders, especially those who plan to trade short term, should pursue an education in reading and understanding charts. Not every short-term trader uses charts to the exclusion of every other trading tool, but you should know more about them before you make that decision for yourself. Using them is your personal decision; however, many short-term traders couldn't imagine trading without charts.

Technical Indicators

Not all proponents of technical analysis rely on chart patterns. Many technical traders, as they are sometimes called, use technical indicators to help spot trading opportunities. Indicators are mathematical calculations usually related to price changes over time. They may also include volume and other factors. Indicators may be plotted on a chart to see how they change or move over time, especially in relationship with other indicators or over different periods.

Indicators can be used to confirm chart patterns or by themselves as buy or sell signals. Most technical analysts like to have more than one confirmation of a signal. Although chart patterns have a visual appeal, they can become complicated because price movements don't always follow patterns precisely. That is why having an indicator confirm a pattern's signal is a wise step.

Leading and Lagging Indicators

Indicators are either leading or lagging. Leading indicators are more predictive and work best when prices are not following an obvious trend—they may be moving in a choppy or sideways fashion. Leading indicators are known as oscillators, meaning they move in a set range that goes from overbought to oversold. As the oscillator moves between these two ranges, it will generate buy and sell signals.

Lagging indicators work best when prices are trending. They are less predictive and produce fewer buy and sell signals, which helps traders stay with the trend longer. These indicators focus more on historical price movements to confirm trends.

Trading Tip

Technical indicators are rooted in mathematical relationships of past price and volume patterns. Many technical indicators can be used without charting as they produce a numerical score that can be a buy or sell signal.

Using Technical Indicators

Technical indicators are used to create buy and sell signals. Indicators generate signals through either *crossovers* or *divergence*, both of which are the result of plotting the values on a chart. This may sound like a return to chart reading, but the difference is indicators don't require you to recognize special patterns or combinations of patterns. Because the indicator is a computed value, its interaction with a price level or moving average, for example, is significant without the need for detailed interpretations. Some indicators, as we'll see below, can be interpreted without a chart simply by their value—above a certain level is considered bullish and below that level is bearish.

def•i•ni•tion

Crossovers occur when an indicator crosses a major marker such as a moving average or a price trend and can signal a buy or sell situation.

Divergence occurs when an indicator moves away from or in the opposite direction of a price trend. This usually signals a reversal of the trend.

Using technical indicators that diverge from major levels or moving averages quickly shows that the direction of the price trend is losing support. The divergence can be either positive or negative. If the price of the stock is going down, but the indicator is trending up, it suggests that interest is building in the stock and the price may soon reverse its direction and begin moving up. Negative divergence is the opposite—the price is trending up, but the indicator is headed down. This suggests that support of the stock's price is weakening and sellers are gaining strength. The stock's price is likely to begin falling.

Examples of Major Technical Indicators

In this overview of technical analysis, there is only room for a brief introduction to indicators. We'll look at some of the most popular indicators and how they are used. For a more comprehensive overview and other resources on technical indicators, visit Appendix A.

On-Balance Volume Indicator

The on-balance volume indicator (OBV) measures the effect of volume on price and the strength of price trends. The indicator measures a running total of volume that is adjusted by price movement—rising price on volume is added in while decreasing price volume is subtracted. The calculation can be found in the reference material in Appendix A. This indicator tells traders whether there is support for price changes (as reflected in volume).

> **Trading Tip**
>
> Volume is an important indicator for traders to watch. If there is low volume associated with what appears to be a change in price trend, be careful of a false signal. Trend change signals with strong volume are much more valid.

If a stock's OBV is rising, it is predictive of a price increase, while a declining OBV signals a drop in the stock's price. Volume is the driver in this indicator and precedes any price change. An OBV moving in the same direction as the price trend confirms the direction, while the opposite indicates the trend is weakening.

Accumulation/Distribution Line Indicator

The accumulation/distribution line captures the money or demand for a security. Supply and demand (as represented by money or buyers for the stock) are the basic determinants of a stock's price in the short term. When there is money coming into a security (buyers), the pressure is on the stock's price to rise. When the sellers take over, money is flowing out and the price must soon decline.

The accumulation/distribution line can confirm a trend if it tracks the same direction or it can signal the end of a price trend by reflecting the money flowing in a different direction. For example, if a stock has been trending up, but the accumulation/distribution line begins to trend down, it is telling traders that support for the stock at that price is eroding and the trend will soon end.

The calculation for the accumulation/distribution line is found in resources listed in Appendix A. However, traders will find this important tool calculated for them in most direct access broker packages and in dedicated charting software.

MACD Indicator

The moving average convergence divergence (MACD) fits in the category of must-know technical indicators. It is composed of two moving averages—one for 12 periods and the other for 26 periods. The two are referenced against a nine-period signal line. The indicator notes a stock's momentum by comparing the short-period moving average to the longer period's moving average.

The MACD generates signals several ways, including crossing the signal line, diverging from the price trend, and when the short-period line crosses the long period line. There is not room to discuss all of the signals MACD can reveal, but you'll find more information in Appendix A. All technical traders and those who want some confirmation of price trends or changes should master this indicator.

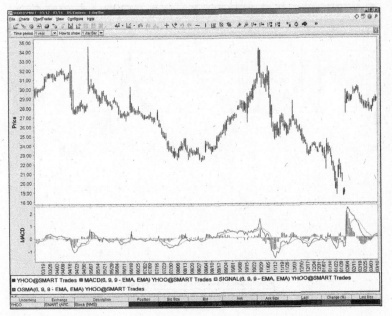

This is a one-year moving average convergence divergence (MACD) chart for Yahoo! from Interactive Brokers's Trader Workstation. The MACD chart is one of the most important confirmation tools traders use to verify breakouts.

(Photo courtesy of Interactive Brokers.)

Relative Strength Index

The relative strength index (RSI) is an important technical indicator that is used with charts, but can also be helpful as a standalone calculation. The RSI calculation generates a number between 0–100. Traders consider an RSI of 70 or more overbought and any value under 70 as oversold. As values move away from 70, the degree of intensity changes.

> ## Market Place
>
> RSI is an important indicator and one active traders should add to their toolkit because it follows the money—and where the money goes, the stock's price will follow.

This number is helpful by itself as a trading tool because it gives traders a sense of what direction the stock may be headed and where the money is. For example, a stock with an RSI in the 90s could be headed for a price reversal as that number indicates the stock has heavy buying pressure, pushing the price up. RSI can also be used to confirm trends or signal reversals. Check out the resources in Appendix A for more information on using this important indicator.

This is a one-year relative strength index chart for Yahoo! from Interactive Brokers's Trader Workstation. The RSI chart is an important technical indicator that can generate buy and sell signals.

(Photo courtesy of Interactive Brokers.)

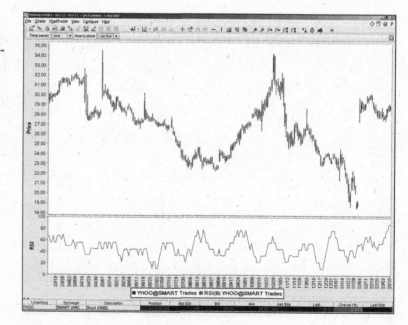

The Stochastic Oscillator

The Stochastic Oscillator is another popular momentum indicator favored by technical traders. It tracks closing prices on the theory that they should follow the prevailing price trend. For example, a stock in a rising trend should close near the high end of the trading range. In a declining trend, the stock should close near the low end of the trading range. When a stock begins a pattern of closing in variance with these norms, it signals a change in the trend.

The Stochastic Oscillator is too complicated to explain in this limited space; however, you should know it registers a numeric score between 0–100. A score above 80 is considered overbought, while under 80 is oversold. With this number alone, traders have useful information. The value of this indicator extends when it is plotted on a chart. There you can see if it confirms a price trend or signals a coming change in direction. Like other indicators, this information generates buy and sell signals. Appendix A has more detailed information on the Stochastic Oscillator and how active traders use it.

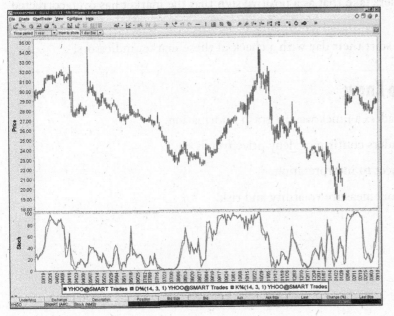

This is a one-year Stochastic chart for Yahoo! from Interactive Brokers's Trader Workstation. The Stochastic chart is an important technical momentum indicator that traders use to spot a change in the prevailing price trends.

(Photo courtesy of Interactive Brokers.)

Market Indicators

Most active traders, especially short-term traders, are more concerned about immediate price trends and don't pay too much attention to overall market activity. However, even very short-term traders keep an eye on certain market indicators that may influence prices.

One of the most important market characteristics traders watch is volatility. Is the market overbought or oversold? Too much volatility may lead to a market correction that can affect virtually all stocks. Three main indicators track major stock indexes: the VIX tracks the S&P 500; the VXN tracks the Nasdaq 100; and the VXD tracks the Dow.

One of the main uses of these indicators is to measure risk in the market. This means the higher the risk the lower the indicator will be, while the lower the risk the higher the indicator. Traders can gauge the perceived risk (is the market bearish or bullish?) by following the appropriate indicator. If the indicators are very high, while the market index is low, traders take that as a positive sign that the market has over-corrected and will reverse.

Many active traders start their day with a check of these market indicators.

The Least You Need to Know

- Charts offer traders a quick way to grasp information.
- Charts help traders confirm or deny price trends.
- Charts are subject to interpretation.
- Market indicators measure volatility and risk.

Part 4

Strategies for Active Traders

Active traders look for profits in price changes. Those changes can happen over a very short period (seconds, minutes, or hours), or they can happen over longer periods (days, weeks, or months). How long you choose to hold a security before trading defines where you fall in the active trading strategy spectrum.

Short-term trading, swing trading, and position trading are considered active trading strategies, but each has a different holding period.

Chapter 17

Short-Term Trading Strategies, Part 1: Day Trading

In This Chapter

♦ What you need to be a short-term trader

♦ Scalping as a trading strategy

♦ A closer look at shorting

♦ Fading as a short-term strategy

A combination of switching stock pricing from fractions to decimals and the bear market following the collapse of the dot.com bubble were thought by many to be the end of short-term active trading. Also known as day trading, this once robust part of the trading industry took a one-two punch. The conversion to decimals in pricing stocks reduced the spread between the bid and the ask, which was an important source of revenue for day traders. The bear market put an end to most of the big intraday gains that were the norm during the dot.com bull market.

However, the short-term active trader is still very much in the game and making money. Tough times weeded out many of the traders who were riding a bull market but lacked the experience to survive a more difficult trading environment. We have used the term short-term trader to

---

> **Market Place**
>
> Short-term traders, also known as day traders, don't get the press they once did, but they are still active in the market.

distinguish the traders of today from the shoot-from-the-hip day traders of the dot.com boom. Today's short-term traders must be smarter and more professional about their business if they want to succeed. Many of the techniques used by today's successful short-term traders are the same as day traders have used for years with updates to include new products and new markets.

The New Short-Term Trader

The one characteristic that has remained constant from the era of day traders is the rule that no trade carries over a trading day. This means traders close out all their positions at the end of the trading day. In this regard, short-term traders remain true to the day trader philosophy. While some view day trading as very risky (and there is risk involved), short-term traders feel holding positions open overnight is riskier.

The other characteristic that is common to short-term traders is a rigid trading system that defines entry and exit points for each trade. The short-term trader may make up to 100 trades per day, but each is organized with definite entry and exit strategies.

Finally, short-term traders use a high degree of leverage to accomplish their goals. When you are only making a small profit on a trade, it helps if that small profit is multiplied by 1,000 or more shares. Short-term traders must balance this need to make small profits with the expenses of multiple trades.

The Importance of Technical Analysis

Short-term traders may use technical and fundamental analysis to guide their trading. However, most use the charts provided by technical analysis to provide buy or sell signals. (We sampled a few of those in Chapter 16.) Thanks to advancements in electronic delivery of news and information, short-term traders have access to information that may change a stock's price trend and can trade on that movement—or at least protect their positions.

> **Trading Tip**
>
> Many short-term traders find most of their buy and sell signals in charts. However, watching the Level II quotes and additional indicators can yield buy and sell signals, too.

If you are going to succeed as a short-term trader, you will need to find a trading system—whether it is based on technical or fundamental analysis or both—that provides you with reliable buy and sell signals quickly and accurately. No system is perfect in all market conditions, but without a working system, it is difficult to survive as a short-term trader.

Be Flexible

While most short-term traders continue the pure day trading strategy, others have chosen to let profit opportunities drive whether the trade is closed at the end of the trading day or not. New short-term traders take a less rigid view of closing all trades at the end of the day and may shift into another strategy if they are holding a trade that has more profit to be made. In this scenario, day traders may become momentum traders (Chapter 18), swing traders (Chapter 19), or even position traders (Chapter 20).

To be certain, this can be a more risky strategy because your position is exposed for longer periods and you may not have done much, if any, fundamental research on the company. However, if you have strong indicators that there is more profit to be taken by holding on, the new short-term active trader is free to carry over trades from one trading day to another.

What You Need to Succeed

Short-term trading is not a get-rich-quick scheme, despite what you may have seen on the Internet. Most people who try it do not succeed. It is not the type of activity you can do when you feel like it or when there is nothing else to do. If you plan to make a living with short-term trading, you should plan to spend months learning the trading platform of your direct access provider (see Chapter 12). This exercise should include paper trading and using all of the platform's features.

You will also need a significant amount of risk capital—that is, capital you can afford to lose without ruining your life. Regulations for day traders call for an account minimum of $25,000. Some brokers may require a higher minimum. You will lose money in the beginning, so it is important to have enough capital to see you through your learning process. Many advise a $50,000 minimum.

Margin Call _____

You will lose money when you begin short-term trading. You must have discipline to keep your losses to a minimum while you are learning. If you can't tolerate losing money, short-term trading is not for you.

With your investment capital, you will be using a high degree of leverage to make large trades. As we'll see later in this chapter, small profits on large trades can add up over the course of a day, as can small losses. Leverage is a two-edged sword, but one we must use to be successful.

Later in the book, we'll look at legal and tax issues as well as setting up your office, time management, and other issues directly related to active trading.

What You're Looking For

Short-term traders look for a stock that has liquidity and volatility. Because most, if not all, trades will be closed out in a single day, the short-term trader wants a stock that trades in a broad intraday range. This means that the difference between the day's high and low is significant enough to allow the trader to profit on up or down swings in the trading range. These swings may only be a point or less, but if the trader puts together a 500-share trade, the net could be impressive.

Say the trader made $0.50 per share on a trade within the intraday range. At 300 shares, that's $150, minus commissions, fees, and so on of $50, for a net of $100 for the trade before taxes. If the trader could do that several times a day, always at a profit, it would be a good day. Unfortunately, not every trade will be for a profit—some will be losses. Not every trade will deliver this much profit. In fact, as we'll see in the section on scalping, many profitable trades make much less.

The bottom line is the more trades you make, the better your chances are of ending the day with a profit—and the greater risk that you will lose more of your investment capital.

The liquidity requirement of good short-term trading candidates means there is an active and ready market for the security. This gives short-term traders good entry and exit points, which are important for capturing profits or cutting losses. With poor liquidity, it may be difficult for traders to get the price they want in a timely fashion. This is one reason most short-term traders stick with well-known actively traded stocks.

> **Trading Tip**
>
> Stocks that are actively traded are said to be highly liquid. This will help keep the spread narrow, which means you are paying less for the product.

A stock with good liquidity will have narrow spreads, meaning there will be little difference between the bid and ask price. This is important because you are not giving up much to the market maker in the stock.

Using the Right Tools

The short-term trader needs the fastest, most reliable technology available. A direct connection to markets via a direct access broker and a trading platform that allows the trader to execute preprogrammed trades with a single click are essential. In addition, the short-term trader should have Level II prices, Time and Sales charts along with TotalView (see Chapter 14) to have a complete picture of the market. Charts beyond a one- to five-minute period are too old to see set-ups for the short-term trader.

Of all active traders, the short-term trader needs the best information technology to be successful. This is not an area to cut corners or save pennies. Buy adequate equipment, software, and services and learn how to use it all completely before you invest a dime in actual trades (we'll discuss tools in detail in Chapter 22). There is nothing more frustrating than failing because you are stumped by a hardware or software question.

Scalping

The best-known trading strategy of short-term active traders is scalping—one that day traders have been using for years and perfected during the dot.com bull market. The essence of scalping is to grab small profits in trades that may last minutes or less. Scalping is the primary trading strategy for a number of short-term active traders. When done correctly, scalping is a moderately low-risk strategy because your exposure to the market for any one trade is so short.

On the other hand, scalping requires strict discipline and endurance. Short-term traders may have to enter many trades every day to make a decent profit, and one slip in discipline can wipe out a big piece of their profit.

The traditional scalping strategy is to buy on the bid and sell on the ask. These orders are entered simultaneously by the traders in mimicking the role of the market maker. This strategy works if there is enough of a spread between the *bid* and *ask* to produce a profit that will cover trading expenses.

In this strategy, the trader buys and immediately sells at prices that guarantee a small profit. To make enough money to cover

def•i•ni•tion

Bid is the price a market maker is willing to pay for a security. **Ask** is the price a market maker is willing to sell the security. The ask price will always be slightly higher than the bid. The difference between the two prices is the market maker's fee per share.

expenses, the trader may have to buy 2,000 or more shares. If the spread between the bid and ask prices is sufficient, the trader can do this repeatedly throughout the day and build up a nice daily profit. This strategy works best with stocks that don't change price frequently during intraday trading.

The switch to quoting stock prices in decimals hurt scalpers. When prices were quoted in fractions, scalpers were almost always assured of at least a spread of one-sixteenth point, which meant a profit of $0.0625 per share. On a 1,000-share trade, this gave the trader $62.50 profit before expenses. With prices quoted in decimals, the spread may be down to $0.01 per share or $10 on the 1,000-share trade. This has made it more difficult to profit by playing market maker, although there are still stocks with larger spreads than $0.01.

Despite the increased risk, scalping remains a major source of income for many short-term active traders. By looking for larger spreads and increasing the size of their trades, active traders may compensate for the more difficult environment.

> **Market Place**
>
> Many short-term traders keep up on several different securities so if one market (stocks, for instance) seems bereft of opportunities, they can switch to another security (Forex or futures, for example).

Although we've used stocks as our example, active traders can apply many of the same techniques to other securities including trading e-mini stock futures, the Forex, and so on. These nonequity markets may offer a different opportunity that you will find more attractive than pure stocks. For example, the Forex trades 6 days per week, 24 hours a day.

Take a Large Position

Scalpers who have been frustrated by the small spreads in the decimalized stock market have taken another approach. They will take a large position in a stock and wait for a small movement in price before selling. Unlike traditional investors who let their profits run, the short-term trader will fix a profit target and exit when that goal is reached. They believe the longer you are in the market, the more danger you face. Still they are out of the trade quickly. A volatile stock will likely move enough during intraday trading for a scalper to grab a profit.

This strategy is much riskier than the market-maker tactic because you are counting on the price to move in the direction of your trade. You must have protective stops in place to prevent large losses. It is not unusual for a volatile stock to move 10 to 50 cents or more during a trading day. Scalpers set their profit goals that reflect the risk and sell when the price hits the target. This strategy may "leave money on the table" by selling out of a stock that is increasing in price beyond the trader's profit target. However, the strategy assures a profit and reduces the risk that instead of continuing an upward climb, the price reverses and destroys your profits.

Scalpers use charts and Level II pricing to watch for price reversals and pressure building on the buy or sell side with pending orders. If they get good signals from their charts with confirmation from volume and Level II information, traders will buy near the low for the day (up to that point in the trading day) and sell when the price is close to the high for the day.

While it is tempting to let a winner run, it is also risky. Intraday prices on volatile stocks can change direction without warning, despite what charts may indicate.

> **Margin Call**
>
> Trying to follow Level II quotes on a very volatile stock can be challenging as the numbers change faster than you can track them. If a stock is moving too fast, it may be time to back off and wait for the action to slow down. Don't be caught in the excitement at the expense of common sense.

While this strategy may entail fewer trades than traditional scalping, you still need discipline to set entry and exit points. Many short-term traders fail because they do not stick to a disciplined exit plan. They will either get greedy and try for a few more cents per share profit on too many trades or will take high-risk trades in an attempt to compensate for losing trades. Either course of action (or a combination) of the two will lead to failure.

Playing the Down Side

Scalpers can make money in other ways besides the traditional "buy low, sell high" strategy. One of the more popular ways is to take the other side of a trade and short stocks that the trader believes will fall in price. Many of the technical tools and charts discussed in Chapter 16 point toward reversals of upward trends. This signal gives the trader the opportunity to short or sell the stock prior to the price fall. We discussed the mechanics and risks of shorting in Chapter 3.

Although the terms are slightly different for traders who close short positions in a matter of minutes or hours, the risks remain the same. Because short-term traders are highly leveraged, the risks of shorting are multiplied. If the stock's price continues up, instead of dropping as anticipated, traders had better have a stop in place to close out their positions in a hurry.

Trading Tip

Shorting is a popular and potentially profitable activity for short-term traders. Following a large run-up in price, some traders will short the stock, feeling acorrect, they profit. If not, they are forced to cover their positions and lick their wounds.

However, with short-term trades not open over trading days, the risks are usually much less than a normal shorting strategy that holds open a position overnight.

Traders may use charts to spot upcoming reversals and make their move based on those signals. Other traders may take a less analytical approach and short stocks that have a quick run-up in intraday price on the belief that toward the end of the trading day (or perhaps before), others will be taking profits and those sales will drive down the price.

On intraday trading, an eye on Level II orders will give the trader an idea when selling pressure is beginning to build. As profits are taken and the price drops, the trader should watch for buyers coming back into the market to pick up shares at a bargain off the day's high. That is a good signal to cover the short position and take your profit. If you feel the price is headed back up to a daily high, you might jump back into the stock as a buyer at this low point and ride it up to a point you are comfortable with and take more profits.

This all sounds very easy when you read it in a book, but in practice, it is far from simple. Volatile stocks that trade in a broad range don't necessarily bounce up and down with any regular pattern. If they all did (and some do), you could make a nice profit following the price up and down as a buyer and seller. In reality, prices don't follow a nice predictable pattern every day. When they don't, you get clobbered with losses if you place trades in the opposite direction.

A Higher-Risk Strategy: The Fade

Despite what many think, short-term investors believe they employ strategies that minimize risks rather than exaggerate them. Holding positions for only short periods is seen as a safer move than exposing yourself to all the bad things that can happen when you hold a security for an extended period. While that attitude is debatable on several levels, it is a fact that closing all your positions each day does eliminate exposure to many market factors that can work against you (and some that work for you).

However, some traders are attracted to the possibility of extraordinary gains made possible by taking more risk. The market rewards risk, but also penalizes traders in proportion. It is important that we be clear that taking a higher risk position is not the same as gambling. If a trader has a clear head, entering a high-risk position is a legitimate strategy. If greed or fear is pushing the trader to take extra risks, the situation is dangerous and the trader is headed for financial disaster. In Chapter 24, we'll examine some of the emotional requirements necessary for successful active trading.

> **Market Place**
>
> Short-term active trading offers many opportunities for traders to get their feet wet in the world of fast decisions and big money. Many find this a more comfortable invitation than traditional investing and its much longer holding periods.

Playing the Fade

You'll find that trading terms often are shared by other endeavors. One of the terms you may hear in trading circles is fade, which is a term that appears in a number of environments from sound to haircuts to shooting dice. It is the definition used in dice that may be most analogous to the meaning in trading. To fade someone in dice is to bet they will not make their point—in other words, to bet they will lose.

In trading, to fade is to bet the prevailing price trend is going to reverse (or lose). Traders employing this strategy buy as prices trend down and sell short as they trend up—a *contrarian* strategy that pays handsome profits if things go your way, but the odds are against you.

def•i•ni•tion

> **Contrarian** strategies suggest that the crowd is probably wrong or will be soon and take positions that are opposite what the market is doing. If prices are trending up, the contrarian shorts. If prices are dipping, the contrarian buys.

Fade Strategies

One of the ways traders play the fade is when a stock gaps at opening. A gap is the difference between the previous close price and the next day's opening price. A gap of a few cents is nothing unusual; however, when there is a significant news event or economic news, a stock may have a large (more than a point) gap either up or down at opening.

Traders with a tolerance for risk can fade those gaps. If a stock gaps up—meaning the opening price is higher than the previous close—a trader can short the stock. If the stock gaps down, the trader would buy. You can see these are contrary moves.

If the stock gaps up, the initial reaction is that it will be moving up for the day. The trader who shorts the stock is betting that won't be the case and the gap will close, but back toward the lower close. When that happens, his short position stands to make a significant profit when covered. Likewise, the trader anticipates that a down gap will close back up to the previous close, making his shares worth more for a nice profit.

> **Margin Call**
>
> Fading is one of the more high-risk strategies available to short-term active traders. While holding out the possibility of high returns, it can fail more often than succeed.

Obviously, the danger in fading is that a stock could gap up and continue to rise. This will put a short seller in a tough position very quickly and the trader will have to exit before the losses become too large. If a stock that opens with a down gap continues the trend, the trader who bought betting the stock would go up is now holding a losing position and must also exit in a hurry to reduce losses.

One clue for traders who want to play the fading strategy is the volume at the opening gap. If a stock gaps with a heavy volume, traders should be cautious that the price will continue the opening direction. However, a gap on weak volume is a clue that the direction at opening may not hold a trend and would be a good fade candidate.

Fading is not a strategy for beginning active traders. However, with some experience in the market, and practice, you can take calculated risks for larger returns.

For Additional Short-Term Trading Strategies

Short-term trading is a challenging way to make a living. We have only scratched the surface of the different strategies that traders use. If you choose to make short-term trading a career, an investment in more in-depth resources and training is required to be successful. There is a wealth of material available to help you get started. If what you've read so far sounds like it is something you would find challenging, continue reading and consult Appendix A for additional resources.

The Least You Need to Know

- Short-term trading is confined to opening and closing positions the same trading day.

- Scalping or taking very small profits is a central strategy to short-term trading.

- Short-term traders short securities for additional profit opportunities.

- Fading is a contrarian strategy favored by some short-term traders.

Chapter 18

Short-Term Trading Strategies, Part 2: Momentum Trading

In This Chapter

- How momentum traders make money
- Finding entry points
- Moving with the market and news
- When to exit—the key to success

Momentum traders might be called the surfers of short-term trading—they ride the wave price movements, then bail out just before the wave crashes on the beach. Okay, the surfer metaphor is a stretch, but momentum traders do share something important with surfers: they stay with the stock until it begins to lose its momentum before exiting.

How Momentum Trading Works

The key for momentum traders is identifying a stock that is rising (or falling) on strong volume and then getting in early. But that's only part of the success formula. The momentum trader must know when to exit to avoid losing any profits. This is definitely not a contrarian strategy because traders are relying on the flow of the market to provide the energy for pushing prices in the direction they want. While scalpers may shoot for many small profits, momentum traders look for fewer but larger profits. It's a risky but rewarding, strategy if done correctly.

Trading Tip

Momentum trading is higher on the risk scale than many other forms of trading because you wait for an uptrend to end before exiting. The trend may last only a few minutes or it could stretch out for hours.

Keeping an Eye on Volume

Momentum traders look for stocks making a strong move on high volume. The price increase or decrease would be above the normal daily trading range and would exhibit signs of sustainable strength. Traders would confirm the move using technical and fundamental tools we'll discuss below and take the appropriate position. Traders know that once a price trend is in motion it will continue until it encounters something to stop or reverse it. Traders will stay focused on the activity around the stock, watching for signs that the momentum is slowing. When they spot the warning signs of slowing momentum, traders exit the position.

While this sounds easy, it requires a careful set-up, patience, and extreme discipline to be successful. In many ways, it is riskier than scalping because momentum traders make fewer trades with higher potentials for reward and loss. A scalper may be happy with a trade that yields a $0.25 per share profit, but many momentum traders shoot for trades that make in excess of $1 per share profit. With the potential for larger profits comes the possibility of large losses.

Finding Stocks for Momentum Trading

The momentum trader's big task is finding the right stock to trade. Each day, that may be a different stock, depending on what is happening in the market and to the company. News developments such as quarterly earnings reports or announcements from the company can produce dramatic price changes. Action for or against the company by a government regulatory agency can also have a serious effect on stock prices. Many of these events intentionally happen after the market closes so their impact on prices is not reflected until the next day's opening. The stock may gap up or down depending on the announcement. We'll discuss gaps later in this chapter.

Volume is a critical piece of the selection equation, as we have noted in other areas of the book. Volume is a confirmation of the strength or weakness of a trend. Momentum traders will avoid stocks that show big price changes on weak volume because it is unlikely that the trend will hold.

Momentum traders begin their search before the market opens by looking at news wires and consulting various news groups they trust to see if any stocks or industry sectors are getting a lot of attention. This begins the narrowing-down process that will help the trader eventually focus in on a short list to trade. While it is easier to follow an upward trend, momentum traders can work the short-sell side of trading, too, by looking for stocks that are breaking down and not up. In some markets, you will find more "new lows" and "new highs."

Momentum traders aren't afraid of stocks trading at or near record highs (or lows). After all, the whole premise of momentum trading is that prices will continue in the same direction until there is a reason for a reversal. Traditional investors are told that the road to riches is to buy low and sell high—a formula that works and has made investors such as Warren Buffett extremely wealthy. The problem occurs when you buy low and the stock stays low or goes

> **Market Place**
>
> Momentum trading on price increases works best in a bull or flat market. Traders can use the same strategy and short (sell) stocks on downward trends, although many find it easier to look for rising price candidates.

lower. Momentum traders, like all traders, are impatient and will not wait for an investment to mature to profit. They are willing to buy an overbought stock if they believe it will rise higher still because they plan to sell as soon as there is any whiff of slowing momentum.

The Breakout

Traders call a strong departure from a previous trend a *breakout*. The problem for momentum traders is knowing what a true breakout is and what is just an excited blip that's going to fizzle in a matter of minutes or seconds. There is no absolute indicator

def·i·ni·tion

Breakouts are strong divergences for existing price trends. They signal a new and powerful direction for the stock. The direction may be bullish or bearish and will continue until it runs out of energy.

that will guarantee a breakout is for real. Momentum traders can use several indicators to confirm as best they can that a breakout is going to have some sustainability. None of these is foolproof, which is why we'll discuss emergency exit strategies below in detail.

This is one of the major risks of momentum trading—misidentifying a trend and taking a position only to have it reverse on you almost immediately. There are protective measures you can take to minimize your losses, but you'll take a loss just the same. The loss may be small (if you're disciplined it will be); however, small losses add up over time and become a drain on your investment capital. In addition, the time you spend on losing trades is time you are not spending on winning trades, so you have a lost opportunity cost in addition to the actual monetary loss. Paper trading for an extended period will help you hone your skills before risking real money.

The Momentum Indicator

Momentum traders use the momentum indicator to confirm a breakout. This calculation offers insight to the trader if the price trend will continue or is about to break. It is plotted on a chart with a moving average to spot movements up or down. The momentum indicator is a simple mathematical calculation in which the closing price of X periods in the past is subtracted from the most recent closing price. If the answer is positive, then momentum is positive. Conversely, if the answer is negative (meaning the most recent closing price was lower than the price of X periods in the past), then momentum is negative.

$$\text{Momentum} = \text{Most recent close} - \text{close of } X \text{ periods in the past}$$

The Rate of Change

Traders can also use the same two numbers to calculate the rate of change. Take the most recent closing price and divide it by the closing price of X periods in the past. If the most recent closing price is higher, the answer will be greater than one. The higher the positive number, the faster the rate of change.

$$\text{Rate of change} = \text{Most recent close} \div \text{close of } X \text{ periods in the past}$$

The period in the past should not be too far back since you are interested in what's happening now.

There are actually many momentum indicators in technical analysis. You will find resources in Appendix A to help you learn more about technical analysis and leading and lagging indicators.

How Long Do Breakouts Last?

The most difficult question facing momentum traders is how long a breakout or upward trend will last before running out of energy and reversing itself. Some breakouts will collapse almost immediately as sellers take quick profits and drive the price down. Other breakouts will last for minutes or hours. Going into the trade, there is no way of knowing for sure how long it will last. Traders can use some technical indicators that may give you an idea to the strength of the breakout, but a reversal could come at any time.

Momentum traders make it a rule to not worry about getting in on the absolute ground floor or be concerned about holding out for the last nickel of profit before selling. If you jump in immediately on the first signs of a breakout, you will probably lose more money over time than you will gain. Smart momentum traders are not concerned about the first few price jumps, because they may confirm or deny the trend. Likewise, traders would rather exit early than wait too long and have the market turn on them.

> **Margin Call**
>
> Technical indicators, including momentum indicators, are not perfect. You may see a nice pattern on your chart for a breakout toward rising prices only to have prices move in the opposite direction on some bit of news no chart could anticipate.

Keeping Watch

Momentum traders can't afford to be away from the market for long if they hope to retain their profits or keep losses to a minimum. Once they have done their preliminary research and scoured the news sites for potential investing opportunities, momentum traders finally pull the trigger and buy (or sell). Now comes the time for vigilance. Breakouts, despite what charts or indicators may tell you, can collapse in the blink of an eye. Traders can protect themselves by keeping focused on their charts, but also on their Level II screens, to note when volume on the ask side starts growing.

The trader has no way of knowing whether the breakout will last three minutes, three hours, or three days (or three seconds, for that matter). Material about technical indicators may give you the impression that these signs are as clear as traffic signals. However, that's simply not correct. If they were always correct, traders would never have losing trades. The best you can hope for is guidance—a suggestion about a general direction. This is certainly better than no help at all, but don't read technical indicators or technical analysis as if it were incontrovertible fact.

It is critical that the trader watch for signs that momentum is about to slow, and the sure sign of that is a building list of sell orders on the Level II screen. This will usually correspond with a diminishing number of buy orders, indicating that traders are ready to take profits.

> **Trading Tip**
>
> Advanced trading platforms offer several tools to traders, including alerts when prices of selected stocks move in a particular direction by so much. This automatic monitoring system is a great help, but nothing replaces your attention to the market.

Momentum and Gaps

Gapping stocks present a number of possibilities for short-term traders as we have seen with scalpers who look for them as opportunities. Stocks that gap up or down on opening may also be good candidates for momentum traders. Momentum traders need some patience with gapping stocks to see which way the stock will head after the opening bell. The momentum trader will want to know why the stock gapped at opening and if the cause is still in play. In many cases, company, market, or economic news was the driving force behind the gap. Will the momentum that built the previous day continue into today's trading?

When a stock gaps up—that is, it opens significantly higher than its previous close—one of two things will happen. It may sustain the enthusiasm for a short while, then fall back toward the lower previous close or the momentum will continue pushing the price up. In some cases, the price may retreat briefly, then push ahead. This is a case where the momentum trader should be very sure of what is happening before entering a trade.

> **Market Place**
>
> Many advanced trading platforms offer a stock screener that includes screens for stocks that gap up or down on opening. This is a great time-saver.

Entering too soon may find the trader buying into a stock that is falling back to the previous lower close.

What looked like a breakout was not sustainable. Check volume in early trading for confirmation that this stock is still attractive. If volume is high, check your Level II screens to see where orders are accumulating. If sell orders are piling up, this is not a breakout that is going to last very long. If buy orders seem to be dominating and your technical indicators indicate a bullish trend, the breakout is as confirmed as it can get.

Traders may miss some of the early trading gains, but by waiting, the have reduced the risk that the breakout will blow up immediately after they enter their trade. In a volatile market, traders may find that many breakouts blow up quickly, and momentum traders can't afford long strings of small losses.

The In-Between Approach

The stock market is a place where many strategies are employed. All of the rational strategies work some of the time, but none of the strategies work all of the time. The main reason is that the market itself is a very dynamic and robust mechanism. The market is constantly changing and responding to an economy that is also always in a state of change. Given this background, it is no surprise that trading strategies must accommodate the market because the market never changes to fit your needs.

Some investors employ a strategy that is similar to momentum trading. The biggest difference is that these investors may hold a position for a much longer period—days, weeks, or months—than a trader who always closes at the end of a trading day. Momentum investors recognize the power behind a trend and stay with their position for an extended period. You can buy momentum mutual funds that employ this strategy. However, from the trader's perspective, the idea of holding on for extended periods has two problems. First, it is more difficult to find stocks that will sustain a trend for a lengthy period. Second, the longer you hold a position, the greater the chances are that something bad will happen to your profits.

Undoubtedly, there are traders who argue for an in-between position—not letting profits run as long as they want, but also not closing a good trade just because the market is closing. This is an individual decision each trader must make. There are compelling arguments for holding a good (profitable) trade overnight. However, many short-term traders will testify to all the bad things that can happen during that period between market close and open, when you have no way to protect yourself.

Which Way Is the Exit? Exit Strategies

Successful momentum traders know as much about quitting a trade as they do about entering one. Both steps are equally important to securing a profit or cutting losses. We noted earlier that momentum traders don't necessarily jump on the first hint of a breakout. They may wait to see the price moving up to confirm the breakout before entering the trade.

In the same manner, momentum traders do not wait until the breakout collapses to exit their positions. Smart momentum traders know that it is better to leave the trade early while a profit is assured than to hold on for a few extra pennies. As traders watch their charts and Level II screens, they decide when momentum is beginning to slow and sellers are beginning to line up preparing to take their profits. Momentum traders know that when the price hits those limit orders, everyone will start selling and the price will drop quickly. They exit their positions *before* the crowd heads for the exit.

> **Margin Call**
>
> It is dangerous to attempt to time the end of a trend. If you are caught when the sell orders begin, the price may drop so fast you will see most of your profit disappear before you can get out of your position.

This may mean they could have made more money by staying with the position a while longer, but smart traders take a sure profit and don't worry over more profit that they might have made.

Settling the Score

Fear and greed are the two most dangerous emotions for any trader. They will ultimately cloud your judgment and ruin any trading plan. Momentum traders must understand this completely and be content with taking a nice profit and not be tempted to take more. By waiting for confirmation of a breakout before entering a trade, momentum traders may lose 10 percent or more of the potential profit. Exiting the position at the first signs of weakening momentum may cost traders another 10 percent or more of the potential profit. However, for the traders' 80 percent, they are capturing a more certain profit at a lower risk.

Even though technical analysis cannot provide perfect tools for entry and exit points, you should learn to use the momentum indicators. When coupled with a practiced observation of Level II screens, they can give you an edge that will make momentum trading less risky.

Don't be fooled by traders who tell you they have a "feeling" about the market and can sense when to enter and exit. Either they are telling you a tall tale or they are telling themselves a tall tale. If the latter, the trader won't be around for long. The market is too complex and driven by too many factors for an individual to sense its upcoming changes.

People may talk about the market as if it was alive, but it is not. The market is a complex economic engine that few, if any, completely understand. Don't be fooled by people selling systems that claim to crack the "secret" of the market. There is no secret. There is no single system that will work every time, all the time. The market is constantly changing—it is different every day and by the time you figure out what is moving the market today, it changes and some other factor is more important. That is why momentum traders—and other short-term traders—are willing to take a certain profit even if it is less than was theoretically possible.

Protect Yourself at All Times

Momentum traders spot an upward movement on strong volume, confirm the trend, and take a position. Now the waiting and worrying begins. Traders are concerned that the trend will end before they can make a profit or even enough to cover their expenses. They can watch their charts and the Level II screens for any sign of slowing momentum and sell to protect any profit or reduce any loss. What if traders don't want to sit glued to their screens, or more likely, what if they have several positions open at once? How can they protect their positions?

One way to protect your profits and limit losses is to use a technique called trailing stops. Trailing stops is a way for you to automatically protect a position that is rising. A stop is an order that only executes when a certain price is hit. In this situation, the trader wants to protect a profit, so the stop is set behind the current market price by a small margin. If the price of the stock falls to this stop, the stop order becomes a market order to sell and is immediately executed.

> **Market Place**
>
> Market orders don't guarantee you will get the current market price, but they do guarantee you will go to the head of the order list for execution. This is not the most elegant way to exit, but it is fast and, if the price is falling, the safest way out.

For example, if the current market price is $35 per share and you bought the stock at $28 per share, you might set a stop at $32 per share. This would give the stock some room to fluctuate up and down without tripping the stop order. However, if the stop came under heavy selling pressure and began to fall, you would want to get out with some of your profits. When the price hits $32 per share, your stop order becomes a market order to sell and you get (hopefully) close to $32 per share.

Trailing stops take the protection one step farther and work with stocks that continue to rise. Trailing stops follow the price of the stock as it rises. They are sometimes expressed as a percentage of the market price. For example, you might set a trailing stop at 10 percent of the market price. This means no matter how high the stock rises, if it ever falls by 10 percent of its current market price, the stop is activated and becomes a market order to sell.

The advantage of trailing stops is that you don't have to watch the stock's price every minute the market is open. As long as the stock continues to rise or stays flat, the stop order just sits there. Only when an event triggers a reversal in the upward trend will the stops be activated. Some traders prefer alerts to using stops. Alerts are offered by a number of vendors and come to you via e-mail, text messages, and other vehicles.

The Risks of Momentum Trading

Momentum trading can be a very profitable endeavor. It works just as well on the downside as it does on the upside. However, momentum trading is also risky. There are a number of things that can and do go wrong. Most of the problems are "operator error" and can be avoided with practice, patience, and discipline. Most momentum traders fail because:

Trading Tip

Momentum trading is not a good place to start your career in active trading, but it is worth considering once you have some experience in other forms of trading.

- They miss the right entry and exit points.
- They try to extend their profits and hold a position too long.
- They refuse to close a bad position in a hurry.
- They become distracted and miss key signals from charts and Level II screens.
- They fail to close a position at the end of a trading day.

If you believe you have the patience and discipline to be a momentum trader, try your hand on paper before committing real money to the process. Appendix A has some resources for getting you started.

The Least You Need to Know

- ◆ Momentum traders look for trends on strong volume.

- ◆ Momentum traders confirm the trend before taking a position.

- ◆ Momentum traders watch the stock closely and exit when they see momentum slowing based on indicators.

- ◆ Momentum trading can be very profitable, but it carries a higher risk.

19

Swing Trading Strategies

In This Chapter

◆ Swing trading is a strategy that complements other trading strategies

◆ How to identify swing trading candidates

◆ Swing trading captures intermediate trends

◆ Making money with swing trading strategies

Swing trading is not a new trading strategy, but it has enjoyed a resurgence of sorts. Thanks to a stock market that has been all over the place, short-term traders have needed more than one way to make money. Bull markets, bear markets, and flat markets may require a different approach if traders are going to be successful. Swing trading is one strategy that can work well in a flat market, which comes along ever so often and frustrates those strategies that thrive on volatility.

Like other forms of trading, swing trading is not precisely defined in the investment community. Some lump it and momentum trading together, while others, including this book, separate the two. Swing trading can be less risky than very short-term trading, although some strategies, such as pursuing news-driven gains, can be just as risky.

Swing Trading Goes With the Flow

Swing traders, like their shorter term associates, momentum traders, understand the power of the trend. While there are valid and successful contrarian strategies, most successful traders work with the energy behind trends and not against it. Trends push stocks up (or down) until something stronger stops them. The "something" is always sellers outnumbering buyers. Swing traders follow a stock up and exit before it hits the wall of sellers. They may reverse their strategy and short the stock as it slides back down before hitting a floor of buyers. The traditional swing trader will cover their short before the price begins to rise on buying pressure and begin the cycle all over again.

> **Trading Tip**
>
> Swing trading makes sense to active traders who need an additional tool for opportunities that stretch beyond typical short-term trading situations.

Advantages of Swing Trading

It sounds simple, but finding the right stock in the right market makes swing trading a bit more complicated than this summary. However, swing trading is not as intense as scalping, momentum, or any other form of day trading. The longer holding period allows positions to mature and offers the possibility of larger profits. Along with that increased potential for a higher return is the risk that holding open positions brings. Most active traders believe the longer they hold a position open, the longer they expose themselves to the possibility that business, economic, or market factors could undermine profits. With proper safeguards in place (discussed below), swing trading doesn't have to entail unnecessary risk.

> **Market Place**
>
> There is a lot to consider when it comes to holding a position open for longer periods. On one hand, the longer it is open, the greater the chances are that something bad will happen. On the other hand, keeping a position open often lets fundamentals play out, which can lead to higher prices.

A Place to Start

Swing trading is often recommended to beginning traders as a way to gain an introduction to the markets without the intense pressure of short-term trading. It is possible to execute swing trading strategies without a direct access broker and expensive technology. You can do swing trading on a part-time basis while holding a regular job—something not recommended or even practical for short-term traders.

Not every trader approaches swing trading as a part-time strategy, however. Some traders use it as their full-time trading strategy and they use many of the same tools that short-term traders use. If the market is right and you want to build to this level of involvement, swing trading offers large potential profits. However, like all forms of active trading, you should ease your way into the strategy by learning as much as you can through paper trading.

Swing trading has an advantage over short-term trading because you don't need to watch every tick of the market to be successful. That takes much of the pressure off beginning traders.

Swing trading and momentum trading are sometimes confused because they both take advantage of trends. However, there are several differences. Momentum traders close out their positions at the end of the trading day, if not before. Swing traders

> **Margin Call** _____
>
> Trading terms can be confusing. Some use momentum and swing trading interchangeably, while others do not. Be sure you understand what your source is talking about when reading about investing styles because there are no absolute definitions that everyone accepts.

may hold a position for several days or weeks while an intermediate trend exhausts itself. Momentum traders look for a stock that is headed in one direction with strong daily volume pushing it. Swing traders look for a stock that is trading in a range or channel and try to profit as the price rises and falls in a broad range.

Finding the Right Stock

One of the most important tasks for a swing trader is finding the right stock combined with the right market, which we discuss below. Many swing traders find that large-cap stocks work well for their strategy. Large-cap stocks tend to be more stable companies that trade in a somewhat predictable range. Unlike smaller companies, these giants set the market rather than bend to it. Because of their size, most of these companies are highly liquid and trade millions of shares on a typical day, which is helpful to the swing trader.

Depending on the market conditions and how traders employ their strategy, swing traders will look for a trading candidate with certain attributes. In a flat market where the major indexes are drifting up and down with no obvious direction, swing traders may focus on large-cap stocks that will follow the indexes and coast along, sometimes up and sometimes down, but within a trading range.

News-Driven Trading

Company news such as earnings reports can create an opportunity for swing traders to pick up on an upward (or downward) trend in prices that often overshoot the ultimate price. For example, if a company reports better-than-expected earnings, the market may bid up the stock over several days. Sometimes the enthusiasm drives the price past the point where sellers want to take profits and the price falls. Swing traders can capitalize on both swings, if they have a clear view of both movements. The upside requires a quick entry or you will miss the early gains. Traders should plan on an equally quick exit, when selling pressure begins to build and the swing looks to reverse direction.

Swing traders can also "fade" the market by taking a position that is contrary to the bump created by news. The play here is that the market will overreact and when it corrects, swing traders will profit as prices swing back. For example, if a company announces a merger possibility, the market may bid the price up quickly. Swing traders would short the stock near the top in the belief that when reason returns, the price will fall back as it often does. When the price does retreat, swing traders cover their position for a nice profit.

> **Trading Tip**
>
> Swing trading is traditionally thought of as a less risky practice. However, some traders use news-driven prices to practice a form of swing trading that is quite edgy.

This is a risky strategy. The price may continue to rise or not retreat. In either case, traders must cover their position quickly to avoid further losses.

When the markets are more volatile, swing traders spend a lot of time studying news wires and industry reports to identify companies that may have a special situation such as major economic, sector, or business news that will push them out of a flat trading range into a new channel. These present an opportunity to ride a trend up to new highs and back down to a higher low. This is a riskier form of swing trading because you can't know when a new trend will end abruptly, forcing you out of your position before you have made enough to cover trading costs. This form of swing trading is best done with access to Level II screens, although it is possible with just information from your online broker.

Using EMAs

When the market is flat, swing traders can use exponential moving averages (EMA) to create a baseline price for a trade candidate. EMAs for the previous 10 to 20 periods may be sufficient to establish a baseline. You'll remember that EMAs track closing prices, giving more weight to recent entries. This indicator is more reliable than a simple moving average and traders can use it to look for variances.

Plotting the baseline on a chart gives the trader a way to see if prices are trending above or below level. When prices push above the baseline, swing traders will go long after confirming the trend or short if the price dips below the baseline.

A relatively flat market prevents prices from bumping above or below the baseline in simply following the market's influence. The trader wants to see the stock moving on its own rather than floating with the market. It is easier to spot trends and reversals if the stock is moving under its own energy (supply and demand) rather than getting a push from the market.

While most swing trades do not need precise timing (see trading on news for an exception), swing traders must still enter as soon as they are comfortable a swing is confirmed and exit when they see signs the swing is about to stop. The right stock will help make this possible.

> **Trading Tip**
>
> If you are not using a direct access broker for your swing trades, see if your regular discount broker provides after-hours charts. If not, you may want to subscribe to a charting service, such as Big Charts.com.

Finding the Right Market

Traders must trade in the market as it is. While many hope for the bygone days of previous markets, practical traders deal with what's before them now. Although it is not always easy to tell what type of market you are in until after it is over, an observant trader can adjust strategies to accommodate reality. It is important to master a particular active trading strategy, but you will find having more than one tool in your box is helpful in dealing with different markets.

Swing trading seems to work best when the market is moving sideways—that is, it drifts up and back down as measured by the major *stock indexes*. Swing traders look for those stocks that will mirror the market in rising and falling with a significant point spread between the high and low. Significant may mean different things to different people, but three points would be a good spread between the high and low points in the swing. If traders are fortunate, it could be more. Traders want a stable market to keep the swing going back and forth, so they can profit on price movement in both directions. In a choppy market, swing traders are less certain of a swing and prices tend to be more erratic.

def•i•ni•tion

> Stock indexes are baskets of stocks designed to represent all or certain segments of the market. Most financial professionals consider the S&P 500 index representative of the market, while the Dow is still the best known.
>
> A set-up is trader talk for identifying particular market or price situations that have profit potential for the active trader. Active traders are always on the lookout for a set of circumstances that lends itself to the trader's game plan.

Consequently, short-term traders prefer volatile markets and don't have as many opportunities in flat markets. That is why many short-term traders use swing trading as an alternative to match the market or *set-up* rather than forcing all their trades into one strategy. Seasoned short-term traders can spot a swing trade opportunity among their set-ups and switch strategies on the fly. Beginning traders should stick with a single strategy until it is mastered before moving to another. The value of having more than one way to make money in the market cannot be overstated. You will be presented many opportunities. Part of becoming a successful trader is understanding which strategy will work best on the opportunity in front of you.

Capturing Profits

In a market where there is no well-defined direction, major indexes may drift up and down without moving very far in either direction. For swing traders, this creates a good environment to find stocks to trade. This is not an absolute requirement because you can find stocks that will trade in a good range regardless of what major indexes are doing. Swing traders are looking for stocks that will move over a period of several days in one direction and then reverse back down to a previous level. This ideal stock gives swing trading its name as its price drifts back and forth from a high to a low over a short period of several days.

Like all set-ups in trading, you don't always find the ideal situation. However, with some practice in learning what to look for, you can often find good swing trading candidates. In many cases, you may find that the stock doesn't swing to a regular rhythm, but may swing up and hold for days or longer before drifting back down. This is not the ideal trade because traders lose the multiple profits of playing the swing both ways. However, if traders are clever, they will take their profits and not wait for a swing downward that may not be coming, especially if there are no technical indicators showing a break in the trend. At this point, traders can't be sure whether the stock will continue up at some point, stay on hold, or retreat. Your best bet is to exit the stock until there a clear indication of where the stock is going.

Trading Tip

The most important step you can take is to practice or paper trade until you are comfortable recognizing swing-trade set-ups. Practice identifying entry and exit points. Keep a journal of your progress so you can identify any consistent mistakes you are making.

Trade Size

In our discussions of short-term active trading, we noted that because of thin bid-ask spreads and other factors, traders often have to increase the number of shares traded to make a profit large enough to cover expenses. In that venue, trades of 1,000–2,000 shares are not uncommon. Swing traders hope for larger per share profits and usually don't need to trade as many shares (unless you want to) as short-term traders. This opens swing trading up to many people who can't afford the $25,000 minimum that pattern day traders must maintain in their accounts. If you are going to be trading frequently, you'll want either a deep discount broker that offers breaks for traders or a direct access broker that has favorable arrangements for heavy traders. You will also want to consider how much margin you want to use because holding a position for several days will cost you something (but not much) in interest expense.

Protect Yourself by Using Stops

Swing traders can protect profits and reduce losses by using trailing stops or manually moving stops as the trend plays out. Either way, you build a floor of sorts under your profits in the event the trend experiences an unexpected sharp reversal. Unless you are attempting to time your entry and exit as close to the limits as possible, you shouldn't have to worry about watching every tick of the market.

This will not be true for those less risk-adverse traders who want to fade the market on news-driven events. These traders should keep an eye on price movement to avoid a nasty surprise. Even with stops in place, it is not possible to be completely safe if you are trading close to the border between profit and loss.

Market Place

If you don't understand stops and trailing stops, spend some time becoming comfortable with the concepts before investing real money. This is insurance you can't afford to be without.

Swing Trading Systems

A short visit to the Internet via Google will reveal page after page of swing trading systems—most boasting certain success. Can they all work as well as they claim? Probably not. Like most trading systems, swing trading systems offered for sale on the Internet or through other venues come in varying degrees of quality. Some are good quality, but only work well under certain market conditions, while some are so complicated it is a wonder they work at all.

> **Margin Call**
>
> Beware of get-rich-quick plans and systems that promise they have discovered a "secret" to market success. Legitimate systems should let you try them or offer some type of money-back guarantee. Are they easy to use? Do they work in up and down markets? Ask questions and get answers.

This is not to say you shouldn't use a system prepared by someone else. There are some good packages available on the market, although it is doubtful that any one system works in every market condition. If you are just starting out in swing trading, you will need a system of some type. Whether you develop your own or subscribe to one of the available commercial systems, you will need something to bring order to the world of swing trading.

Whether you develop your own system through practice and refinement or use an existing system, plan on paper trading for some time to become familiar with how the system works. Your trading system should evolve with your trading style. Don't make changes during the heat of the trading day because you will not be thinking clearly at that point.

A Technical Point of View

Most of the systems on the market use technical analysis to spot entry and exit points for swing trades. You will find proponents of technical analysis who insist there is no other way to trade. While technical analysis can improve your odds of finding good trades, it won't guarantee them. Don't be led to believe that charts and lines can predict something as uncertain as tomorrow's stock prices with any consistency.

Given that warning, it would be a mistake to not learn the basics, at least, of technical analysis and how it can help you make better short-term and swing trading decisions.

Technical analysis can improve your chances of better entry and exit points. You would be foolish not to use these tools, but they come with a learning curve, so take the time to study and practice before committing money.

Evaluate and Reflect

The end of each trading day is a good time for evaluation and reflection on the day's activities and trades. How would you rate your performance as a trader? What tweaks (if any) do you need to make in your trading system? To help this process, it is important to document your trades and outcomes during the day. Most brokers provide reports covering your activity; however, those reports don't say why you performed a task in a certain manner.

The Least You Need to Know

- ◆ Swing trading is often used in concert with other short-term trading strategies.
- ◆ It is possible to start swing trading part-time using a regular discount broker.
- ◆ Swing traders not adverse to more risk can fade price swings driven by market news.
- ◆ Traditional swing trading works best when markets are trading flat with low volatility.

Chapter 20

Position Trading Strategies

In This Chapter

◆ Position traders compared to investors

◆ Fundamental research drives stock selection

◆ Important business, market, and economic cycles

◆ Holding a position until the trend reverses

Position trading anchors the other end of the holding spectrum from short-term trading. Instead of a holding period of no more than one day and sometimes no more than a minute, characteristic of the short-term trader, the position trader is in for the long haul. The long haul in this case is as long as the stock is doing well and the price is moving up, even gradually. Position trading, also known by some as trend trading, looks to ride an upward (or downward) trend for as long as it runs, which could be months.

Active traders, which as a group are not known for their patience, may find the pace of position trading too slow for their taste. In fact, some refer to position trading as short-term investing. However, if practiced correctly, position trading departs dramatically from short-term investing. Position trading gives traders an alternative when a stock appears to have longer term prospects.

Trading, Not Investing

Active traders by definition remain engaged with their positions. They remain aware of price changes, trend reversals, and other factors that could increase or decrease profits. Traders have little patience for securities that don't produce profits. As we have seen in exploring short-term trading, momentum trading, and swing trading, when the trade shows signs of reversing a profitable position, the trader exits and moves on to the next opportunity.

> **Market Place**
>
> Position traders are prepared to exit their position any time it appears the price trend is reversing. This distinguishes them from investors.

Investors, by contrast, are less concerned with daily pricing and more concerned with long-term growth and value. They pick investments based on the fundamentals of the company and the relative price of the stock. If they get the stock at a reasonable price, investors will stick with the stock for years, even if the price is battered by market or economic factors. As long as the business fundamentals remain solid, "buy-and-hold" investors will stick with a company. If the price should stumble because of market conditions, investors might consider that an opportunity to add to their holdings.

This "buy-and-hold" philosophy is a sound and proven strategy that has been borne out over years of experience. Warren Buffett, one of the richest men in the world, became so, in part, by using this strategy. Of course, for a strategy of buy and hold to succeed, investors have to choose a great company that is going to remain great throughout their holding period. This is no small task in itself. The other problem occurs when investors need cash (as in retirement) and the stock is the victim of market doldrums. Investors are faced with selling at a loss or hoping the stock will rally in the near term—and neither are welcome prospects for a retiree needing cash to pay bills.

> **Market Place**
>
> Many traders speak disparagingly of buy-and-hold investors, but the facts back up the philosophy when executed correctly as a superior long-term wealth-building system.

Because the anticipated hold time may be months, position traders must have a better understanding of the company, its products, and markets than other types of traders. The longer holding period means the trader is exposed to more risk that events in the market, economic, or business cycle could have an adverse effect on the stock.

As with all trades (and investments, too), it is important that the position trader enter the trade at a good price. If the stock has already been bid up in price, there may not be much left in growth possibility before it becomes overbought and profit-taking begins pushing the price down. Ideally, the position trader will catch the first part of a stock's upward trend and take a position. If the trend is built on solid fundamental growth (as opposed to a single event, such as an earning report), the stock should be in a groove for a sustained growth. Technical analysis and charts will help you determine where the stock is in a price trend.

The position trader may be more tolerant of small retreats if the overall trend remains upward. Weekly and monthly charts of moving averages among other technical analysis indicators will help the position trader keep an eye on the trend's progress and spot any potential reversals.

The trader's position is safer if the stock doesn't attract much market or media attention. A run on the stock may hike the price in the short run, but it will almost certainly kill the long-term growth trend, at least for the immediate future.

Fundamental Analysis Is Key

Position traders can't rely on technical analysis to give them answers to which stocks have longer term growth potential. For that information, traders must turn to fundamental analysis, which is the study of a company's key financial ratios along with an understanding of the company's business and market.

This is an area investors are familiar with, and if you are coming from that discipline, you know what is required to identify companies with growth prospects. However, position traders are not interested in value investing. A *value investor* will pick up the stock at a cheap price and sit on it, often for years. When the market does correct its underpricing, the stock often records an extraordinary gain. Successful value investors do very well over time. However, the risk is the company's true potential will never be recognized and the stock price will remain stagnant.

def•i•ni•tion

Value investors look for companies that have been overlooked by the market or had their stock beaten down for no good fundamental reason. Value investing is not about buying cheap stock. It is about buying stock that is underpriced by the market, meaning it is trading for less than its fair market value.

Position traders are more interested in growing companies with immediate potential. Growth investors look for companies with prospects for growing their business and hope to share in that growth through long-term appreciation of the stock's price. In many cases, growth companies reinvest any profits back into the company to fund more growth, rather than pay dividends. The danger of investing in growth stocks is that at some point the company may stop growing. When that happens, the market often punishes the stock with a sell-off that dramatically reduces the price.

Active traders are by nature interested in trades that exhibit activity. There is a certain amount of skepticism that traders can sit still long enough to let position trades play out to their full potential. Although position trades don't require the oversight of other more rapidly moving strategies, you can't doze off either.

Using Both Technical and Fundamental Analysis

The position trader more than any of the other active traders uses tools from both fundamental and technical analysis. Technical analysis proponents are almost fanatical in their faith in charts and indicators. They turn to them for guidance on all their trades. In many situations, technical analysis can prove helpful to traders and investors. However, some things technical analysis can't predict, and some decisions are best left to the tools available through fundamental analysis.

Trading Tip

Volume is the best way to verify a trend or indicator. If you are unsure whether a trend is forming or reversing, volume is one key point to consider. Without strong volume, most indicators are questionable in their guidance.

Technical analysis is best used to look at price and volume patterns. These factors when combined with other indicators help traders determine buy and sell signals. They also help traders spot trends and trend reversals. Technical analysis is not a perfect predictor, but it can be helpful when position traders have identified a stock and needs to determine when to enter or exit their trade.

Fundamental analysis will tell the position trader whether the company behind the stock has the credentials to carry a growth agenda into the near future. Charts may tell you a stock has done well in the recent past, but they can't tell you whether the president of the company has just been indicted for looting the pension fund. Less facetiously, charts can't tell you whether the company is financially healthy or in a dying market or about to merge with a competitor. All these factors would be considered in fundamental analysis and would have a bearing on whether this was a growth stock.

If position traders are looking for a stock with upside potential, they will need to confirm that with fundamental analysis. Technical analysis can only suggest an upside if history repeats itself (which it does sometimes). While fundamental analysis can suggest the intrinsic value of the stock, it can't tell you where the market will price it tomorrow. Certain financial ratios reflect what the market is paying for the stock, but only guess at what it should pay in the future.

Fundamental analysis doesn't reveal pressure building on the sell side or the possibility that a trend is about to halt or reverse. You can't use fundamental analysis to plot your exit strategy as effectively as you can with technical analysis.

If your stock candidate is particularly suscep-
tible to certain market or economic events,
you can use technical analysis as a historical
tool to gauge how the event affected the stock's
price in the past. For example, homebuilders
are sensitive to changes in interest rates. If you
anticipate an interest rate change, you could
go back to a previous change and chart prices
along with moving averages to see what

Market Place
Most charting software services will provide historical prices so you can construct charts. If not, Yahoo.com Financial offers historical stock prices so you can build your own charts.

happened. A hike in rates is usually not good for interest-rate sensitive companies, so what happened to the stock the last time rates went up? What happened when rates went down? Depending on the economic environment you are trading in at the moment, an anticipated hike or cut could influence whether you bought the stock or shorted it (also a viable strategy for position traders, but not often, because of interest charges).

Choosing the Right Cycle

Position traders can find candidates in just about any market. However, it is easier in some situations than others. A full-blown bear market, when very few stocks are rising, is a tough market for the position trader. Still, this market sets the stage for some great opportunities when recovery begins.

Analysts who study the market's behavior and follow technical analysis are fond of breaking the market into four phases: accumulation, markup, distribution, and markdown. These phases each hold a special opportunity for position traders. The most significant problem is identifying which phase is presently in control at any particular moment. Think of these phases as part of a circle that rotates at various speeds.

Sometimes we zip through one phase, but are hung up in another. Here's what they mean to position traders.

The Accumulation Phase

The accumulation phase is where smart buyers are bottom fishing for good stocks that have been beaten down in price. At some point during the accumulation phase the market bottoms out, but that point is usually confirmed after it happens. This may not be a great place for position traders because there is not an easy or effective way to determine how long stocks will be stuck in this phase. You could buy in cheap but sit on a stock that is going nowhere for a lengthy period. This works for value investors, but not position traders who need something on the move.

Margin Call

Position traders should not try to time the bottom of a trend (or the market), but wait until they can confirm the upward trend with confidence. Otherwise, you may be stuck in a stock that goes nowhere and is not even a candidate for a swing trade.

The best buys are going to be found in this phase, but position traders will want to wait until the market is moving on to the next phase and stocks are beginning to head up. In a perfect position-trading world, you would have a good fundamental candidate in mind and watch the charts for the patterns that indicated the stock was breaking out of this phase. As this phase ends, prices of leading stocks begin moving up when more buyers come into the market. Position traders should be among the buyers who have seen the technical indicators that breakouts from the low prices are happening.

The Mark-Up Phase

There is not a sign that says, "The market is now entering a new phase," so you'll have to be sensitive to the news. However, during this phase you will see a continuation and acceleration of price increases that marked the end of the previous phase. One of the indicators that the market is in the next phase is a substantial increase in volume. At this point, many investors who left the market during the dark days of the accumulation phase are coming back in and driving up prices on premium stocks—the type position traders should own. The early part of this cycle is where position traders want to establish their trades, because the people waiting on the sidelines for a sign will begin to buy.

Prices will increase throughout this phase and accelerate toward the middle and end. You will soon be witnessing the less intelligent money jumping on after many stocks have already posted substantial gains. Stocks will become over-valued and that will begin setting off technical alarms of a pending price reversal. Position traders should watch the smart money and begin moving when they see institutional investors do the same.

As the unsophisticated money moves into the overbought market, it is time for the position trader to plan an exit. While it doesn't always happen, the end of the markup phase may be capped by an artificial surge driven by unreasoned buying—such was the case toward the end of the dot.com boom in the late 1990s. This unreasoned feeding-frenzy of buying is for amateurs only, but if you are confident of where the market is headed, this is a great time to establish short positions in the most volatile and overbought stocks. It's a risky play, but if you are right, the bottom will drop out and your shorts will produce a nice profit when the market moves into the next phase.

> **Trading Tip**
>
> Active traders make money off amateurs who jump into the market at all the wrong times. This may seem harsh, but trading is not a game where everyone wins.

The Distribution Phase

The distribution phase is when things begin to turn ugly. Sellers take control and prices begin to fall. Note that this is not an across-the-board reaction. Some stocks may not fall as fast as others do. Big-cap stocks may hold their prices longer than more volatile smaller cap stocks. If an industry sector is hit with bad news, those stocks may fall faster than other stocks. Fewer stocks are hitting new highs than in previous phases, while the number of new lows begins to grow.

Investors grow increasingly pessimistic, even if there are several false starts that make it look like the market is bouncing back. Concern drives some out of the market and into cash. This lowers prices even more and the "it's going to get worse before it gets better" feeling grows.

Position traders, except those who shorted stocks at the height of exuberance, are out of the market unless they see more short opportunities.

The Mark-Down Phase

The mark-down phase is when all the wheels come off and prices drop to their lowest. True buy-and-hold investors will be tested during this phase. If their time frame is long enough and they have chosen quality firms, their best strategy is to wait out this phase and hope prices come up as the market cycles through its phases. Other investors will finally give up and sell, often at a loss. These are the folks who bought near the market top in the accumulation phase and now choose to sell near the bottom. They will complain the loudest about the stock market being unfair.

While this phase can be difficult for investors, it sets the stage for position traders and others to pick up stocks at deep discount prices.

> **Market Place**
>
> No one wants to see bear markets, but the fact is there would be no bull markets if there were no bear markets. Bear markets squeeze the excess out of the market and prepare it for the next expansion.

Timing Cycles

A market cycle (all four phases) doesn't have a fixed length. Some cycles are short, while others are longer. Some categories of stocks may fall into a fast cycle, while other stocks just poke along through one or more phases. Stocks have their own individual phases and you can see them in charts of various periods. These indicators help traders understand where the market or an individual stock is at a particular moment and what that might mean for future price changes.

When looking at an individual stock, remember that it can jump through a particular phase very quickly. It takes more time for the larger market to move through a cycle, but count on it happening. When you can identify where the market (or stock) is in its cycle, you have an edge in predicting where it may be headed next. For the position trader, this is very helpful information.

Economic and Market Cycles

You can match market and economic cycles to some extent with the understanding that the market usually leads the economy by several months. The point of matching cycles is to look for industry sectors that might do well in the various economic cycles. Like the market, the economy periodically cycles through phases that you can roughly match to the market's phases for purposes of identifying investment candidates.

Politicians, especially around elections, do what they can to avoid downturns in the economy. However, there is ample evidence that relatively mild recessions, like mild bear markets, are good for the economy and the financial markets. Excess is eliminated and weak companies purged, making way for new entrants into markets.

Here's how market and economic phases line up and the industry sectors that do well in each.

Trading Tip _____

Economic cycles are affected by election-year cycles. Politicians want the economy humming around election time and will often do what they can to make that so. There is some evidence their efforts do more harm in the long run and help in the short run.

Accumulation—Economic Downturn (Recession)

The economy is in trouble and the Fed is cutting interest rates to get things moving. Unemployment is high and manufacturing is down. *Noncyclicals* and service sectors may produce candidates.

def·i·ni·tion _____

Noncyclical stocks are from industries that are not as subject to the condition of the economy as other industries. For example, health care is non-cyclical since people still get sick even if the economy is bad. On the other hand, the automobile and housing industries are cyclical. When the economy is weak, cyclical industries suffer. However, they can experience significant growth in a robust economy (people have more money to buy cars and houses).

Mark-Up—Beginning Recovery

The economy is coming around and people are beginning to feel good about their personal financial situation. Interest rates have leveled off and companies are hiring. Look for opportunities in industrials, energy, and technology.

Distribution—Waning Recovery

The boom is off the economy and growth may be slowing. Businesses and investors who aren't paying attention will act as if the economy is still booming, setting themselves up for a harsh fall when it slows down even more. Look for continued opportunities in energy, services, and staples.

Mark-Down—Early Economic Downturn

The market will generally drop off first, followed by the economy. Consumer sentiment will shift from cautious to concern and politicians will be in denial. Look to utilities for safety as well as noncyclicals.

Playing Market Cycles

Market cycles are not always as neat as outlined here, but because position traders may hold trades open for months, it is possible they could span a phase or two of a market or economic cycle. Knowing where the economy is in the business cycle will give the position trader a hint about which industry sectors may hold likely candidates.

For other active traders, this type of information is generally not important. As we have noted, today's active trader is likely to employ more than one trading strategy depending on the market conditions and opportunities that present themselves.

The Least You Need to Know

◆ Position trading is not investing but usually requires a longer hold than other active trading strategies.

◆ Stock selection is driven in large part by fundamental analysis.

◆ Technical analysis plays a role in determining entry and exit points.

◆ Position traders must be aware of economic and market cycles when selecting stocks.

Part 5

What It Takes to Be an Active Trader

Active trading as a profession requires all the preparation of starting your own business because that is what you are doing. You will want to explore the legal and tax consequences because there are particular codes that apply to traders.

Most active traders work from their homes, so you will need to fashion an office and equip it with the proper tools of the trade. However, the most important tool is your emotional and intellectual capacity to be a successful active trader.

Chapter 21

Tax and Legal Issues

In This Chapter

- Organize yourself as a business
- Taxes for traders
- Keeping records straight
- Organizing for success

The assumption of this book is that you plan to pursue active trading as a full-time career. You can certainly take some of the information from here and other sources to dabble at it part-time, but most active traders want to go full-time as soon as possible. Active trading, as we have seen, encompasses several strategies. The most intense strategies and those with the most promise for supporting you and your family require a full-time commitment.

You should start your active trading career the same way you would start a business—with legal and tax advisers on hand to make sure there are no missteps. Your biggest concern is going to be taxes and accounting for your income (and losses) and expenses to the satisfaction of the IRS. You are safer if you know what the requirements are from day one rather than learn too late that you have run afoul of the tax code. The IRS does not count "I didn't know" as a valid excuse. Get your mind set that this is a business and run your trading operation like one.

Consider Active Trading a Business

If you make all or most of your income from trading, you should seriously consider organizing yourself from a legal and tax perspective as a business. The best strategy is to do this from day one, with the help and guidance of competent legal and tax counsel. It is important, especially of your tax adviser, that your counselors have experience with the intricacies of trading as a business. As we'll see below, there are special considerations for securities traders by the tax code, but, as always, you must meet certain tests.

> **Market Place**
>
> If you mentally and physically structure your trading activities as a business, it will help you keep focused on the important aspects of record-keeping and controlling expenses.

Your accounting system should capture the information necessary to satisfy tax code requirements for the most favorable treatment. If you are a short-term trader making dozens of trades each day, your accounting system must be robust enough to handle the profits, losses, and expenses of each trade. Your broker may provide this information, but ultimately you are responsible for its accuracy and reporting it correctly to the IRS. Homemade systems from scraps of paper won't get the job done.

You may want to consider incorporating yourself for legal and tax reasons. Whether this makes any sense for you is a decision that you will have to make with your tax and legal advisers. However, there may some advantages to a legal structure beyond a sole proprietorship.

A Taxing Business

As we dive into everyone's favorite subject—taxes—let's get one thing very clear. You may call yourself a trader and your spouse may call you a trader (or traitor, but that's another story), but until the IRS declares you a trader, you aren't one for tax purposes. Like most other issues with the IRS, there are certain tests you must meet to be declared a trader. You definitely want this designation because it means you are eligible for certain deductions not available to others.

The IRS says you are a trader if:

◆ You make your money from daily price changes in securities and not dividends, interest income, or appreciation.

◆ Your activity is substantial, meaning trades numbering in the thousands per year, although the number is not specifically noted.

◆ You trade more or less full-time. If you have another job, trade part-time or don't trade continuously, as the IRS will not allow the trader designation.

A good tax adviser with experience in this area can tell you what will stand up under an IRS audit. You want to be nowhere near the edge on this one. A ruling against you in this area will cost you dearly in deductions the IRS will not allow, which means a big tax bill.

What Type of Tax Adviser Should You Get?

You can find several different types of tax advisers in most phone books, but for this type of reading of the IRS code, you should only consider the most qualified. That means a Certified Public Accountant (CPA). Some CPAs specialize in tax work and advice. You will pay more to use a CPA than some of the other designations, but your business will be set up correctly and you should not have to worry about the trader designation (assuming you meet the qualifications).

> **Margin Call** _____
> Taxes for an active trader can be one of your biggest expenses if you aren't careful. You can't afford to be wrong in this area. Follow the rules and set up your books as your tax adviser suggests.

Those Pesky Tax Rules

If the IRS says you must have thousands (3,000 is considered a good number, but that is subject to change and interpretation) of trades each year to qualify as a trader, they all must be recorded for tax purposes. Unfortunately, it is not just a simple matter of putting winners in this stack and losers in another stack. The IRS has special rules that will make you crazy if you don't follow them carefully.

Traders don't have earned income the same as people with regular jobs. Earned income is a salary, commissions, and such. Traders live in the world of capital gains and losses.

> **Trading Tip** _____
> You won't earn the qualified trader status from the IRS your first year of trading, so you must pay attention to capital gains and wash-sale rules.

Along with some special rules for traders, capital gains and losses require special attention, not just at tax time, but also as part of your trading strategy.

Two Types of Capital Gains, Losses

When a trader sells a security for a profit that is a capital gain. As you might guess, if the sale is for a loss, it is a capital loss. The fun doesn't stop there, however. If the trader held the security for less than one year, which will be most of the time, the capital gain or loss is considered short term. If the security was held for more than one year, it is a long-term gain or loss. The time designation is important because long-term capital gains (as of this writing) are taxed at a much lower rate—15 percent—than short-term gains. Short-term gains are taxed as ordinary income, which could be much higher.

Most traders deal in short-term gains, so it is extremely important to take advantage of any help the tax code gives you. Some gains can be offset by losses, but the rules are complicated and here is where your tax adviser will earn his fees.

The Wash-Sale Rule

One of the biggest headaches for short-term traders is the wash-sale rule. The rule says you can't deduct a loss if you also have a gain in the same or substantially similar security within a 61-day period. What does this mean? Many short-term traders will buy and sell the same security several times during a trading day and may do this day after day. The wash-sale rule has the effect in many cases of not allowing any of the trader's losses in those trades to be deducted from her taxes.

> **Trading Tip**
>
> Your direct access broker should provide comprehensive records of your transactions. However, you need to capture your trades in your own accounting software for tax purposes.

You are allowed to add the loss to your basis of the stock, which may end up giving you a deduction in the long run. However, this is a complicated rule that requires precise record-keeping to justify.

If you qualify as a trader, there are some things you can do to offset the negative impact of the wash-sale rule. Whatever your strategy, it requires comprehensive record keeping or the IRS will chuckle while making out your tax bill.

If you meet the IRS's definition of a trader, you are eligible to request a change in accounting methods that will save you money and hassles with the wash-sale rule. The catch is you can't use it the first year you're a trader. You must complete a year

as a trader and submit the request form
with your tax form for the year. If approved,
you will be allowed to use the mark-to-
market election when figuring your capital
gains and losses.

This election, if allowed, lets you forget
about the wash-sale rule. You convert all
your capital gains and losses to income. For
active traders, this is probably not a big deal
since they are unlikely to hold a position
open more than one year anyway. By giving
up any chance for a long-term capital gain, you get to forget about the wash-sale rule.
Your paperwork is greatly reduced and most traders will see a reduction in taxes.

Margin Call

Most active traders are self-employed, which means paying estimated taxes on a quarterly basis. The IRS expects these payments to be accurate. This means your books must be current at least quarterly—no more waiting until the week of April 15 to do taxes.

Your tax adviser can explain the finer points of mark-to-market accounting and what
it means in terms of bookkeeping and so on.

Expense Deduction Boost

In addition to tax benefits, this election also allows you a greater deduction of business expenses. Those expenses are important deductions when it comes time to do
your taxes. Be sure you document all of the expenses directly related to your trading
business. You can do this in a journal or better still through a software program such
as QuickBooks.

If you decide to adopt a formal business structure (partnership or incorporation),
there may be other considerations—your legal and tax advisers will help you there.

Following are some of the major expense categories you can deduct.

Office Space

Most active traders work out of their home. If you do, you can claim a deduction for
dedicated space to your trading business. Ask your tax adviser how to do this. If you
rent space in a commercial business, the process is somewhat more straightforward as
long as you don't run any other businesses out of the same space.

Office Expenses

You can deduct related office supplies and equipment up to an amount set each year
by the IRS. This includes furnishings, computers, and so on. There is a limit to how

much you can deduct, so don't go crazy. Remember, deductions are not dollar-for-dollar reductions in your tax bill, but at your prevailing tax rate. If your tax rate is 28 percent and you spend $1,000, you get to deduct $280 from your taxes. You will need receipts to prove you actually spent the money.

Fees

Most consulting fees associated with your trading such as accounting and legal services are deductible. If you use a bookkeeper or other services directly related to trading income, those are probably deductible, also.

Interest

You can deduct interest you pay on margin loans. It may not be much for most traders, but interest paid on loans for trading is a deductible business expense.

What the IRS Says No To

The IRS says you can't deduct commissions on trades, which many traders simply can't understand. Isn't that a cost of doing business, just like a telephone or computer? Actually, you do get to deduct commissions, just not in a straightforward manner.

The IRS allows you to add commissions to the cost and deduct them from the sale. This has the effect of reducing the amount of tax you owe, while avoiding any limits deductions.

The IRS also says attending investments seminars and annual meetings are not deductible. The reason is both usually involve travel and could easily become ways for taxpayers to subsidize vacations. Imagine how many investment seminars would pop up in vacation resorts if the expenses were tax deductible?

> **Market Place**
>
> One difference between operating as an individual and organizing as a formal business is the deduction of expenses. Businesses are able to take expenses as a direct deduction from gross revenue, which reduces net income and tax liability.

The IRS also notes that it will not allow tons of deductions for a hobby that loses money year after year. If you lose money three out of five years, the IRS will probably revoke your most favored trader qualification and you will lose the accounting and expense deduction benefits.

A Big Caveat

Tax laws are complex and change frequently. Nothing in this chapter should be read as a definitive interpretation of tax code. Please use the services of a qualified tax professional, preferably a CPA, before making any tax decisions.

Keep It Legal

How you decide to organize your trading business depends on several factors. That decision should come after a conversation with your tax and legal advisers to consider all the benefits and pitfalls. Ideally, the entire team would be in the same room so each option could be discussed and evaluated. You will make the final decision; however, it should be made with a full understanding of the consequences. The greatest impact will be on your potential tax liability, because it's safe to assume your attorney would not let you do something that is illegal.

> **Trading Tip** _____
>
> Congress and the IRS are constantly tweaking the several million lines of IRS code. A good tax adviser will help you stay out of trouble by alerting you to changes that may affect your trading business.

As we have already seen, those tax consequences can have a real effect on your trading policy, which can alter basic profitability assumptions.

Get Organized

There are a few minor rules and regulations that you should pay attention to as you are getting your office organized and located. Many active traders work from home, as noted previously. Unfortunately, many homes are not up for hosting a business. Often a spare bedroom or a room in the attic or basement becomes command central for the trader. We'll talk about outfitting your office in Chapter 22, but before we get to that point, we need to do some legal work. You may be able to do some of this yourself or have your attorney do it for you.

In the Zone

The popularity of home businesses has led some communities to enact zoning laws covering what you can and can't do from your home. In some cases, communities have enacted very strict zoning laws to prohibit home-based businesses that have an unusual number of shipments or deliveries. Other communities have restricted the number of employees a home-based business can have. Other ordinances require fire inspections and other commercial inspections. Along with these additional services will come additional fees, licenses, and other ways of parting you with your money.

> **Market Place**
>
> The devil is in the details, some say. Don't let the details such as zoning ordinances, business licenses, and such be a stumbling block to your trading business. Most simply require patience to file the paperwork.

Most active traders work alone, so many of the activities that regulators fear (customers, deliveries, employees creating traffic problems) aren't going to happen. However, if your local government requires you to get a permit or license of some type, don't think you can ignore it. Violations can result in fines and even shutting down your operations. If you're having a hard time getting answers from the local authorities, check with the Chamber of Commerce for information on starting a business.

Choosing a Legal Structure

As we noted above, the choice of legal structure is a matter you should discuss with your attorney and tax adviser. There are advantages for some traders in formalizing their structure, but there are also additional costs and paperwork to go along with it. Weigh the costs and benefits to see what is best for your situation, but rely on advice from your attorney and accountant, not generic pronouncements you may read on the Internet.

The Sole Proprietor

Many traders don't choose a formal structure for their business, which means by default they are sole proprietors. Being a sole proprietor simply means you are the business and the business is you. There is no stock issued and no legal papers to file in many cases beyond any business permits or licenses your local or state government may require. Any income or loss from your trading goes on your personal income tax form along with any special forms your tax adviser provides.

The sole proprietor has the big advantage of simplicity. Beyond business licenses or fees, if any, there is usually nothing to do. If you want to give your trading business a name and have a separate checking account—which is a good idea—you may need to file an assumed name with your county clerk or other local authority. This is usually a simple matter of going to the courthouse, filling out a form, and paying a small fee.

The assumed name filing tells the public that you are doing business under a name other than your own. Many banks will not open an account under a fictitious name without a certified copy of the assumed name certificate. Once you have this done, you can get business cards and so on printed with your company name.

The sole proprietor is also the easiest form of business to quit. You simply close the checking account and pay off any outstanding bills and you're done.

The downside of the sole proprietorship is that it offers no protection at all from creditors or anyone who wants to sue you. If you don't pay your bill at the broker, they will come after you regardless of whether you have an assumed name or not.

Be sure to keep business expenses separate from personal expenses. This will make it easier and cleaner at tax time.

Trading Tip

Assumed names are not the same as trademarks. They aren't protected and you can't use a name that is already in use. The best idea usually is to keep it simple, something like Joe Smith Trading.

Partnership

A partnership, which is the next step up in legal organizations, doesn't make much sense for an active trader unless you are going to form some type of trading group to pool expenses. This is a real possibility for some traders who want to share facilities with other traders, but run their own trading activity. Partners can share office, equipment, and service expenses, which might allow each trader more resources than would be practical for them to own alone.

An attorney needs to draw up the partnership agreement to make certain that all aspects of the relationship are covered. How will decisions be made? What happens when a partner wants to leave? How are partnership assets valued? All of these questions and many more should be addressed in the partnership agreement.

Don't assume because you have known the future partners for years that you will be able to work things out without spelling everything out in writing. That's a good way to destroy a partnership and lose friends.

The concept will work, but it requires a complete, written understanding of every detail and a plan for every circumstance to be successful. Generally, profits and losses to the partnership flow through to the individual members.

Corporations

If you think you want to incorporate, there are several possibilities. However, the benefits of incorporating for the active trader are limited compared to most businesses. When you incorporate your trading business, it becomes a separate legal entity from you. This has some benefits and drawbacks. For one thing, the corporate tax rate may, in some cases, be lower than individual tax rates. If you incorporate your trading business, you can become an employee of the business who draws a salary, has benefits paid for by the corporation, and a retirement plan jointly funded by the company. You don't pay self-employment taxes.

> **Margin Call**
>
> Be sure a partnership makes sense for you. They can be complicated to run and manage. It may seem straightforward in the beginning, but there will be problems and if they are not addressed in the partnership agreement, conflict will strain relationships.

Is this a better situation than being a sole proprietor? Only your tax adviser can answer that question. However, forming a corporation is more expensive and does require filing two tax returns (yours and the corporation's). The corporation may be able to take some expense deductions that you can't as an individual. The corporation can hire your children to do legitimate work and pay them a market rate for that work, while writing off the expense. Don't do anything your tax adviser doesn't approve of, but these are legitimate benefits.

The Bottom Line on Organization

How you organize your trading business is a decision that will make itself after you talk it over with your tax and legal advisers. The bigger issue beyond that is how you think about your active trading business. If you approach it with the mindset that you are running a business that has profit goals, expense concerns, and a business plan, it will help you be a better trader. We'll discuss this process in more detail in the following chapters.

The Least You Need to Know

- Consider your active trading as a business.
- Taxes are a primary expense for active traders.
- Your trading strategy can affect your taxes.
- How you legally organize your trading business is an important decision.

Chapter 22

Tools of the Trade

In This Chapter

- ◆ Begin with the basics
- ◆ Technology for traders
- ◆ Connecting to the market
- ◆ Information resources

Active trading is mentally, emotionally, and physically demanding as a full-time endeavor. If you have dreams of lazy days in your pajamas, sipping coffee, and playing the stock market, you should wake up to the reality that active trading is hard work. At least it is if you want to make money.

Because the business is so intense, it is important that you prepare every aspect of it for maximum efficiency and comfort. This means a comfortable, but efficient office, top-of-the-line technology, access to the best news and information resources, and the time to put all of this together. When you begin trading full-time, you should know all aspects of your technology and trading account, so making those work are not a distraction from your main job, which is finding profitable trades. Every step you take that isn't directly related to finding and executing profitable trades is wasted. The tools of your business are there to help you avoid any wasted steps.

Your Domain

Most active traders work out of their homes in a spare room they set up for an office. This arrangement usually works fine if you take the time and spend the money (if necessary) to make sure it is outfitted for your active trading business.

Trading Tip _____

Your friends may be jealous of your work-at-home lifestyle, but if you are to be successful, you will probably work harder at active trading than any other job you have ever had.

If you have a choice, pick a room that is not too cramped, but isn't huge either. It should be large enough to hold all of your equipment and supporting resources, but not so big that you have to get out of your chair to reach important items.

It is best if you don't share the room with anyone else or any other function—not the laundry room, for example. It is understandable that not every residence has extra rooms that are not used for anything else, but do your best to claim the space as your exclusive domain. This is especially important if you have young children in the house. Don't even think about being an active trader and caretaker of young children at the same time. Do one or the other, but if you try to do both at the same time, you will not do a good job of either and raising young children is too important not to give your full attention. You should also be careful that you do not try to take a home-office deduction on your taxes if

Margin Call _____

Finding a good balance between work and your home life is more difficult when work is at home. You may find it difficult to leave work, but set regular hours just as you would in a regular job to keep life in balance.

you use the room for other purposes. A dedicated room for trading may let you claim a home-office deduction, but check with your tax adviser because the tax code is constantly changing.

A good compromise is to set certain times aside during the day when you close your trades and spend uninterrupted time with the children. This only works if there is another adult in the residence whose primary job is looking after the children. You might consider a special, age-appropriate sign for your office door that tells the children you are busy.

The Furnishings

You will need plenty of desk space for reading material, computer keyboards, and other tools. You can go as fancy or plain as you wish and can afford; however, there is no need to spend thousands on expensive tables in the beginning of your trading career. Simple folding tables from any office supply will do. After you're making six-figure profits you can move up to oak tables.

One furnishing you should not scrimp on is your chair. Plan to spend 10-plus hours a day sitting in this chair, so buy a good one. It should provide good back support, be adjustable in height and tension on the back. Consider the covering for wear and how comfortable it will feel after sitting in it for hours. Your back will feel better after a long day if you have a supportive chair.

Other standard office items such as a file cabinet (for records, receipts, and such), bookshelves, and so on can be bought strictly for utility value when you are starting out. However, make sure your work area has adequate lighting that doesn't cast a glare on your computer monitors or work surface. This may mean desk lamps or other additional lighting to illuminate your work area. If your office has an exterior window, be careful how it is oriented to your work. A bright exterior light can sometimes obscure monitors or other work areas. On the other hand, natural light will keep your sense of connection to the outside world. It is easy to become consumed in trading to the exclusion of all else.

> **Market Place**
>
> When you are starting your business, focus on spending money on those items that will contribute to your profits and buy everything else as inexpensively as possible. Before you buy an item for your office, ask yourself, "How will this help me make profitable trades?"

Technology

Technology has made active trading possible from your home. Hoping a three-year-old computer will not crash is a bad idea, so you'll want to upgrade if your system is more than one year old—your old system can serve as a backup. This is the main tool of your business, so don't cut corners when upgrading.

As you are deciding how to equip your computer, consider the software and services you will be using. You'll want a significant over-capacity to accommodate multiple programs running at the same time. The most important areas of upgrading are in internal memory (RAM), the hard drive, and the video card.

A good rule of thumb: if your most intensive program requires 2 gigabytes (GB) of RAM, equip your computer with 4GB. The hard drive should be the largest you can buy with a desktop and the video card should be the top one offered for the computer. You will need this processing power to crunch numbers and, if you use charting software, to quickly draw charts for fast-moving markets.

If this sounds like overkill, it probably is, but it is better to have too much processing power rather than too little. Besides, you have no way of knowing what services or features you might want to subscribe to after trading for six months that will require extra processing power.

Screen Test

One of the most important decisions you'll make in buying your computer will be in selecting monitors. Notice the plural—"monitors." You will need and want more than one monitor. Stick with flat-panel LCD screens for your monitors. They take up less room and are easier on the eyes. For active traders, bigger is better in monitor size, so go with at least 21-inch screens.

> **Trading Tip**
>
> Before you begin your active trading career, get a good physical checkup, including an eye exam. Tell the eye doctor what you will be doing and, if you need glasses, get a special pair just for watching monitors. Don't be concerned about fashion in your office at the expense of eyestrain.

On one screen, you will have your direct access broker account screens open and ready to trade. Most advanced trading platforms have multiple windows you'll want open, such as Level II screen, Time and Sales Screen, an Order Screen, and your account screen.

On the other monitor, you might have charting screens (either your broker's or a separate charting service), news wires with alerts on, and other information sources, such as respected chat rooms.

Your job will be to monitor these screens while identifying potentially profitable trades. You won't be able to juggle this much information the first time you try, which is why it is important to do enough paper trading to get familiar with the technology and information, before you actually begin trading for real. These dry runs will help you acquaint yourself with the software, but also with the hardware. When you are trading real money, you don't want to get stymied by a software or hardware problem.

Doubling Up

Do yourself a big favor and have a duplicate of just about everything ready to swap out or replace a broken component: that means a spare keyboard, mouse, and, yes, even another computer. If you had a computer before you upgraded and it is fairly new, you can use it as a backup. Have it set up with the essential software you need to carry on trading if your main computer goes down. You may not want to load every piece of software, but enough so you can connect with your broker and either continue trading or close your short-term positions.

You can use the backup computer for e-mail and other non-trading activities, leaving the main computer dedicated to your trading business. Many of the newer laptops are capable of serving this capacity and let you take your trading business on the road.

Power Play

Most computer users know about power strips and surge protectors. Active traders need to take their office one step further and install an emergency power backup supply. These systems, which are available in most office supply stores and online, provide a period of backup electricity should power go out to your house.

Your computer and any high-speed Internet modems should be connected to this backup. You can buy systems that will provide various amounts of backup time. The more equipment you have attached to the system, the less time it will provide. You need this protection to close out any positions you have open in a power failure. Since you never know how long power will be off, the safe action is to close your short-term positions. Longer positions with appropriate stops can be left open.

> **Margin Call**
>
> If you have several highly margined trades opened, count on a disaster striking at some point in your trading career. If you are prepared with a backup strategy, you may be able to get out of your positions without major losses. With no backup plan, you leave yourself open to two disasters.

Using Your Connections

Short-term trading (scalping, momentum, and some forms of swing trading) require lightning-fast execution. This requires a high-speed Internet connection. You must have a DSL or cable Internet connection to transfer data at the speeds necessary to keep pace with the markets. In many markets, cable connections are faster than DSL and that should be your primary connection.

However, knowing that bad things can happen, you should also have a DSL connection to your backup computer. If your cable connection goes down, you can switch your main computer to the DSL connection or jump on the backup computer to keep working.

If you live in an area where neither cable nor DSL service is available, consider a commercial satellite Internet connection. Satellite Internet connections are not as reliable as cable or DSL because of atmospheric conditions, but rapid improvements are being made. If all you can get is a satellite connection, be very careful about the types of active trading you do until you are comfortable with the performance and reliability of your service.

Fail Safe

As a last resort, when a major disaster strikes, be sure you have a cell phone that works and written instructions (including your account number and other necessary information) handy. If you can't connect to the Internet by your primary or backup systems, you'll have a way to call your broker. Having all the phone numbers and account numbers in writing will save time when you need to make that call in a hurry.

> ### Market Place
>
> If your system goes down or the power is lost for an extended time and you can't get to your account, call your broker and close all your orders no matter what. This way you are out of the market until you can see what's going on when you are reconnected.

Two Trading Accounts

In the spirit of doubling up on everything, you should also consider having two different trading accounts. There are several reasons for this redundancy that relate back to protecting your positions in the event of a disaster on either end of the trading equation.

We have discussed the ways you can protect yourself from a disaster at your office due to equipment failure, loss of power, and other problems. But what happens if your direct access broker goes down with its own problem in the middle of the day?

Although it is unlikely—modern brokerages have multiple backup systems and emergency power supplies—the unthinkable can and does happen. If you have a large position open and your direct access provider crashes, you could be in big trouble.

A second brokerage account won't let you reverse a position opened by another broker, but you can take an offsetting trade to limit your risk until your primary broker comes back online. For example, if you were long in a stock when your broker became unavailable, you could check the price via your backup brokerage account and short the position to offset any loss if the stock dropped. If the stock fell, you could cover your short and short the stock again further up. You could also buy an in-the-money put option. There are other steps you could take to protect an open position, but you would be at risk if you had to set up a new account and wait for all the paperwork and money to clear before your could use it.

Having a second trading account, especially one with low commission, may also be useful for placing some swing and position trades that don't require intra-day pricing. Depending on the fee structure, it may be cheaper to do the trades on that account. Conversely, you could do your long-term investing on that account and keep those transactions separate from your active trading strategies. There may be some tax benefits in this separation, so check with your tax adviser.

Trading Tip

Your second brokerage account should be accessible by your computer or cell phone in the event you need to connect that way. With the proliferation of "smart phones," that is a viable way to connect to your account.

Shopping for Your Trading Account

Here are some of the larger online brokerage accounts that also have special arrangements for active traders. They would make good second accounts after a direct access provider for most active traders. Some traders who will only do swing and position trading could use one of these as a primary account. (Note: The website addresses for the sites mentioned in this section are listed in Appendix A.)

Schwab

Schwab is the granddaddy of discount brokerages and is carrying this tradition to its online offering. It offers its own research and clients can work with an investment adviser or Schwab will manage their account for them. It offers a section for active traders.

E*Trade

E*Trade gets high marks for its range of offerings including banking and mutual funds. The company has absorbed several other brokerage firms and is now a significant player in the online stock-trading market. Like its competitors, it offers active traders lower rates on their trades.

Fidelity

Fidelity shows up at the top or near the top of almost every ranking of online stock-trading brokers. They are not the least expensive, but top most lists in customer satisfaction. Fidelity is known for its research and investors can talk to advisers face-to-face at one of the many Fidelity investment centers.

Muriel Siebert

Muriel Siebert may not have the marketing muscle of other online stock-trading sites, but it is a solid brokerage house worth your look. The company receives high marks for customer service and research. The fee structure is straightforward and easy to understand.

Scottrade

Scottrade's claim to fame is superior customer satisfaction as noted in J.D Power and Associates's survey of online brokers. Commissions are on the low side and transactions are processed quickly.

TD Ameritrade

TD Ameritrade is another brokerage that is the result of mergers The company has a good education section and is known for customer service.

TradeKing

TradeKing is an online stock trading site to check out for low-cost trading. This is their thing, and SmartMoney.com, Barron's, and Kiplinger all agree. If you are looking for the low prices on trades, this is a good place to start.

Market Place

Low commissions are very important, but so is ease of use and customer service if you have a problem. Most of these brokers will let you try a demo before you open an account.

Vanguard

Vanguard made a name for itself as the low-cost leader in mutual funds. Vanguard is a solid company that excels in providing value to their customers and in consolidating investments in a brokerage account.

Wells Fargo

The financial services powerhouse Wells Fargo has an online stock trading site that fits its image of offering comprehensive services. You are offered five different levels of accounts depending on whether you want a strictly independent trading account or a version of their managed accounts.

Information, Resources, and Training

Your computer may be your main physical tool, but it is your knowledge, training, and access to research that will make you a successful trader. No one should consider starting active trading without solid preparation in the form of training, research, and practice.

Fortunately, you can do most of your preliminary training and preparation before you quit your "day job" and plunge into active trading on a full-time basis. The Internet offers a large selection of training courses and resources, many free of charge or for nominal fees. Even if you are an experienced investor, it will be helpful to explore the resources dedicated to trading since this is a different discipline.

> **Trading Tip**
>
> There are many good online courses, but, as you might suspect, there are also a number of snake-oil peddlers who promise unlimited wealth with 30 minutes a day of work. Trading scams are a real problem, but remember, the only secret to success is hard work and education.

Free Information Sources

The Internet offers a treasure trove of free information on trading and investing. While some of the information on investing works for active traders, much of it does not. For example, the major exchanges, Nasdaq and the New York Stock Exchange, have educational material on their sites. However, most of the information is geared to investors rather than traders. Both websites are worth a visit for their free information even if most of it targets investors.

While the major exchanges are noted markets for stocks and bonds, other exchanges are markets for derivatives and commodities. These securities are not investments, but are traded for the most part. Options, futures contracts on commodities and indexes, and assorted combinations of other derivatives are all traded securities. The websites for the exchanges that clear these securities want you to be familiar with the products and how to trade them.

> **Margin Call**
>
> Always consider what organization is offering free education and what its motive might be. Brokerage firms want customers who trade, stock exchanges want investors, and software vendors want customers.

The exchanges offer Web-based classes, tutorials, and other training opportunities online. Some exchanges offer in-person training for more advanced traders.

The Stock Exchanges

The major stock exchanges cater to investors, so the information you find there is geared toward the long-term holder. However, it is important to know how the exchanges work, and the educational material is top notch.

The New York Stock Exchange (NYSE)

The NYSE is the most prestigious exchange, but not the oldest—that honor goes to the Philadelphia Stock Exchange. The NYSE offers information on stocks, bonds, and exchange traded funds. Its recent overseas acquisitions will made it a truly global market, a fact revealed in its new name: NYSE Euronext.

The Nasdaq (Nasdaq)

The Nasdaq pioneered the electronic market that was the blueprint for modern trading. The edgy market was dismissed for years by the Wall Street crowd as a place for stocks too small for the real stock market to trade. Since then it has grown to become home of some of the largest companies in the world. Still, Nasdaq is more for investors than traders, although you'll find plenty of free information.

The American Stock Exchange (AMEX)

The American Stock Exchange slipped into obscurity for a number of years, but one product—the exchange traded fund—has brought it roaring back. As the popularity of these products (over 350 are traded on the AMEX) has exploded, so has the fortune of the AMEX. The exchange could never compete with the Nasdaq or NYSE on stocks and bonds, but has carved out a significant niche with structured products. That has been enough to make them a takeover target for NYSE, which should conclude in late 2008. The AMEX site is rich in information on structured products and ETFs.

Options and Futures Exchanges

While the major stock exchanges cater to investors, the *derivative* exchanges are more focused on traders, because their products are designed to be traded. You will find comprehensive educational information on these sites, which are targeted at traders. In addition, some classes are offered in person.

def•i•ni•tion

> **Derivatives** are securities that are based on other investment products. For example, stock options are based on the underlying common stock, so the option's value, in part, is tied to the value of the stock.

Chicago Board of Trade (CBOT)

The Chicago Board of Trade provides educational information on trading futures, commodities, and a variety of financial futures. Online information and tutorials are offered along with live workshops. A recent listing offered a 3-day workshop for the "Active Futures Trader."

Chicago Board of Options Exchange (CBOE)

The Chicago Board of Options Exchange is the place to go for information on trading options. The CBOE offers an extensive educational program through its Institute, which includes online courses, live online tutorials, and classes taught in Chicago. The site also offers a variety of calculators and other tools helpful to options traders.

The Chicago Mercantile Exchange (CME)

The Chicago Mercantile Exchange offers online and live educational and training events in trading futures. You can learn about their unique weather futures as well as traditional stock index, single stock, agricultural, and commodity futures contracts. From this site, you can link to brokers' sites, which will allow you to paper trade.

The stock and commodity exchanges are in the midst of a consolidating period, so some new names may appear because of mergers and takeovers.

Nonprofit and Government Agencies

In addition to the exchanges, several nonprofit trade groups and government agencies have websites that offer training or educational products that are either free or available at a nominal fee. Here are some of the main offerings:

- ◆ **The Institute for Financial Markets.** This nonprofit group provides resources for people trading options and futures. It is geared primarily toward industry professionals, but does offer courses that work for individuals. Some of its material is available in print form.

- ◆ **The National Futures Association.** This trade group has an extensive investor education section that deals with futures and options of futures. There are online courses and some written publications. The group also provides training and information courses and publications on forex trading opportunities.

- ◆ **The Investor's Clearinghouse.** This site covers more information for investors than traders. However, if you need a refresher on investing basics or want more information on bonds, for example, it's a good source. The site is an aggregator of information, so you'll be taken to other sources for the various courses.

- ◆ **The Securities and Exchange Commission.** The Securities and Exchange Commission (SEC) is the ultimate federal agency charged with regulating investing and the markets. In addition to links to educational material, you can find information on companies that have violated SEC rules. The site also explains how to file a complaint.

> **Market Place**
>
> Nonprofit groups tend to be fairly conservative in their educational approach and focus on investing ideas. However, they do offer good information on securities and the investment process.

Brokerage Firms

Many brokerage firms offer educational materials on their sites—obviously, it is in their best interests to encourage you to trade. Those firms that cater to active traders will have more and better material that is specific to trading. In addition, many firms offer live workshops or seminars in major cities. These are obviously client-building opportunities for the firms, but they are usually a good time to get a feel for the people behind the brokerage. They can also give you expert tips if you are a customer of their online software.

The Least You Need to Know

◆ Spend an adequate amount on the technology you need for your trading business.

◆ Set your office up as a professional work environment.

◆ Be redundant in all critical office equipment, Internet connections, and trading accounts.

◆ Take advantage of free or low-cost online educational resources.

Money and Time Management

In This Chapter

- Plan your business with a business plan
- Profit goals and expenses
- Constructing a money-management plan
- Your time is your money

Your trading business is physically set up like a home-based business, but you can't stop there. Before you begin full-time active trading, you need a plan for how you will transition from a money-losing startup to a profitable business that will provide the financial support you and/or your family needs. It could happen accidentally, but it will more likely happen intentionally if you plan for it to happen.

Your business is simple compared to most businesses, so your business plan doesn't need to be 100 pages with charts and supporting documents. It does need to lay out what your goals are, how you plan to reach them, and when you plan for all of this to happen. You may not know precisely how long it will take, but you can make adjustments later. One of the other benefits of having a business plan is that it should describe your time commitment to the business and to yourself and those close to you. How you manage your money and your time are the most important business tasks you face.

Why a Business Plan?

It is easy to think that a written business plan is overkill for a one-person business, but that would be a mistake. Once you begin active trading, you may easily get lost in the daily struggle and lose sight of the goals you have set for yourself. A written plan lets you back off periodically to see if your business is still on track toward those goals. If you're not, what has changed? What do you need to do to get back on track, or do the goals need to be modified in the cold reality of actual trading?

Beginning active traders, especially those doing short-term trading, often overestimate their abilities and underestimate how hard ending the day with a profit is. This wakeup call can be disheartening, but if new traders learn from their mistakes and stick with sound money-management practices (discussed later), they can turn things around.

Your business plan should also include strict rules on money management. These rules will prevent the emotions of greed or fear from taking hold and ruining you financially. These money-management rules will not guarantee you will succeed as an active investor, but if you don't follow them you can be almost certain to fail.

Your business plan doesn't need to be an elaborate document, but you should put some time into it well before you begin trading. The primary parts of the plan are goals, deadlines, and strategies. If you want to include information about your physical setup, feel free, but the main focus should be on goals, deadlines, and strategies.

> **Market Place**
>
> Constructing a business plan requires you to put in writing goals, objectives, and timelines that are important to keeping your business focused.

You can approach the business plan several ways—the format is not important as long as it works for you. Here are some questions to help you create a business plan that fits your goals.

What Are You Going to Trade?

What securities are you going to trade: stocks, bonds, futures, options, and so on? We have focused primarily on stocks because that's where many beginning active traders start out. However, there is no rule that says you must start with stocks.

It's best to focus on one security type in the beginning and then expand when you become competent with that product. What you decide to trade may influence several other factors in your plan such as when you are going to trade, what strategies you'll use, and so on.

How Are You Going to Trade?

Do you plan to trade short-term (day trading) or pursue one of the other strategies? Many active traders get into trading for this reason. If this is your plan, it has implications for how much investment capital you'll need, what type of broker you'll use, and so on. You don't have to start this way. Some active traders make a living swing trading a variety of securities. Plan your business on what works for you, not on someone else's vision of active trading.

What Training Do You Need?

Are there areas of your business you need to focus on before beginning trading? The answer should be yes for almost everyone beginning a career in active trading. You'll need a lot of practice with your trading software, including charting and reading Level II screens. Spend enough time paper trading that when the time comes, you aren't stumbling over how to enter a stop-loss order or some other basic function.

Trading Tip

One of the reasons many beginning traders start with stocks is that they come from an investment background, so they have some knowledge of the process and product.

What Are Your Short-Term Financial Goals?

Most active traders will lose money in the beginning. Don't set yourself up for failure by planning to be profitable from day one. One way to approach your initial goals is to set a percentage of profitable trades in the beginning and increase the percentage until more trades make money than lose money. It makes sense to space this process out over a six-month period. If you practice

Margin Call

If you can't stand the thought of losing money, drop the idea of becoming an active trader. There is no way you will start out as a truly active investor and not lose some money.

good money management, even though you are losing money, you will not lose everything in the process. If you learn from trading mistakes, you may turn the corner sooner than six months.

What Are Your Long-Term Financial Goals?

Depending on how many trades you make and their size, you can work toward a long-term goal of building an income from your business that meets your needs. If you need a huge income from your active trading business, be prepared to make large frequent trades. As you grow your business, it will be tempting to up the size of your average trade—say from 500 shares per trade to 1,500 shares per trade. Obviously, the more you have at risk, the greater your potential reward and loss. It will become clear that your income is a factor of how often you trade and the size of those trades.

How Long Will You Trade Unprofitably?

It is possible to become just proficient enough to more or less break even in your trading business, but never quite turn a profit. This is a place many active traders find themselves (or worse). Statistics indicate that 80 percent of the people who try active trading don't succeed. Include in your business plan a reasonable period for you to begin showing success or commit to close shop before you lose too much money. If you have been at active trading for a year and still can't turn a profitable week, but aren't suffering big losses either, it's time to reconsider this as a career. Too many beginners will become desperate and begin making risky trades. In a short period, they will usually go through most of their investment capital. If it's just not working for you, quit while you still have some of your investment capital left.

> **Trading Tip**
>
> There is no shame is admitting active trading is just not working for you. Better to walk away with some money in your pocket than stubbornly try to be something you are not.

What Will Be Your Trading Hours?

If you are not careful, you will find yourself trading around the clock. This is a bad idea for several obvious reasons. Your business plan should set your trading hours, which will be driven in part by the products you trade and when those markets are open. Office hours are a good idea and should be in your business plan. Since you don't have a boss to ask, schedule vacation when you like, but do schedule vacation—at least two weeks per year. If you have a family, you can schedule it around their schedules. The important thing is to take vacation, no matter what. Close all your positions, leave your laptop at home, and get away from the market. You'll be a better trader for it. If you are having a run of bad days, take a day off and clear your head.

What Is Your Schedule?

Your business plan doesn't need to map out each minute of the day, but it should outline a pre-market opening routine of checking any open positions, doing research, looking for trading opportunities, and so on. Do a general schedule for the rest of the day, including a wrap-up after the market closes (if you are trading on the exchanges). There are two purposes for this. First, it gives structure to your day, especially those times when the market is closed. Second, if you share your residence with someone who may be tempted to pop in the office and ask you to run an errand or want to chat, you can have him or her review your business plan. They'll see, hopefully, that your day is full and you are not available for errands or chitchat until your work is completed.

> **Margin Call**
>
> One of the pitfalls of working at home is that loved ones may feel free to pop in whenever they like for whatever reason. If you are doing short-term active trading, it is impossible to carry on a conversation and fully watch the market at the same time.

Investing in Your Business

An important part of your business plan is the financial section. Here you detail how much money you plan to invest and the expected return on that investment. While you may spend several thousand dollars upgrading your computer equipment, the real investment is in trading capital. If you plan to be a short-term trader, you will probably meet the SEC requirements of a pattern day trader. This means you must maintain $25,000 equity in your account. Some direct access brokers may require more, as short-term traders usually trade on margin.

You will want enough investment capital to keep you trading through your learning period and to maintain the $25,000 minimum in your account. It would be prudent to have $50,000 on hand as your investment in your trading business. Open your trading account with $30,000 or so and add to the account as needed to maintain the minimum equity balance.

You should also have another fund separate from your investment capital of at least three months (six months is better) expenses (mortgage, food, utilities, everything) in cash. This is your escape fund. If you decide active trading isn't for you and there isn't much left of your investment capital, this fund will give you a cushion while you plan your next step.

You might balk at this much capital for your trading business, but one of the main reasons new businesses fail is they are undercapitalized. That is true of active trading, also. It would be a shame if, just as you were getting the hang of things, you ran out of money.

It is true that you can start out trading in other securities or markets and avoid the $25,000 minimum equity requirement. For example, the dealers in the forex market tout the fact that you can open an account for $1,000 or so. Using the tremendous leverage available to forex traders, you can build a sizable trading account very quickly. This assumes you are making winning trades of course. If you don't make the best trades, your $1,000 stake won't last very long. Other markets don't require a large minimum investment either.

However, a strategy that attempts to enter active trading on a minimum budget and build up a pool of investment capital through profitable trades is a high-risk, low-probability plan. One of the main reasons 80 percent of the people who attempt active trading fail is they don't have enough money to get through losing trades. Beginning active traders will lose money, no matter what market or security they choose. Despite what you may hear on infomercials or see on the Internet, there are no easy ways to make money trading securities.

Your Source of Investment Capital

The best source of your investment capital is money you have saved from earnings or some other business activity. Don't use money from:

♦ **Your retirement fund.** You should never put your retirement at risk for any potential gain. Borrowing money from or cashing in IRAs or your 401(k) plan is a very bad idea. The knowledge that if you lose money trading, you are sacrificing your retirement, puts extra pressure on you that you don't need.

- ◆ **Your home equity.** Home equity loans are easy to obtain and the interest may even be tax deductible. If a vendor selling a trading system or encouraging you to trade a certain market suggests that you get a home equity loan to fund your trading, report them to the authorities. It is unethical and a very bad idea. You don't need the pressure of knowing your house is at risk to cloud your judgment.

- ◆ **Your credit cards.** Obtaining a credit card with a high line of credit and willing to give cash advances is easy. However, the sky-high interest rates charged for cash advances make it almost impossible to earn enough to repay the interest.

- ◆ **Any loan of any kind.** Don't use borrowed funds from any source, including friends, family, or commercial sources.

It is difficult enough trading and losing your own money, although some people have less regard for borrowed money than they do for their own money. In either case, you should put up equity to fund your business, not borrowed funds.

> **Margin Call** _____
>
> Many Internet scams promise instant profits for day traders. You will end up spending thousands on trading systems, upgrades, and a variety of other fees and services for mostly worthless offerings. The only short-cut to success is hard work and patience.

Setting Profit Goals

You need to set profit goals for your trading business even if you have no idea how long it will take you to begin executing more profitable trades than losing trades. If you don't have a goal with a date to reach the goal, it is harder to measure your progress. Don't expect too much too soon, but also set goals that are challenging so you push yourself to master the trading strategy. A little pressure is usually not a bad thing.

One way to consider your goals is by percentage of profitable trades. In other words, of all your trades for the day, what percentage was profitable? You can assume that number will be low in the first weeks. You will probably not execute a large number of trades each day the first few weeks. As your skill and confidence grows, the number of total trades will increase and the percentage of profitable ones will climb. It is not possible to say when you should be making more profitable trades than losing trades, since that will depend on each individual's skill and the active trading strategy they pursue.

It's common for new active traders to take several months and maybe as many as six months before breaking into profitable trading percentages. Active short-term trading is the most intense and most difficult to learn correctly. Active traders who pursue this strategy may face months of negative returns before finally pushing through to the positive side. Traders who survive this initial trial may go on to very successful careers. However, they won't survive if they don't learn and adjust from their mistakes, practice sound time management, and closely protect their money with a management system.

> **Trading Tip**
>
> While it varies for each individual, you should plan to spend at least three months and as many as six months toiling away before you hit any profitability.

What Is a Money Management System?

A money management system is a plan for how you will structure your trading business and how much money you will invest in trades. You need to include this system in your business plan and stick with it, especially when times get tough and you are tempted to alter the plan to recoup losses.

A money management plan spells out how much you will place on each trade and answers the "What are you going to trade?" part of your business plan. No matter how difficult the market, you stick to your plan, which may mean, in some markets, you have days when there is nothing to trade. For short-term active traders, the market can present days when there are few opportunities and days when there are too many opportunities. Sticking to your money management plan means you have a fixed trade size no matter the market conditions. The worst mistake is chasing hot tips or what appear to be super trades.

How much of your investment capital are you willing to risk on each trade? This is a question you'll have to answer personally because everyone has a different threshold. The answer we are trying to get to is how big of a loss on a trade are you willing to suffer before closing your position? There is plenty of mathematical evidence that using a small percentage of your total investment capital as the maximum will keep you from losing all your money in a hurry.

Many active traders use 1 or 2 percent of their investment capital as the maximum they will lose on any single trade. Remember, with stop loss orders, you can keep your losses from getting completely out of control in most markets. If you follow the percentage rule, you will keep your losses to a small amount. Many traders expand on that rule and limit losses in a single day to 5 percent or less. If their losses for the day hit that mark, prudent traders close positions and quit for the day. The natural impulse might be to attempt to catch up by increasing the size and frequency of trades. This just increases your risks because you are forcing more trades to recoup losses.

Traders who use this risk management technique keep their losses under control and preserve investing capital for another day of trading. More experienced traders can use hedging techniques such as opposing trades or options to offset risk, especially on large positions. For beginning traders, sticking to a trading plan is critical. The other critical way short-term active traders control risk is to close all of their positions at or before the end of the trading day. It can be tempting to let a winning trade run or to hold on to a losing trade hoping it will turn around. Both steps more often than not lead to losing situations.

> **Market Place**
>
> Traders make calculated trades using a system of allocating their investment capital. Gamblers employ whatever strategy is working, while traders stick with the planned strategy that is successful.

Using Your Leverage

One of the characteristics that distinguishes short-term active trading is the use of margin, or leverage. When the market shifted to the decimal system of pricing stocks, it took much of the profit out of the bid-ask spread. As we have noted in other parts of the book, this has meant short-term traders have much thinner bid-ask spreads to trade. Where a short-term active trader may have been able to make money before decimalization with a 500-share trade, she now has to trade 1,000 or 2,000 shares to make the same profit.

These larger trades usually mean a much greater use of margin. The broker lends a large percentage of the trade amount to the customer so she can buy a larger block of stock just to make the same return under the new rules.

Margin allows traders to buy large blocks of stock, but not all traders are comfortable with using leverage that can work against them if the trade goes bad. There is no rule that says you must use leverage or a large amount of it in your trading business. When you are preparing your business plan, include in the financial part a section on margin and how much you plan to use. Without margin, you may need to seek out

> **Trading Tip**
>
> Margin is an important tool for active traders, but it is not a required tool. Some traders use more than other traders do. What is important is a complete understanding of the benefits and dangers of using margin. Traders can then decide for themselves.

trades where you have the potential to earn substantially more than the bid-ask spread. This may mean fewer trades with a slightly elevated risk factor.

After you have some successful experience behind you as an active investor, you may want to rethink your use of margin, but that's a personal decision.

Your Daily Tally

One of the most important tasks in the daily routine is to review the day's work and determine if you made a profit or loss for the day. If you are using an advanced trading platform, you should be able to review your account statement and see each transaction along with the associated commissions and interest charges, if you used margin. It will be easy to see a gross profit or loss number using this information. However, you need to get to a net profit or loss, which will include some accounting for your overhead and tax liability. That may be too fine a point on a daily basis, but you should have your accounting software (or a spreadsheet) set up to give you that number on a weekly basis.

You'll want a report that shows percentage of profitable trades (to relate to your goals), how much was traded, and the return you earned. This information will be invaluable as you move forward. It will tell you whether your trade size is right (does it need to be higher for a higher return?) and it will track the percent of winning trades.

You should also review your trades to see if you can determine why they worked or didn't work. Sometimes you will clearly see in retrospect what you didn't see at the time of the trade. Often, only experience will help you "see" the market with greater clarity. You can also note why trades worked and how you might recognize those patterns again. This recap is not a time for beating yourself up over mistakes or for gloating over smart trades, but for expanding your knowledge. The day you think you're smarter than the market is the beginning of the end of your career as a trader.

> **Market Place**
>
> It is more meaningful to track your progress in percentages rather than raw numbers. This gives you the perspective of how well or poorly you are doing relative to your total trades.

Trading With Discipline

Your business plan will help you stay focused on nurturing the two most important resources you have as an active trader: your time and your money. If you waste either, you are asking for trouble and may be looking for something else to do soon. In Chapter 24, we'll look at some of the emotional and intellectual characteristics necessary to be successful as an active investor. We'll mention one now because it is so important in making your business and money management plans work.

Discipline is the ability to stay focused on the task at hand and follow a plan when there are many distractions that encourage you to shift your attention elsewhere. For example, if your trading plan calls for short-term trading of large cap stocks, don't drift over to small cap stocks just because they are hot today. It may seem like the logical thing to do, but the two stocks don't react the same way in the market, and in the afternoon tech stocks may get hot. The point is without discipline, a trader will be jumping all over the market in search of the "next big deal."

Here's an insider's tip: there's always another "next big deal." If you listen to the hucksters, they will make it sound like they have the inside track on the last big deal and, if you don't get on board now, it will be too late. Discipline is being patient and waiting for your trade. It doesn't need to be the perfect trade, a good trade will do. If you have discipline, your trade will come and you will make money. Inexperienced traders will trade just to be in the game and that is a mistake. Sit out the whole morning if you must, but wait for a good trade. You'll make more money than jumping at bad trades and hoping they turn out okay.

If you make a bad trade, let it go and move on to the next one. Don't let fear restrain you from trading. If you are afraid of losing, your judgment will be clouded.

The Least You Need to Know

- Run your trading business from a business plan with goals and timelines.
- You should set profit goals and specify when you plan to achieve them.
- A money management plan brings discipline to your trading and protects your investment capital.
- Managing your time requires discipline and organization.

Chapter

24

Is Active Trading Right for You?

In This Chapter

- ◆ The traits you need to be a successful active trader
- ◆ Personality traits that could work against you
- ◆ Practice on paper before investing your money
- ◆ Alternatives to trading full-time

Active traders can make a lot of money. If you have the tolerance of risk and the willingness to learn, active trading can be a successful business. It won't be an easy business and you will lose money in the beginning. However, if you have enough investment capital to see you through the startup and learn from your mistakes, you have a chance at success.

Unfortunately, most active traders don't succeed at full-time trading. They don't have enough investment capital or are overcome by fear or greed or simply lack the discipline necessary to get out in the market every day and give it their best shot. Closet gamblers looking for a quick jackpot are soon out of money as are those too timid to make trades. Active trading is not for everyone, and if it isn't for you, it's better to find out now than after risking your savings. There is no precise formula for what you must do to succeed in active trading, but there are some personality traits, emotional characteristics, and mental capabilities that will make it easier.

Today's Active Trader

In the stock market, you will see largest gainers and losers lists along with the most active list of stocks. Each stock on these lists represents a potential large gain for active traders. It is not unusual to see stocks that moved up or down three or more points in one trading session. Admittedly, some of these stocks represent obscure companies that won't easily show up on anyone's radar, but others could be spotted by astute active traders.

A three-point move in a single day when you are holding 1,000 shares is a $3,000 gross profit. Do active traders make this type of money every day? Some do, but most do not. Those who do have spent a lot of time studying the market and the securities they trade. They learn from their mistakes and remain objective in their trading practices.

Trading Tip _____

Deciding if active trading is for you is a personal decision, but some personality traits will make it difficult to succeed. Be honest with your self-assessment.

When the market was rocking and rolling during the dot.com boom of the late 1990s, day traders were hauling in big profits. A great many of them confused a market anomaly with trading genius. When the market correction came, they were lost because they did not have the discipline to trade in a market that fought back. The active traders who survived the ensuing bear market came out stronger and smarter—and humbler.

Understand New Strategies, Products, and Markets

One of the differences between the active trader of today and those in the past is that more trading strategies, products, and markets are being used. While most active traders still focus on one type of trading strategy, many have expertise in alternatives in case the market is not right for their primary game plan.

New technology and connections with providers have made trading from home as easy as being at an office. With Web-based services, traders can take their business wherever there is access to high-speed Internet connections. Advanced trading platforms have brought together the technical analysis, fundamental analysis, and news feeds along with an order system that provides super-quick executions. Traders have access to a vast array of tools to help them identify and act on profitable trades almost as fast as market professionals.

Markets such as the forex and products like the e-mini securities have opened new opportunities for active traders that weren't as common a few years ago. Alternate ways to trade provide new profit opportunities for active traders willing to expand their business into new products or markets. This is a change from the days when active trading meant day trading exclusively.

Market Place

Everyone is a trading genius when the markets are shooting up, but it takes a real professional to survive and thrive in all types of markets.

Margin Call

New markets and new products mean new opportunities for active traders. However, it also means there is an opportunity for traders to spread themselves too thin by attempting to master too many products.

Prepare for Different Markets

If you are going to succeed as an active trader, you must be able to turn a profit in all different types of markets. This means adapting your trading style and even what you trade to different market conditions. Your trading plan that worked well in last month's market may not work so well this month. What needs to change to get your trading back on track? Earlier in the book, we talk about going with the trend. You may face more than a trend if the market turns from bull to bear or neutral to bullish.

Trading Tip

The preparation for beginning an active trading business should be substantial. Much of it can be done at night and on weekends so you can remain on your present job. This preserves investment capital and lets you prepare without the pressure of bills to be paid and no income.

If the market is very volatile, it may be hard to determine what kind of market you are in—one day it's up, but the next day it's down. When patterns are hard to discern, you may have to move back and forth to find profitable trades—remember, active traders make money on declining prices as well as rising prices. There will be other times when the market is coasting in a narrow range, without moving up or down. These markets require a special touch and frequently the use of a swing trading strategy.

At other times, your best strategy may be to go play golf or engage in something other than trading. Active traders know when to walk away and not force trades. The market is always right, no matter how smart you are. When you understand that fact, you'll be on the road to success. That doesn't mean the market is always rational, far from it. The market reflects its participants and people aren't always logical. There are times when this is glaringly apparent, but no one wants to admit it. The dot.com boom of the late 1990s was a perfect example of a market gone mad. However, no one wanted to say anything because they were making so much money. The smart traders made a lot of money, but constantly pulled profits out of their account, so when the bubble burst, they didn't lose everything.

> **Market Place**
>
> There are still big gains to be had, but it is slow and steady that wins the race. You lower the risk profile of your business and raise the reward potential by increasing the number of trades.

Active traders were scoring big gains during that time, but if you try for a big gain on every trade, you will soon be out of money. In a normally irrational market, your best strategy is always many small gains (and small losses) rather than trying for the big score every trade.

Behaviors That Will Cause Trouble

There are certain behaviors and emotions that will cause problems for active traders (these apply to investors also, by the way). Some are attitudes you can leave behind, while others may be a part of your personality that may cause serious problems in your active trading business. It is important that you take an honest assessment of your personality because kidding yourself won't solve anything. In a regular business, you can hire someone who is strong in the areas where you are weak. However, in your active trading business it's only you. If you have a weakness in a critical area, it could be fatal to your active trading business.

Emotional Issues

Emotions are your enemy in active trading. Emotions cloud your judgment and force bad decisions. Many active traders are competitive people—they want to win. The competitive nature of trading is one of the things that attracted them to the business.

Wanting to win is a good thing. Having to win every trade is not. Your goal is to win more trades than you lose, but you are going to lose some trades. If you let your competitive nature gain control of your actions, you'll stay in losing trades too long trying to turn them around or take other actions that prolong the inevitable, rather than close quickly and move on to the next trade. Your goal should be at the end of the day to say you have more winners than losers and you have net earnings for the day.

If you are an active trader for very long, sooner or later you will have a trade go very bad. A market maker will fool you with a phony order and you'll take a beating, an order will be screwed up, or something else will happen that will cost you a lot of money. If you have ever thought of revenge when you've been treated unfairly, forget it—revenge doesn't happen in the market. If your pursue revenge, you waste valuable time and energy in a very negative activity.

> **Margin Call**
>
> When emotions rule your actions, you are out of control and you will never make the best decisions. If you find yourself in a rage or depression over a bad trade, it's time to close all of your positions and take the rest of the day off. If this happens often, you should question whether active trading is the best career choice.

Fear

Fear is one of the two deadly emotions of trading (greed is the other). Fear drives you to bad decisions or it drives you out of the market altogether. Fear usually pops up after a bad loss or series of losses. The fear of losing money is one of the strongest emotions many people experience. If it is so for you, consider another line of work, because you will lose money and maybe a lot of it before you learn active trading. When active traders become fearful, they are very tentative about their trades. They lose confidence in their ability to spot a potentially profitable set up. Some active traders who've had their confidence shaken sit out the market for a period and go back to paper trading to affirm their trading plan and skills without the emotions of using real money. When they get their confidence back, they go back to trading with real money. Some people will never overcome the fear of losing their money.

Greed

Greed is the other deadly emotion of trading. Greed happens two ways. The first is when you have had a good streak and want more. Rather than stick with your money management plan, you begin doubling or more the size of your trades. If things don't continue to go well and you suffer some losses, you may up the size of the trades even more just to recover your losses. The other way greed ruins active trading careers is

Trading Tip

Active traders need more than a financial incentive to stick with the business. Most who are successful deeply enjoy the markets and learning about them. They want the financial rewards, but there is more to it than that.

by being the motivating factor for getting into the business. If the only reason you are becoming an active trader is to get rich, you are probably off to a bad start. Sure, everyone wants to make money, but if your focus is way down the road and not right in front of you, it will be hard to succeed. The way to get rich is by being successful one day at a time. Greed wants it all now and, despite what you may hear or read, active trading seldom works that way.

Gambling Issues

People with issues around gambling often find their way into active trading because is seems like a legitimate way to satisfy their needs. Active trading is not gambling. Traders make rational decisions based on evidence, not rolling dice or flipping coins. If you find the casino thrilling and get the same feeling when discussing active trading, that should be a warning sign of trouble ahead. If you approach active trading with the same mindset as gambling, the result will be the same: the house always wins.

Low Tolerance for Risk

A low tolerance for risk will cause trouble for an active trader. This may seem like stating the obvious, but with the number of trading systems being touted as almost "risk-free," it is important to note that active trading entails risk. In many cases, you are quickly buying and selling in a market that is dominated by professional traders who have access to more information and better technology than you do. These professionals are happy to take your money. You will have a steep learning curve before you can adequately protect yourself from their tactics.

What Will Help You Succeed

Active trading as a business offers many positive qualities to the right people. While some emotions, experience, and behaviors will be obstacles, other personality characteristics will be helpful in your success.

Technological Curiosity

Active trading is about technology. You don't have to be a computer nerd, but almost everything you do is driven by technology, and as a self-employed business owner you are also the chief technology officer. You should be comfortable learning new software, unafraid of trying out a new online service, familiar with how your computer is set up, and able to perform basic maintenance and repairs. You will place your trades online, do research online, track expenses in an accounting program or spreadsheet, use charting software, and work with other applications. The key applications you use every day, such as the trading platform, should be second nature to you before you begin trading with real dollars. You will be in big trouble if you have to click on "Help" or call tech support every time you want to place a trade or close a position.

 Margin Call

If you are a techno-phobe, be careful about a career in active trading. People who are afraid of new software and uncertain about basic computer maintenance will be at a big disadvantage.

Decisiveness

A good active trader is decisive. They see an opportunity that fits their trading strategy and they act on it. Success, particularly in short-term trading, depends on quickly entering and exiting a position. Hesitating or second-guessing will cause traders to miss the window of opportunity. If the trader makes a mistake, he tries to figure out what went wrong so it doesn't happen again, but a loss doesn't slow him down.

Independence

Some people thrive when they are in a group, while others prefer to go their own way. Neither is right or wrong, that's just the way they are. If you value your independence, that will serve you well as an active investor. You want to do it yourself, and that's why we encourage active traders to organize as a business—to put a structure in place that allows the independent trader to keep focused on trading. If you value the input of a group and seek advice from others before making a decision, active trading as a full-time career is probably not for you.

Investing Experience

People with previous investing experience have an edge when it comes to succeeding as an active trader. Although investing and trading have little in common, they both operate in the same markets and, in many cases, work with the same securities. Some knowledge of the securities markets and products is helpful background information.

Market Place

Investing won't teach you much about active trading, but you will share some common language, and a basic knowledge of how the markets work will be a big help in getting your active trading business started.

Practice on Paper First

One of the ways you can measure your ability and aptitude as an active trader is to paper trade. Paper trading is practicing using a demonstration account, usually though a broker, but often using real market data. Many of the direct access brokers offer demo accounts, as they are often called. You can sign up for free and try out their software. This will also give you a feel for active trading.

If you are serious about active trading, try out several direct access brokers and choose one that seems most comfortable to you. Go ahead an open an account if there is a limit on how long they will let you paper trade (if you decide active trading is not for you, just cancel the account). Practice paper trading until you learn their software or you decide you are not interested in pursuing active trading. Try out all of the strategies discussed in this book with the exception of position trading, which doesn't require a direct access broker.

Trading Tip

Paper trading extends beyond your trading platform. If you subscribe to a charting service, spend time using it so you are familiar with how the interface works. The same goes for news feeds and any other software. All of this prep work should be done before placing your first trade.

Many of the direct access brokers populate their demo account files with real market data from several days or weeks past. This gives you a feel for what it would be like if you were really trading during market hours.

Of course, paper trading is never the same as having real money on the line. The emotions discussed above can change a challenging exercise into a time of terror if you are not cut out for this type of trading. On the other hand, you may find you have the focus, patience, and determination to be a successful active trader. You may never know until you try.

Is Active Trading Right for You?

Is active trading right for you? Only you can answer that question honestly, and that's exactly how you should answer it. As noted earlier, some 80 percent of the people who become full-time active traders don't succeed. The odds say you are one of them. However, you control most of the factors that determine whether you will succeed or fail as an active trader.

Assuming you want to pursue active trading on a full-time basis, we have outlined what is required. You will need adequate investment capital, which could be as much as $50,000. You will need an office equipped with computers, a high-speed Internet connection, and the proper software. You will need an account with a direct access broker and possibly other subscriptions to news feeds, Level II quotes, and charting software. You will also need a personal reserve fund that will cover your personal expenses (food, mortgage, clothing, and so on) for you and your family for at least three months.

Anyone with enough financial resources can get meet these requirements. Beyond these physical and fiscal requirements, you must be a quick learner and unafraid to lose money in the start-up phase of your business, which could last up to six months.

If you are prepared to spend long hours every trading day in your office with the door closed, learning the market and the securities you trade, you may succeed as an active trader. It is hard, lonely work and if you are used to working in an office full of people, the solitude may be disturbing.

However, the rewards of success can be substantial. In addition to the money, there is the satisfaction of being your own boss and choosing when and where you want to work. That independence is worth a great deal to many people.

Trading Tip

Active trading may appeal to many people, but only a few will have the determination and energy to make a career of it. With adequate resources, above-average intelligence, and determination, you can be one of those who enjoys the life of a successful active trader.

What Are the Alternatives?

We have focused in this book on working full-time as an active trader of stocks. We did this because many active investors trade stocks or at least start with stocks. We focused on full-time because it is ill advised to attempt almost any form of short-term trading (day trading) on a part-time basis. The exception to this might be the forex because it trades around the clock and is oriented towards day trading.

We have noted earlier the reasons a part-time effort at short-term trading is problematic (high cost of needed services). That same argument may not be true for other forms of active trading. Swing trading can be practiced as an intraday strategy or as a multi-day strategy. The multi-day swing strategy that follows broader price changes is a popular form of active trading. It does not require you to watch every tick of the market to participate. Because it is not as intense, you could practice swing trading as a part-time business while you keep your current job. It is not necessary to have a direct access broker to execute this strategy, so you could use a regular discount broker.

The same would be true of position trading, which many would suggest is only called active trading because the hold times may be less than one year. Position trading is something you could absolutely do part-time through a regular discount broker. It requires fundamental research, which you could do in the evenings and on weekends. Since you would not be trading often, unless you held a large number of open positions, checking on your position would be a simple matter. Stops and trailing stops could prevent a loss if you had to be away from access to your broker.

Where Do You Go From Here?

As noted in the introduction, this book is not about selling you on the idea of becoming an active trader. It has laid out an overview of what an active trader is and does. It has touched very briefly on some of the important areas you will need to know in detail, such as technical analysis.

If you wish to pursue the idea of a career further, there are many resources listed in Appendix A that will help you uncover more information about specific areas of active trading.

Active trading can be a financially and emotionally rewarding career, but it is not for everyone, so do your homework. The best decision you can make is the honest one.

The Least You Need to Know

◆ Today's active traders have an array of products and markets that weren't available to traders in the past.

◆ Some personality traits and behaviors, such as fear and greed, will make success difficult, while decisiveness and persistence can help your active trading career

◆ If you decide full-time active trading is not for you, consider alternatives such as position trading part-time.

◆ Practice or paper trading before you invest any money will help you decide if active trading is for you.

Appendix A

Resources

List of Exchanges

The following is a list of major securities exchanges and their websites:

The American Stock Exchange (AMEX)
www.amex.com
Home of over 350 exchange traded funds.

Chicago Board of Options Exchange (CBOE)
www.cboe.com
Largest options market.

Chicago Board of Trade
www.cbot.com
One of the oldest commodities exchanges.

The Chicago Mercantile Exchange (CME)
www.cme.com
Futures market.

The Nasdaq (Nasdaq)
www.nasdaq.com
An all-electronic exchange that is rapidly growing.

The New York Stock Exchange (NYSE)
www.nyse.com
The most prestigious and largest exchange.

Nonprofit Government Websites

The following websites offer regulatory or educational resources for traders.

The Financial Industry Regulatory Authority (FINRA)
www.finra.org
Polices the securities dealers.

The Institute for Financial Markets
www.theifm.org
Nonprofit educational resource.

Internal Revenue Service
www.IRS.gov
Taxes.

The Investor's Clearinghouse
www.investoreducation.org
Good source of educational material.

The National Futures Association
www.nfa.futures.org
Self-regulatory futures association.

The Securities and Exchange Commission
www.sec.gov/investor.shtml
Chief federal regulatory of the securities markets.

U.S. Savings Bonds
www.savingsbonds.gov
Information about U.S. Savings Bonds.

U.S. Treasury
www.treasury.gov
Sells U.S. Treasury bonds, notes, and bills.

Investing Resources

Internet sites with resources for traders:

Bank Rate
www.Bankrate.com
The single best source of information on interest rates for investments.

Investopedia.com
www.investopedia.com
Investing terms and tutorials.

MorningStar.com
www.morningstar.com
One of the most valuable investing resources.

Yahoo! Finance
www.yahoo.com
An investing site full of free information.

Charting Software

These websites are excellent resources for charting.

E-Signal
www.esignal.com/
Offers a variety of charting packages.

Sierra Chart
www.sierrachart.com/
Comprehensive, third-party charting software.

Financial Software

This software will help you keep track of your business or prepare your taxes.

Microsoft Money
www.microsoft.com
Personal financial software that helps you organize your money.

Quicken
www.quicken.intuit.com
Personal financial software that helps you organize your money.

Taxcut
www.taxcut.com
A personal tax-preparation software program.

Turbotax
www.turbotax.com
A personal tax-preparation software program.

List of Electronic Communications Networks (ECNs)

Electronic communications networks (ECNs) provide another way for active traders to execute trades. Some of the more prominent ones include:

BATs Trading ECN
www.batstrading.com

Direct Edge ECN
www.directedge.com

NYFIX
www.nyfix.com

SmartECN
www.networkliquidity.com

TrackECN
www.trackecn.com

Market Makers

When you are looking at Level II prices, it may be helpful to know what market makers are lining up on either side of the trade. You can find a complete list of market makers and their four-letter symbols at:

Allstocks.com
www.allstocks.com

Online Broker Sites

Here are some sites for some of the top-rated online brokers:

Charles Schwab
www.schwab.com

E*Trade
www.etrade.com

Fidelity
www.fidelity.com

Muriel Siebert
www.siebertnet.com

Scottrade
www.scottrade.com

TD Ameritrade
www.tdameritrade.com

TradeKing
www.tradeking.com

Vanguard
www.personal.vanguard.com/us/home

Wells Fargo
www.wellsfargo.com

Advanced Trading Platforms

If you are going to do short-term trading, you will want and need a direct access provider, also known as a direct access broker. These brokers provide advanced trading platforms and connect you directly to the market.

Here are some for your consideration:

CyberTrader (now part of Charles Schwab)
www.cybertrader.com

Interactive Brokers
www.interactivebrokers.com

RealTick
www.realtick.com

Technical Analysis

Technical analysis is a complicated subject, but there are numerous resources on the Internet and in books to help you learn this important form of analysis.

Websites

The following websites will help you understand and use the tools of technical analysis (some of the site will include links to other sites for even more information):

Candlesticks and Oscillators for Successful Swing Trades
www.investopedia.com/articles/trading/06/swingtrades.asp

eSignal
www.esignal.com

MetaStock
www.equis.com

StockCharts
www.stockcharts.com

Technical Analysis: The Basic Assumptions
www.investopedia.com/university/technical/techanalysis1.asp

Books

The following books on technical analysis may be helpful in the learning process:

Achelis, Steven B. *Technical Analysis from A to Z*, 2nd Edition. New York, NY: McGraw-Hill, 2000.

Murphy, John J. *Technical Analysis of the Financial Markets: A Comprehensive Guide to Trading Methods and Applications.* Paramus, NJ: Prentice Hall Press, 1999.

Tinghino, Mark. *Technical Analysis Tools: Creating a Profitable Trading System.* New York, NY: Bloomberg Press, 2008.

Appendix B

Glossary

Actively managed mutual funds   Open-ended funds that employ a portfolio manger who buys and sells stocks and bonds in an attempt to post a better return than the market. Usually represented by some stock index, such as the S&P 500.

Ask   The price at which a market maker is willing to sell the security.

Away from the market   A phrase that means the bid or the ask price on a stock is not the best order available at that moment. There are lower bids or higher asks currently available.

Ax   A market term for the main market maker for a Nasdaq stock. The market maker is responsible for creating an orderly market for a stock and must be willing to either buy or sell the stock if needed. You usually get the best prices from the ax.

Back testing   A process of running a trading system through sets of historical market data to see how the system would perform. It can be helpful when used objectively, but it can also be manipulated by commercial providers to elicit the results they want.

Baseline   A price that a stock has been trading at recently. It is often a short period moving average. It gives the swing trader a reference point for gauging when a stock may be moving up or down at the beginning of a swing.

Bid   The price a market maker is willing to pay for a security.

Breakouts   Strong divergences for existing price trends. They signal a new and powerful direction for the stock. The direction may be bullish or bearish and will continue until it runs out of energy.

Buy-and-hold investing   A strategy that says investor success is a result of identifying quality investments and holding them rather than actively trading in and out of the market.

Buy to cover   An order you can execute that will buy an equal number of shares of the stock you shorted. Buy to cover is often a simple click of the mouse on an advanced trading system.

Channel   The price zone between resistance and support that a stock will trade in. Depending on the stock, that zone can be wide or narrow. If a stock breaks above the channel, that's a bull signal, and if it falls below the channel, it's a bear signal.

Consolidation   When a stock trades in a narrow price range without any clear direction from buyers or sellers. The active trader has profit opportunities when the stock breaks resistance or support as the volatility usually increases markedly.

Contrarian strategies   Strategies that are opposite what the market is doing. If prices are trending up, the contrarian shorts. If prices are dipping, the contrarian buys.

Crossovers   When an indicator crosses a major marker such as a moving average or a price trend. Can signal a buy or sell situation.

Derivatives   Securities that are based on other investment products. For example, stock options are based on the underlying common stock, so the option's value, in part, is tied to the value of the stock.

Discount brokers   Brokers who focus on quick trades and straightforward execution. They offer their services for much less than full-service brokers, but don't provide personal advice or research.

Divergence   When an indicator moves away from or in the opposite direction of a price trend. This usually signals a reversal of the trend.

Diversification   The reduction of risk by spreading investment dollars over numerous stocks and/or bonds to minimize the impact should one of the investments turn bad.

Dividends   Cash payments (usually, but not always) to shareholders by companies. Dividends are a distribution of profits to the owners. Companies that pay regular dividends are valued for that extra return they provide shareholders.

Dollar cost averaging   Investing a fixed amount on a regular basis in a mutual fund, usually monthly and through an automatic debit to your bank account. This investment method means you buy fewer shares when prices are high and more shares when prices are lower, resulting in an overall lower average cost.

E-Mini Stock Index Futures or e-minis   An electronically traded futures contract. The e-minis are a smaller size than normal future contracts and are issued on stock indexes such as the S&P 500, Dow, and so on.

Earnings   A word that can have several meanings when used to describe accounting activity. However, it generally means profits when used without a modifying term to describe some other function.

Earnings per share (EPS)   A way of reporting earnings or profits on a per share of stock. The number is found by dividing the annual earnings by the number of shares.

Emergency cash reserve   A ready supply of cash in bank products or a money market mutual fund that you can tap in a hurry in the event of an emergency such as the loss of a job, a big uninsured medical expense, or some other financial crisis. You should have enough to keep your household running for six months.

Exchange Traded Funds (ETFs)   Funds that are similar to mutual funds in that they are baskets of stocks or bonds, but they are traded on the open market like stocks.

Gap   A term used to describe a jump (up or down) in price from the closing price to the next day's opening price. Gaps also occur during intraday trading when prices skip up or down. Several factors, both good and bad, can cause a gap. Gaps are warning signs to active traders to pay attention.

Growth stocks   Stocks that represent companies that are growing at a faster pace than the market in general. They often plow profits, if any, back into the company to finance more growth. Investors count on continued growth to keep stock prices increasing. If the company stops growing, even for a quarter, the stock market may lose confidence in the company and the stock's price can plummet.

Intraday price   The price quote of a security during active trading. It is neither the opening nor closing price and will change many times in the course of the trading day.

Leverage   The use of borrowed money to increase your purchasing power. If the value of the asset rises, your return on investment increases dramatically. If the asset loses value, the borrowed money that must be repaid magnifies your loss.

Liquidity   The relative ease at which a trader or investor can buy or sell a security. Stocks are highly liquid because there is a ready market for them. Real estate is not liquid because it may take months to find a buyer.

Margin   The ability to borrow against the value of a security to extend your investment capital. Margin accounts with brokerage firms usually let you borrow up to 50 percent of the account value for a reasonable interest rate. Short-term traders may have higher limits on margin accounts.

Market capitalization or **market cap**   Calculated by multiplying all of a company's outstanding shares (those shares available for trade on the stock exchanges) by the current per share price.

Market makers   Broker dealer firms that make a market for a particular stock by holding a certain number of shares in inventory. They display bid and ask quotes—offering to buy or sell the stock. The Nasdaq has more than 500 market marker firms that keep the exchange working.

Penny stocks   Generally stocks of very small companies that trade outside established exchanges. They may sell for several dollars per share and are considered very speculative.

Retail stockbrokers   Stockbrokers who provide general brokerage services to non-professional investors and traders. Retail brokers can adequately serve the majority of people who invest or trade. Advanced trading platforms provide sophisticated services for professional traders and investors.

Securities and Exchange Commission (SEC)   The main regulatory agency responsible for monitoring the stock markets and the securities industry. It must approve all IPOs and requires frequent and regular filings from publicly traded companies. It is a watchdog for investors to protect them against unethical investing practices.

Short position   In futures trading means you have sold a contract anticipating its value was going to decline. Unlike shorting stocks, you don't have to borrow a contract from your broker and there are no restrictions on buying or selling short contracts.

Short selling   A trading strategy that seeks to profit when the price of a stock falls. Traders "borrow" shares from their broker and sell them. When the price drops, traders buys the shares back at the lower price and returns them to their broker. The difference between selling high and buying low is profit.

Slippage   The difference in the bid-ask spread from the time a trader enters an order to the time it gets filled. Another form of slippage involves the market maker upsetting the applecart with a change in price to take advantage of an upcoming market order.

Specialist   An employee of a member firm of the NYSE. This investment professional is responsible for maintaining a market in a particular stock. The specialist matches buy and sell orders, but if the market gets out of balance, may step in and buy or sell out of the company's account to regain balance.

Stock indexes   Baskets of stocks designed to represent all or certain segments of the market. Most financial professionals consider the S&P 500 index representative of the market, while the Dow is still the best known.

Stop-loss orders   Orders that tell your stockbroker to execute a sell order when the price of a stock drops to a specific level. When the price falls to this level, the broker sells the stock at the current market price. This strategy prevents you from losing more than a specific amount.

Spread   The term that describes the difference between the bid and ask price. It is also used to describe other financial arrangements where there is a difference in price or interest rates. The difference or gap is the spread.

Trailing stops   Stops that are similar to stop-loss orders. However, they are used by investors to protect a profit. Investors place a trailing stop behind a profitable stock so that if the price begins to fall, the broker will sell while the price will still produce a profit. If the stock continues to rise, the trailing stop rises with the stock's price, usually followed by a percentage.

Index